The Traditional Music of Thailand

Illustrations from a book, dated circa 1730, saved from the destruction of Ayuthaya in 1767. Left: an early mahōrī (string) ensemble; right: a pī phāt (percussion) ensemble.

The Traditional Music of Thailand

David Morton

University of California Press

Berkeley . Los Angeles . London

1976

University of California Press
Berkeley and Los Angeles, California

University of California Press, Ltd.
London, England

Designed by Vincent Ryan
Printed in the United States of America

(chon dai mâi mī́ dontrī kān nai sǎn dān

ชนใดไม่มีดนตรีภารในสนดาน

pen khon chɔ̂p kon nák)

เป็นคนชอบภลนัก

Anyone who does not have music in his soul
is a very peculiar person indeed.

—Thai proverb.

To the composers and musicians of Thailand
who have made their traditional music what it
was, is, and will be—who indeed had music in
their souls—this work is respectfully dedicated.

Preface

The traditional music of the Thai people has long deserved the attention of musical scholars, both in terms of itself and as a bridge between the various musical cultures surrounding it. But reconstructing its evolution is virtually impossible. Thailand, like many nations of the world, does not have an extensive or lengthy recorded history. Written records such as court annals and regulations in which music may have been mentioned were often destroyed during times of war; in the extant records of the Thai only perhaps a dozen references to music are to be found, and these scattered over a period of more than a thousand years. Also, until recently the Thai had no written notation by which the music could be studied in and of itself.

Since the seventeenth century traditional Thai music has sometimes been commented on in reports of political missions and in travel books; but Western politicians, merchant traders, tourists, and even some musical scholars without an international "ear" are not equipped to listen to and comment on, with any degree of understanding, a music that differs radically from their own. The usual Western writing on Thai music tends to be a hodgepodge of opinions and statements that are often conflicting, generally subjective, and sometimes even patronizing (see for example, some quotes at the beginning of Chapter II), and the writers usually view the music as a deviation from Western standards.

A brief summary of my experience in Thailand illustrates a further difficulty in the study of the traditional music. My introduction to a non-Western music was at the first public concert, in May 1955, of the study group in Javanese *gamelan* started at the University of California at Los Angeles by Dr. Mantle Hood, Director of UCLA's Institute of Ethnomusicology. I joined the group and worked with it until I went to Bangkok in 1958 to study intensively Thai traditional music in Thailand; the transition from Los Angeles to Bangkok was made easier by this acquaintance with Javanese music. My first exposure to the traditional music in Thailand itself happened on the day after I arrived, in a rural locale near the old summer palace at Bang Pa-in, some miles north of Bangkok, at the time of a special Buddhist ceremony. After the ceremony, as we stood around the car eating our lunch, I became aware of a blend of many melodies floating from beyond a clump of banana trees. I could distinguish the bell-like tones of gong-kettles, xylophones, drums, chiming cymbals, and a penetrating oboelike sound. I pushed through the trees and found, spread out on the broken flagstones of the side courtyard of the temple, an ensemble of traditional Thai instruments being played by a group of men of various ages. Some months later, in recollection, I appreciated the rarity of that occasion, for as I pursued my studies of the traditional music I found that since the 1930's its performance in Thailand has become more the exception than the rule, being largely replaced by Western music and Western-style Thai music. Although by the 1950's a move was already under way on the part of a number of Thai to restimulate interest in the traditional music, on returning to Bangkok for a few months from September 1969 to January 1970 to record the repertoire of Luang Pradit Phairo (mentioned frequently in this study) I found the situation unfortunately little changed. From the time I first noticed the traditional music performed so little, I often wondered why. Some possible answers emerged in the course of my study; they appear scattered throughout this work.

This work is based on direct research with a number of Thai instruments, musicians, and other authorities, and on the reading of extant material on the traditional music by Thai and other scholars. It draws in large part on the repertory of traditional music recently put into notation in Bangkok, which I was allowed to microfilm in 1960. My investigations and research were specifically focused on instrumental music and forms; I felt that a study of this area would more likely reveal the fundamentals of Thai music than would a study of some other aspect, such as vocal practice (other than the preliminary investigations of Sidney Moore. By the way, little research has been done in the area of Thai vocal practice). The early chapters of this work, then, contain history and description of instrumental music—tuning system, melody, rhythm, and tempo as well as instruments, ensembles, and aspects of mode; vocal practice is touched on briefly in Chapter V, which deals with forms and compositional techniques.

An explanation of the transliteration system used in this book to put Thai words into Roman letters is given in Appendix A; to avoid undue confusion, tone marks indicating the correct inflection of the words (Thai is a tone language) are not given in the text. A glossary of all Thai words used, giving the complete pronunciation and the word in Thai letters, is in Appendix D. Phonetic transliteration has not been used, however, for personal names or proper place names (except in a few instances) —the traditional transliteration has been retained because it is the one used in most books, on maps, and so forth; for many sounds the two systems are alike, so there is no difficulty where no ambiguity occurs in pronunciation. For a few proper names, phonetic symbols have been used to avoid mispronunciation. For example, the first name transliterated in the old system as "Son" or "Sorn" is pronounced "Sǫn." (A more striking example is the family name transliterated in the old system as "Diskul"—it does not appear in this book—which is correctly pronounced "Deet-suh-goon"!) The correct pronunciation for proper names appears following the entry for that name in the index.

The photographs in this book are mine except where noted. The pictures of the ensembles were made by the Thai Department of Fine Arts and are reproduced with their permission. The three photographs of Balinese instruments from the Colin McPhee collection are reproduced by permission of Mrs. Shirley J. Hawkins, executrix of Mr. McPhee's estate.

I wish to express here my gratitude to Mantle Hood, with whom I have had the privilege and pleasure of working in ethnomusicology at UCLA since 1955, for his unfailing friendship and guidance during the years of my study and for his help in completing this present work. My study in Bangkok was supported from 1958–1960 by a grant from the Rockefeller Foundation, and in 1969–70 by a grant from the American Council of Learned Societies; I thank these organizations for their support. During these two periods in Thailand I met with consideration and cooperation from everyone. I should like particularly to thank Dhanit Yupho, the Director-General of the Thai Department of Fine Arts at the time I was there from 1958–1960, and all the members of the department who aided my work by giving so generously of their time and knowledge—in particular my teacher on the Thai instruments, Chirat Atchanarong, and Montri Tramote, Head Musician of the music section of the department. I am deeply indebted to Prasidh Silapabanleng and his family, who took me into their home and hearts and shared with me their vast fund of knowledge about Thai music, past and present. My gratitude is extended to Supachai Vanij-Vadhana, then Secretary-General of Chulalongkorn University, and his family, who most generously took every opportunity to make me feel at home in Bangkok. Last but not least go my thanks to Rev. and Mrs. Ray C. Downs, Directors of the Student Christian Center (in 1958–1960) in Bangkok, where I lived while I was in Thailand, and to the many students there who treated me as one of themselves.

Los Angeles, California   David Morton

Contents

Chapter I: History 1

Chapter II: The Fundamentals of Thai Music 20

   A. The Tuning System 22
   B. Melody 29
   C. Meter, Rhythm, and Tempo 39

Chapter III: Instruments, Their Idiomatic Characteristics, and Ensembles 44

   A. Melodic Percussion 45

     1. Sets of Gong-kettles

       a. Khǭng wong yai 45
       b. Khǭng wong lek 50
       c. Khǭng (wong) klang 51
       d. Khǭng mǭn 52

     2. Xylophones

       a. Ranāt ēk 54
       b. Ranāt thum 57

     3. Metallophones

       a. Ranāt ēk lek 62
       b. Ranāt thum lek 63

   B. Rhythmic Percussion 64

     1. Cymbals

       a. Ching 64
       b. Chāp lek 66
       c. Chāp yai 67

     2. Gong

       a. Mōng 67

     3. Drums

       a. Taphōn 68
       b. Taphōn mǭn 71
       c. Sǭng nā 71
       d. Klōng khāek 73
       e. Klǭng that 74
       f. Thōn 76
       g. Rammanā 77

C. Woodwinds 77

　　1. Flute Types

　　　a. *Khlui* 77

　　2. Reed Types

　　　a. *Pī nai* 80
　　　b. *Pī chawā* 88
　　　c. *Pī mǭn* 90

D. Stringed Instruments 91

　　1. Plucked

　　　a. *Krajappī* 92
　　　b. *Čhakhē* 92

　　2. Bowed

　　　a. *Sǭ sām sāi* 94
　　　b. *Sǭ ū* 97
　　　c. *Sǭ duang* 100

　　3. Notation for String Parts

E. Ensembles 101

　　1. Development of String Ensembles 101

　　2. Development of Melodic Percussion Ensembles 104

　　3. Standard Contemporary Ensembles 105

　　　a. *Pī phāt* 105
　　　b. *Khrᵾāng sāi* 111
　　　c. *Mahōrī* 111

　　4. Special Ensembles 111

　　　a. *Pī phāt nāng hong* 113
　　　b. *Pī phāt mǭn* 113

Chapter IV: Mode 115

A. An Approach to Modality in Thai Traditional Music 115

B. Classification of Modal Types 126

C. *Metabole* 128

D. Analysis of Representative Compositions of the Classified Types 133

　　Fifth Polarities 137

E. Coda 172

F. Summary 178

Chapter V: Forms and Compositional Techniques 180

    A. *Rɨ̄ang* 180

        "Lā" (Farewell Song) 182

    B. *Thao* 182

    C. Developmental *sām chan* 212

    D. *Tap* 212

    E. Other Forms

        1. *Sɔ̄ng chan* 214
        2. *Sī chan* 216

    F. Ceremonial and Theater Music 216

    G. Vocal Music 216

Chapter VI: Conclusion 223

Notes 225

Appendix A: Phonetic Transliteration of Thai 231

Appendix B: Measurements of Tunings 232

Appendix C: Structure of the Versions of "Lā" (Farewell Song) 238

Appendix D: Glossary of Thai Words 239

Bibliography 244

Discography 252

Index 253

List of Illustrations

Frontispiece. Two early ensembles.

Figure 1. Chinese *yang-ch'in* 2

Figure 2. Thai *khim* 2

Figure 3. Procession carved on Angkor Wat (*a*) and detail from
the carving (*b, c, d*) 5-6

Figure 4. Procession carved on the Bayon, Angkor Thom 6

Figure 5. Procession carved on Angkor Wat 6

Figure 6. Procession carved on Angkor Wat 7

Figure 7. Procession carved on Angkor Wat 7

Figure 8. Procession carved on Angkor Wat 8

Figure 9. Procession carved on Angkor Wat 8

Figure 10. Ensemble with harp carved on the Bayon, Angkor Thom 9

Figure 11. Ensemble with harp carved on the Bayon, Angkor Thom 9

Figure 12. Ensemble with harp carved on the Bayon, Angkor Thom 9

Figure 13. Ensemble with harp carved on the Bayon, Angkor Thom 9

Figure 14. Ensemble accompanying a vaudeville performance in a
carving on the Bayon, Angkor Thom 10

Figure 15. Khmer gong-chime: *a*, detail from figure 3;
b, detail from figure 5 10

Figure 16. Javanese *bonang* 11

Figure 17. Balinese *trompong*: *a*, the instrument alone; *b*, being played 11

Figure 18. Balinese *réong* 12

Figure 19. Chinese *yŭn lo* (gong-chime) 12

Figure 20. Mask for Hanuman in a *khōn* drama (Thai) 13

Figure 21. Detail from a carving at Angkor showing a Khmer mask 13

Figure 22. Hanuman and a giant fighting in a scene from a *khōn* drama (Thai) . . . 14

Figure 23. Female dancer with headdress, carving at Angkor Wat 14

Figure 24. Thai dancer, female in male dress with headdress 14

Figure 25. Three dancers carved on a column, Angkor Thom 14

Figure 26. Learning by rote, the author and his teacher at the
Department of Fine Arts, Bangkok 19

Figure 27. Methods of tuning instruments in Thailand: *a*, adjusting the
wax in the boss of a gong-kettle; *b*, comparing the same
pitch on the xylophone and the set of gong-kettles 31

Figure 28. Tapestry with harp, unearthed in Thailand 46

Figure 29. *Khǫng rāng*, early form of the Thai gong-circle in the form
of a straight rack 47

Figure 30. Carving of a gong-circle on a bookcase, from the Ayuthaya period . . . 47

Figure 31. Contemporary gong-circle 48

Figure 32. Gong-circle being played 48

Figure 33. Inside of a gong-kettle from a set of gong-kettles
showing the tuning wax in the boss 48

Figure 34. *Khǭng wong lek*, small set of gong-kettles   51
Figure 35. Detail of the gong-circle showing the method of fastening
            the gong-kettles to the rack, and the mallets   52
Figure 36. *Khǭng mǭn yai* being played   52
Figure 37. *Khǭng mǭn lek* being played   53
Figure 38. Several *khǭng mǭn* at a cremation ceremony   53
Figure 39. *Krāp sēphā* being played   55
Figure 40. *Ranāt ēk* being played   55
Figure 41. *Ranāt ēk* used in the *pī phāt* ensemble (left) and the one used
            in the *mahōrī* ensemble (right) shown side by side   55
Figure 42. River boat, showing the similarity to the case of the *ranāt ēk*   57
Figure 43. *Ranāt ēk* case without the keyboard   57
Figure 44. The under side of the *ranāt thum* keyboard, showing
            the tuning waxes   59
Figure 45. *Ranāt thum* being played   59
Figure 46. *Ranāt ēk lek,* open case and metal keys in their carrying
            and storage box   62
Figure 47. *Ranāt ēk lek* and *ranāt thum lek*   62
Figure 48. Javanese *saron*   63
Figure 49. Javanese *gendèr*   64
Figure 50. Pair of *ching*   65
Figure 51. The two strokes of the *ching*: *a, ching*; *b, chap*   65
Figure 52. The Chinese *shing*   66
Figure 53. *Chāp lek (a)* and *chāp yai (b)*   66
Figure 54. *Chāp lek* being played   67
Figure 55. *Khǭng rāo* or *khǭng hui*, set of three gongs on a rack   67
Figure 56. *Mōng* (on a stand)   67
Figure 57. *Mōng* (on a tripod)   68
Figure 58. *Taphōn*   68
Figure 59. *Taphōn mǭn* and *taphōn,* showing relative sizes   68
Figure 60. *Taphōn mǭn* being played in a *mǭn* ensemble
            (see also figs. 36, 37)   69
Figure 61. *Sǭng nā* being played   72
Figure 62. Pair of *klǭng khāek* being played   72
Figure 63. *Klǭng that*: *a,* front view; *b,* rear view   72
Figure 64. Chinese percussion instruments   75
Figure 65. Pair of *thōn chātrī*   76
Figure 66. *Thōn mahōrī*   76
Figure 67. Two *rammanā,* head side (left) and underneath side (right)   76
Figure 68. Chinese *pang ku*   76
Figure 69. *Thōn mahōrī* and *rammanā* being played   77
Figure 70. *Khlui phīang ǭ* being played   80
Figure 71. Three sizes of *khlui*   80
Figure 72. Detail of *khlui* mouthpiece   81
Figure 73. *Pī nai* being played   81
Figure 74. Process of making the reed for the *pī nai* (*a* through *m*)   82
Figure 75. *Pī nai*: *a,* closed end with reed and tube holder; *b,* lower end,
            showing tuning wax   85
Figure 76. Different sizes of *pī*   86
Figure 77. *Pī chanai* being played   89
Figure 78. *Pī chawā* being played   90

Figure 79.   *Pī chawā* being played 90
Figure 80.   *Pī mǫn* (see also figs. 36, 37) 90
Figure 81.   *Phīn nam tao*: *a*, side view; *b*, bottom view, showing
 the open half gourd 91
Figure 82.   *Phīn phia* 91
Figure 83.   Two sizes of *krajappī* being played 91
Figure 84.   *Čhakhē*, an old ivory-inlaid case 93
Figure 85.   *Čhakhē* contemporary model 93
Figure 86.   *Čhakhē* being played 93
Figure 87.   *Sǭ sām sāi*, back view, showing the sound box with
 three mounds on the back, with bow 95
Figure 88.   *Sǭ sām sāi*, front view, with bow 95
Figure 89.   Detail of the spike of the *sǭ sām sāi* showing the
 strings entering the spike 95
Figure 90.   Detail of the front of the neck of the *sǭ sām sāi*, showing
 the strings entering the neck 95
Figure 91.   *Sǭ ū* 98
Figure 92.   *Sǭ ū*, bottom of the sound box 98
Figure 93.   Chinese *pan hu* 98
Figure 94.   *Sǭ duang* 98
Figure 95.   *Sǭ duang* sound box, showing the hair of the bow
 passing between the strings 99
Figure 96.   *Sǭ duang* being played 99
Figure 97.   Chinese *erh hu* 99
Figure 98.   *Khap mai* ensemble 101
Figure 99.   Original *mahōrī* ensemble 102
Figure 100. Rubbing of a stone carving showing an early ensemble of
 the Sukhothai period 103
Figure 101. *Klǫng khāēk* ensemble 104
Figure 102. Small *pī phāt* ensemble 106
Figure 103. Small, informal indoor *pī phāt* ensemble with the *khlui*
 substituted for the *pī* 106
Figure 104. Medium-sized or double *pī phāt* ensemble 107
Figure 105. Large *pī phāt* ensemble 107
Figure 106. Small *khrüang sāi* ensemble 108
Figure 107. Medium-sized or double *khrüang sāi* ensemble 108
Figure 108. Small *mahōrī* ensemble 109
Figure 109. Medium-sized or double *mahōrī* ensemble 109
Figure 110. Large *mahōrī* ensemble 110
Figure 111. *Pī phāt nāng hong* ensemble 112
Figure 112. *Pī phāt mǫn* ensemble 113
Figure 113. *Pōeng māng khǫk* being played 114
Figure 114. Back view of *pōeng māng khǫk* 114
Figure 115. Burmese *Anyein* ensemble and ceremonial instruments 114
Figure 116. Burmese *saing* ensemble 114

List of Charts

Chart 1. Comparison of Thai and Western tuning systems 33
Chart 2. Thai pitch levels and pentatonic modes 45
Chart 3. Ching patterns 48
Chart 4. Ching patterns 48
Chart 5. Ching patterns 49
Chart 6. Percentage of occurrences of pitches as a finalis 116
Chart 7. Classification of finalis pitches according to pitch levels 116
Chart 8. "Khāek Sai" (Thao), pitch outline 121
Chart 9. "Tuang Phra Thāt" (Thao), Section 1, pitch outline 131
Chart 10. "Tuang Phra Thāt" (Thao), Section 2, pitch outline 133
Chart 11. "Lāo Sīang Thīan" (Thao), pitch outline 136
Chart 12. "Lāo Khruan" (2 chan), pitch outline 139
Chart 13. "Lāo Chīang Tat Sǫi" (2 chan), pitch outline 140
Chart 14. "Nok Khao Khamāē" (Thao), pitch outline 141
Chart 15. "Khamāē Thom" (3 chan) 141
Chart 16. "Līlā K(r)athum" (3 chan) 146
Chart 17. "Sām Mai Nai" (Thao) 148
Chart 18. Pitch-exchange process for metabole 150
Chart 19. "Hong Thǫng" (Thao), pitch outline 152
Chart 20. "Khāek Thǫn Sāi Bua" (2 chan), pitch outline 153
Chart 21. "Phrayā Khruan" (3 chan), pitch outline 155
Chart 22. "Yǫng NGit" (Thai), pitch outline 158
Chart 23. "Phat Chā" (3 chan), pitch outline 158
Chart 24. "Dǫk Mai Sai" (3 chan), pitch outline 159
Chart 25. "Khāek Mǫn Bāng Chāng" (3 chan), pitch outline 164
Chart 26. "Sōi Mayurā" (Thao) 165
Chart 27. "Rasam Rasāi" (3 chan) 167
Chart 28. "Chāng Prasān NGā" (Thao) 169
Chart 29. Classification of rӯang 181
Chart 30. "Lā" (Farewell Song), pitch outline 182
Chart 31. "Nok Khao Khamāē" (Thao), pitch outline 188
Chart 32. "Khāek Sai" (Rӯang), pitch outline 189
Chart 33. "Khāek Sai" (Thao), pitch outline 189
Chart 34. "Ānū" (Rӯang), pitch outline 190
Chart 35. "Ānū" (Thao), pitch outline 195
Chart 36. "Khamēn Yai" and "Khamāē Thom" (Rӯang and 3 chan),
           pitch outline 197
Chart 37. "Khāek Tǫi Mǫ" (Thao), pitch outline 206
Chart 38. "Khamēn Pāk Thǫ" (Thao), pitch outline 222

Chapter I

History

The ancient history of the Thai is shrouded in myth and legend. Few records or accounts remain of the early Thai kingdoms; consequently almost no information is available on Thai music of the past.[1] As an integrated, unique system the traditional music of Thailand is probably not more than six hundred years old, having begun to evolve in the direction of its present form in the fourteenth century when Ayuthaya became the center and capital of a new and rapidly expanding Thai empire. With the destruction of Ayuthaya most of the artifacts that would have aided, at least partially, in reconstruction of the musical scene of that time were lost. And a comprehensive history of the evolution of Thai music in terms of the music itself is impossible because, oral tradition rather than the printed book having been the carrier of the culture,[2] the Thai have never had a traditional notation system for their music; and of course no recordings from those earlier times exist. Thus what we know today of Thai music is in actuality only of the nineteenth and twentieth centuries—the "classic" or Bangkok period.

In most Asian cultures, however, the process of change until recently has been relatively slow; perpetuation of traditional methods rather than the conscious striving for originality in the Western sense has been the procedure in music as in culture in general. Perhaps, as Montri Tramote suggests (1954), the music played for the celebration of the founding of Bangkok in 1782 was not much different from that performed during the latter part of the Ayuthaya period. Certainly Thai music of the "classic" period of the late nineteenth and early twentieth centuries can be considered a culmination of musical evolution that probably started, as nearly as can be ascertained from the references, in the fourteenth and fifteenth centuries with the rise of Ayuthaya as the capital.

But to understand traditional Thai music and the cultural matrix in which it emerged, one must examine at least the little that is known of Thailand's earlier past: the history of the Thai people themselves, and also those peoples with whom they came into contact. For the mainstream of Thai traditional music as it is known today is probably a composite of musical elements from several cultures. Blended with early Thai music itself are influences from Chinese, Indian, and Khmer (Cambodian) music. Musical elements from other neighboring cultures—Burma and Malay, for example—were possibly also absorbed into the evolving Thai traditional style. Recent influences are discernible from such widely varying sources as Japan and the West. Characteristically the assimilated elements were incorporated into the existing culture of the Thai to suit their own taste, resulting in a culture distinct from those from which these elements were originally acquired.

The earliest homeland of the Thai is said to have been the southern part of present-day China (Blanchard 1958: 1). The most important early Thai kingdom, flourishing by the sixth century A.D., was Nanchao[3] in the province of Yunnan in southern China. For a time Nanchao declared itself independent from the Chinese—"Thai" means "free"—but by the end of the ninth century it had again become a vassal state. It lost its remaining independence in 1253 when China, together with Nanchao, was conquered by the Mongols under Kublai Khan.

The few references seem to indicate that from the very beginning the Thai were a musical people The amalgamation and blend of original Thai musical

1

elements with those from China and India—Nanchao was located along the trade routes between the two countries—probably occurred during the six hundred years this kingdom flourished. The culture of Nanchao was heavily influenced by the Chinese culture to the north through contacts of diplomatic exchange, trade, war, and royal intermarriage (Blanchard 1958: 24), and one may suppose there were musical influences also. And the influence seems to have operated in the reverse: it is reported that during the Nanchao period groups of musicians, actors, and dancers from the Thai capital went to other areas to teach these arts. One must bear in mind that China is a large area whose history extends back to the third millennium B.C.; there is no one "Chinese" music, as there is no one "Chinese" language—even "Chinese" people themselves have differed, ethnically speaking, at different times as a result of the constant absorption of invaders from the north and conquered peoples to the south, including areas of Indochina, dominated from Han times (ca. 200 B.C. to ca. 200 A.D.), until the tenth century. History shows that both China's invaders and those people conquered by the Chinese have been absorbed into, and have been heavy contributors to, the "Chinese" culture.

Although documentation of a similarity between Thai and Chinese music of the period prior to 1250 is impossible, perhaps ancient Thai and Chinese music were similar since there were such close contacts

Figure 1. The Chinese yang-ch'in; a contemporary model being played in the Institute of Ethnomusicology, University of California, Los Angeles.

Figure 2. The Thai khim. Learning by rote. The man at the right is the student, sitting on the correct side of the instrument; the woman on the left is the teacher. The lesson is taking place on the porch of the old Silapabanleng home in Bangkok; the instrument is slightly blurred in the picture because it vibrates when being played.

between the two peoples. Certainly two of the main characteristics of "Chinese" music are also characteristic of a large portion of contemporary Thai music: the minor third pentatonic genus and the prominence of the interval of the fourth (Picken 1957: 86). A similarity also exists between some Thai and Chinese instruments. The ancient Chinese had a drum that they called literally "drum of the southern people," the "southern people" being the Thai in south China. Two Thai stringed instruments, the sǭ ū and the sǭ duang, are practically identical with the Chinese hu hu and hu ch'in. A large barrel-shaped drum with pegged heads (klǭng that), used in pairs in the large Thai percussion ensemble, is similar to the Chinese t'ang ku, and the Thai ching (small hand cymbals) are probably derived from the shing, the Chinese hand cymbals (for illustration of these Chinese instruments, see Chapter III, figs. 50, 52). The Thai also use a table or lap zither, called khim, which they consider to be Chinese and not Thai; primarily a solo instrument, it is not used in traditional ensembles (see figs. 1, 2).

Possible influences of Indian music on Thai music are also undocumented. Certain instruments of the Thai, such as the čhakhē (three-stringed floor zither) and some of the drums, may be derived from Indian models, and the *ching* may be related to the Indian hand cymbals as well as to the Chinese ones. Thai music does not have a complex modal structure such as the Indian *raga* system, and Thai music is a "composed" music in contradistinction to the essentially improvised music of India. Further, in its simple duple metrical division, Thai music is closer to Javanese music than to the Indian *talas*—metrical patterns, often asymmetrical, based on the additive principle. In some of its musical forms Thai music does make use of a division within a single composition into three tempos—slow, medium, and fast—a fundamental of North Indian (Hindustani) music (Popley 1950: 79). South Indian (Karnatic) music does not use this three-fold tempo structure; only in certain *varnams* (a composition somewhat in the nature of a concert etude) is it "customary to increase the speed of the tala at the beginning of the *charanam* (a rondo-like section in which a characteristic melody alternates with contrasting sections), this being the only instance of a change of tempo in South Indian music" (Brown 1960: 51). In the *pallavi* form in South Indian music, on the other hand, a technique is used which may be the origin of, or may have contributed to, the development of what might be called a "telescopic variation" *(Thao)*—the most important and most exploited compositional technique in Thai music of the last hundred years. After certain preliminary sections, the pallavi proper begins "with a line of melody which fills one *avartam,* or cycle of the tala, usually a long or unusual one. The performer then leads his melody through a set of complicated rhythmic variations, doubling and quadrupling the speed of the melody above the constant *tala* . . ." (ibid.: 52). The Thai form is a composed composition, however, while the Indian technique is used mainly in improvisatory style. The Thai adopted the Theravada or southern form of Buddhism, and influences may also have come into Thai music, particularly the vocal practice, from the Buddhist chants. Because no depth study has been made of this aspect of musical relationships between India and Thailand, such influences are still conjectural.

What North Indian influences existed probably came along the northern trade routes and were absorbed into ancient Thai music during the Nanchao period; possible influences from South India would have been brought by the early Indian colonists who settled along the mainland coast of the present-day Gulf of Thailand and the South China Sea and would have traveled inland as the center of culture moved northward, culminating with the Khmer (early Cambodians), from whom the Thai received them.

Thai contact with the Khmer of present-day Cambodia and northern Thailand started in the latter part of the Nanchao period, when the kingdom was still vassal to China. During that time a number of tiny but independent Thai principalities were established in northern Thailand, and in 1238 two Thai chieftains defeated the Khmer at the city of Sukhothai. The invasion of China and the defeat of Nanchao by the Mongols in 1253 caused a major migration of the Nanchao Thai southward; Sukhothai rapidly became an active and vigorous center and by 1257 was the acknowledged capital of a new Thai kingdom. Further expansion to the south involved warfare with the Môn people of southern Burma and central-southern Thailand. Under the leadership of the Sukhothai ruler, Rama Khamhaeng, Thai suzerainty by the fourteenth century was extended south to the Gulf of Thailand and east to the Bay of Bengal.

During the Sukhothai era (1250–1350) the Thai again became a unified people with distinct cultural trends (Blanchard 1958: 25); they also began to absorb a number of cultural elements from the Khmer and the Môn. In 1283 King Rama Khamhaeng created the Thai alphabet from Khmer-Sanskrit models and developed a writing system. Khmer-Môn influences were surely felt in Thai music, of which they "had plenty . . . which 'resounded,' according to Rama Khamhaeng's famous inscription on a stone, 'all over the city of Sukhothai'" (Dhaninivat 1957: 6); references to Thai music of that time speak of simple stringed instruments, bamboo flutes, some drums, and singing.

After Rama Khamhaeng's death Sukhothai began to decline and, starting in 1350, through royal intermarriage was gradually and peacefully absorbed by a new and more powerful Thai kingdom centered at Ayuthaya farther to the south. The next four hundred years saw intermittent warfare and other forms of contact between the Thai and both the Khmer to the east and the Burmese to the west.

Much has been written of the glory of the Khmer civilization and its capital at Angkor; the probably strong influence of the Khmer on Thai music warrants a brief review here of their culture. Khmer culture evolved out of the early Indian colonies established along the coast of the Indochinese peninsula as early as the first century A.D. From the second to the sixth century the center of culture was in the Indianized state of Funan in the south; at the same time another Indianized state, Chenla, was growing strong farther to the north in the middle basin of the Mekong River——these people, of Môn-Khmer stock, called themselves Kambujans. As the power of Funan waned, that of Chenla grew, until in 550 Chenla annexed Funan. Although little is known of the history of the area during the seventh and eighth centuries, the Khmer civilization is said to have been born at this time. Early unification was carried forward by Jayavarman II, who founded the first great dynasty of Angkor at the beginning of the ninth century. The civilization reached its apogee during the twelfth century in the reign of King Suryavarman II (1113–1150), who built the great temple of Angkor Wat; at this time the power of the empire extended from the China Sea to the Indian Ocean.

The carvings at Angkor indicate considerable musical activity among the Khmer, but its style and characteristics can only be surmised. "A distant sound of music gives warning that the king has just left his private apartment. . . . At the head of the procession come the banners and standards, the band, and the gilded bronze insignia carried on poles. . . . From the dancing-hall which occupies one whole side of the courtyard come the strains of music and song . . . . At many religious festivals the common people must have joined the dancing" (B. Groslier 1957: 161–164). Thus run some of the poetic reconstructions.[4]

Though the native genius of the Khmer emerged rapidly and created a distinct cultural identity, the models were Indian in essence.[5] Since practically nothing remains of the Khmer civilization today except some statues and the ruins of stone temples and buildings at Angkor, comparisons are necessarily confined to elements of the plastic arts, but such comparisons do show similarities—and if Indian influences are traceable in this area of Khmer arts, the music also probably had Indian elements. Some of the stringed and wind instruments, drums, and hand cymbals that appear among the carvings at Angkor are similar to early Indian models (G. Groslier 1921: 125–128).

Khmer culture had also been subjected to influences from Java, which was also colonized by India, at least by the fifth century (Kunst 1949: 106); it appears that for a time Cambodia may even have been under the control of Java, for it is known that during the last years of the eighth century, Jayavarman II, before he became the Khmer king, was in exile in Java. Possible evidence of Javanese influences in Khmer music might be found among the carvings on Angkor Wat. In a carving of a series of processions in which a group of musicians with their instruments is taking part, one instrument is a set of eight gong-kettles on a curved rack (figs. 3, 3c, 5, 6, 7, 15a and b). When in ancient cultures an article such as a musical instrument was dignified by being included in an important picture or carving, the assumption is that it had already been in use for some time and had therefore become established. Angkor Wat is dated at the first half of the twelfth century; the Khmer, then, had a set of gong-kettles by at least that time and thus before their culture was contacted to any great extent by the Thai. Was the instrument an original creation of the Khmer, or did the idea for it come from elsewhere? No gong-kettle instruments like the Khmer set appear among the early temple carvings in Java, as reference to Jaap Kunst's book on the music of Java will show; only the "dumb-bell" type of *réong,* still used in some parts of Bali (Kunst 1949: II, illus. 40, 41, and 46), is found. But the Khmer set seems definitely related to the later *bonang,* the gong-kettle instrument of Java (fig. 16), and to the *trompong* and *réong,* the gong-kettle instruments of Bali (figs. 17, 18). The Chinese also used a set of gong-kettles——a small hand-held model the "gongs" of which were suspended on cords on a vertical rack[6] (fig. 19)——but its exact age is unknown; presumably it was an instrument of court music, not of popular or theater music, and therefore may be of no little antiquity.

A great deal of romantic nonsense has been written about the "sudden collapse" of the Khmer empire, but even the few known facts contradict it. After the reign of Suryavarman II the empire began to decline, starting in 1177 with the sacking of the capital by the Chams from the east. The country

Figure 3a. Procession carved on Aṅgkor Wat. Details
from the procession can be seen in the next three illustrations.

Figure 3b. Detail from the procession
shown in figure 3a; the players at the left
are blowing wind instruments (it is impossible to tell whether they are flute or
double-reed instruments), the player in
the middle is playing the Khmer version
of the one-stringed plucked zither (similar to the Thai phīn types), and the player
at the right is playing a pair of hand cymbals.

Figure 3c. Detail from the procession
shown in figure 3a; the player of the hand
cymbals at the left is the same as the one
at the right of figure 3b, in the center are
a drum and two large gongs being carried
on a pole, and to the right are more players of wind instruments.

Figure 3d. Detail from the procession shown in figure 3a; in the center is the Khmer model of the set of gong-kettles in the shape of an arc, at the right are drums being carried on straps around the necks of the players, and behind are players of the conch-shell trumpet and curved horns. The set of gong-kettles does not seem to have any support around the player's neck and is shown here with the flat side to the viewer, similar to the Egyptian style of painting and sculpture.

Figure 4. Procession carved on the Bayon, the central building of Angkor Thom ("Thom" means "city"); hand cymbals, drums, and wind instruments can be seen.

Figure 5. Procession carved on Angkor Wat.

Figure 6. Procession carved on Angkor Wat.

Figure 7. Procession carved on Angkor Wat.

Figure 8. Procession carved on Angkor Wat.

Figure 9. Procession carved on Angkor Wat.

Figure 10. Ensemble with harp carved on the Bayon, Angkor Thom; to the right are dancers, to the left of the harpist the player seems to be playing a stick zither, and to the extreme left the two figures seem to be clapping their hands to keep time.

Figure 11. Ensemble with harp carved on the Bayon, Angkor Thom; also represented are stick zithers, and the player at the left seems to be beating a large stick to keep time.

Figure 12. Ensemble with harp carved on the Bayon, Angkor Thom.

Figure 13. Ensemble with harp carved on the Bayon, Angkor Thom. The position of the stick zither here suggests that it may be played like a plucked lute and may have more than one string. These stick zithers in the carvings at Angkor resemble the early Indian models of the _vina_.

Figure 14. Ensemble accompanying a vaudeville performance in a carving on the Bayon, Angkor Thom.

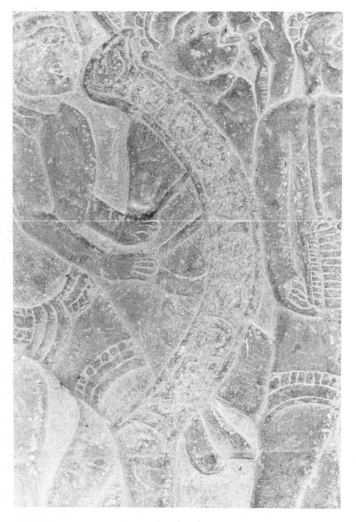

Figure 15a. Detail of the Khmer gong-
chime from figure 3a.

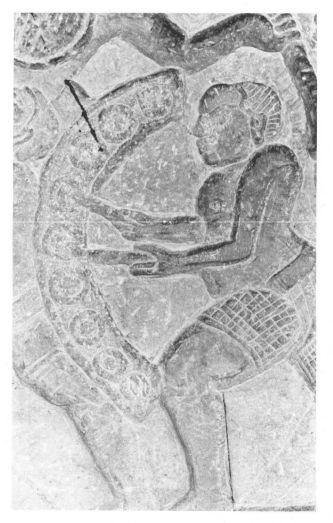

Figure 15b. Detail of the Khmer gong-
chime from figure 5.

Figure 16. Javanese bonang being played at the
Institute of Ethnomusicology, UCLA, Los Angeles,
California. (Photograph from the collection of the
Institute of Ethnomusicology.)

Figure 17a. The Balinese trompong.
(Photograph from the Colin McPhee collection.)

Figure 17b. The Balinese trompong
being played. (Photograph from the Colin
McPhee collection.)

Figure 18. The Balinese réong being played by four players. (Photograph from the Colin McPhee collection.)

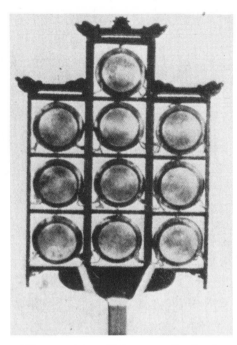

Figure 19. Chinese yün lo (gong-chime). (Photograph reproduced from van Aalst.)

rallied during the reign of King Jayavarman VII (1181–ca. 1219). This king was a devout Buddhist; in a frenzy of pious building he created the city of Angkor Thom, and under his direction many of the temples and buildings in and around the city were erected. The detailed account of the Chinese traveler, Chou Ta-kuan, who visited Angkor about 1296, tells us that the country was bursting with riches, and Angkor apparently enjoyed 'at least two centuries of prosperity after Jayavarman died in about 1219 (B. Groslier 1957: 195). But with this ruler gigantic building projects ended. The kings became more and more detached from the people, reverting to Hinduism and becoming enmeshed in an intricate web of great priestly families. The society of the ruling classes became overrefined and sterile, and more and more of the Khmer people were converted to Theravada Buddhism, which advocates peaceful renunciation. The country became unable to resist the steadily increasing successful Thai invasions that resulted in the absorption of province after province of Khmer territory and, often, mass deportations to Thailand of Khmer people including artisans and high officials; in 1393, for example, 90,000 Cambodians were transported to the Thai capital at Ayuthaya

(Blanchard 1958: 27). The Thai finally defeated the Khmer in the fifteenth century—Angkor fell in 1431—and shortly after that the Khmer abandoned Angkor.[7]

Cambodian and Indian influences were strong in Ayuthaya from the very beginning, as it had once been part of the Khmer empire. Although the Thai conquered the Khmer, the Khmer civilized the Thai: "The Ayuthayans derived benefit not only from the sinews and muscles of captives, but also from their minds. Cambodian prisoners, especially high officials, became to the Thai as Greeks to Romans—the educators of their captors" (Blanchard 1958: 27). Similarities between the styles of Thai sculpture and architecture and those of the Khmer suggest that as this was true on political levels, it was also true in the arts.[8] A great similarity between Thai traditional dance and the style of Khmer dancing can be demonstrated by comparing the dance movements and costumes of Thai traditional dancing with the carvings of dancers on the buildings at Angkor (Strickland 1938: 440), as can be seen in figures 20 through 25. Xenia Zarina, writing of the Thai royal ballet, says, "When the Siamese (at that time a rude people) conquered and destroyed the Khmers, they

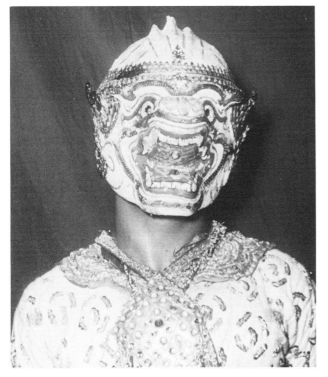

Figure 20. Mask for Hanuman in a
khōn drama (Thai).

documentation exists showing that the Thai had this type of instrumental music prior to their contact with the Khmer. The Burmese have instruments of these types very much like the Thai models. Who had them first is unknown, but very likely the Thai adopted them from the Khmer and in turn passed them on to the Burmese. The four hundred years of the Ayuthaya era (1350–1767) was a period of constant contact also between the Thai and the Burmese. When the Burmese won battles against the Thai and looted Thai territory, they in turn took back to Burma captive Thais, just as the Thai did with the Khmer.

The climax of the Thai-Burmese skirmishes came in 1767, when the Burmese in a surprise attack sacked and razed Ayuthaya. The Thai forces were scattered but were finally rallied some miles to the south by a Thai general, Taksin, who established a

were themselves conquered by the beauty of the Khmer arts, and they took the dance home with them and protected and loved and cultivated it" (Zarina 1941: 285). An even more inclusive statement is made by a Thai musician himself: ". . . the Cambodian cultures in music, dances and architectural arts remained dominant over the Thais" (Silapabanleng 1955: 1).[9]

Montri Tramote states that when "Ayuthaya was the (Thai) capital, it seems that music became extremely popular with the common people everywhere. Besides the musicians whose profession and occupation was music, all the people played music as a hobby and avocation. The principal instruments used were the stringed instruments and the flute. This condition of widespread musical activity continued without limitation until a royal decree appeared in the court regulations in the latter part of the fifteenth century forbidding singing and playing instruments in or near any royal household without royal permission" (Tramote 1954). Also, during the Ayuthaya period a new style of instrumental music arose utilizing melodic percussion types such as xylophones and gong-kettles—no

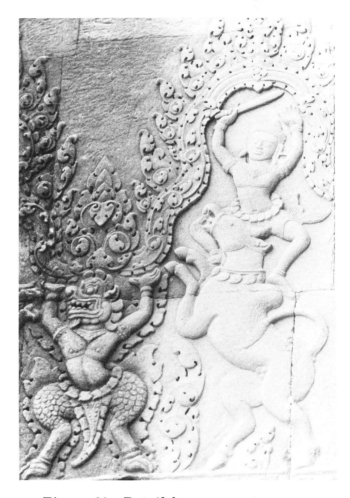

Figure 21. Detail from a carving at
Angkor showing a Khmer mask.

Figure 22. Hanuman and a giant
fighting in a scene from a khōn drama;
the scene is an excerpt from the drama
given by artists of the Phakavali Institute of Dance and Music in Bangkok.

Figure 23. Female dancer with headdress,
carving at Angkor Wat.

Figure 24. Thai dancer, female in
male dress with headdress. (Photograph
taken at the Phakavali Institute of Dance
and Music, Bangkok.)

Figure 25. Three dancers carved on a
column, Angkor Thom.

capital at Thonburi and ruled for fifteen years. In 1782 another general, after having Taksin officially pronounced insane and put to death, had himself proclaimed king. The capital was moved across the Chao Phya River to Bangkok, where it has remained. The new king became known as Rama I of the new Chakri dynasty; the present king of Thailand (Rama IX) is a direct descendant. Four of the Chakri kings, as well as several princes of the dynasty, have been noted for their artistic abilities and have contributed much to Thai culture.

During the colonial period in Asia, England controlled Burma and India on the one side of Thailand, and France controlled the Indochinese peninsula on the other; Thailand itself remained independent, a buffer state between the colonies of the two European powers[10] with no colonial servants domiciled within its borders. Consequently Thai traditional music entered its "classic" period in the nineteenth and early twentieth centuries with few or no Western influences. Since music was always an integral part of Thai court life as an adjunct of ceremonial, official, and social functions, the traditional "classic" or high-art music existed and evolved under the aegis of royal patronage very much as did Western music during the seventeenth and eighteenth centuries. Bowring described a typical scene of the 1850's: "The close of each day, in fact, at every nobleman's house, is the signal for the commencement of singing and dancing; and the concert is continued without interlude till the next day has been encroached upon by some hours" (Bowring 1857: I, 146).

According to Montri Tramote (1954), in Thailand only those trained in music furthered the evolution of musical practice and theory. As soon as a young musician began to be known for his musical ability, he was commandeered by a noble and became attached to his household for its own private use. Here the young musician came under the tutelage of older, more experienced musicians from whom he received formal training. He perfected his technique on the instruments and gradually learned, through listening and imitation, the traditional repertoire. If the young novice showed signs of creativity, he was also able to learn the compositional techniques from the main music master, who was generally a composer as well as a performer. In time the novice became a

teacher, passing on in turn his knowledge to new novices. Thus the wheel of oral tradition turns.[11]

Musicians attached to courts or aristocratic households were in reality servants, as was Haydn in the Esterhazy household, but they were apparently not looked down upon. In 1857 Bowring stated that "the profession of music was esteemed worthy" (I, 150), and Montri Tramote's statement above goes on to say that "amateurs remained amateurs." But the terms "professional" and "amateur" mean different things in the West and East. Perhaps in the days when certain Thai musicians were attached to courts they were considered professionals, and those who were not so attached were considered amateurs; in this case the term referred more to the standard of performance technique than to a salaried job. Be this as it may, it does not in itself preclude the possibility of influences creeping into court music from outside sources, although no music or references remain and so such influences cannot be traced.

Shortly there developed much friendly rivalry between the musical ensembles of the various households, a rivalry that resulted in a period of great technical ability and virtuosity among performers and a rapid development in the creative efforts of musician-composers.[12] This period, perhaps from the late 1800's until the change of government in 1932, might be called the "classic" period of Thai music. Patrons vied with one another to have the best musicians and musician-composers attached to their households, and these in turn vied with one another in composing the best "new" compositions and performing them better than any other group; these musicians and composers were highly respected, and many of them were specially rewarded with medals, titles, or other honors. The custom—as apparently in the past and certainly into today—was to use an old traditional melody as a basis for enlargement and arrangement rather than a new composition per se. Besides Thai melodies, Thai composers frequently used those borrowed from neighboring cultures—Chinese, Burmese, Javanese, Khmer or Cambodian, Môn, Laotian, and possibly Indian—and to show the origin of these compositions, the name of the original country or culture is retained as the first word of the title. But the resulting composition is distinctly Thai; regardless of the strong influences from other cultures and the borrowing of melodies, Thai music has developed into a distinct musical system that is one of the principal members of the family of high musical cultures of Southeast Asia. Ellis writing in 1885 rightly said, "Although their music is entirely different from ours, it must take a high rank among extra-European music, which is not adapted for harmony" (Oct. 1885: 1103).

In 1885 Frederick Verney, the English Secretary to the Siamese Legation in London, wrote a small pamphlet on Thai music and instruments which attests to the popularity of the art in its home country in the late nineteenth century. Since there was little on the subject in print at the time, Verney probably obtained most of his information from the Thai attached to the Legation and from those from Thailand participating in a Thai musical ensemble present at the Inventions Exhibition in London that year. He writes:

> Although in Siam there are musical circles, or guilds professing to train musicians for public and other performances, these guilds seldom prosper, for the simple reason that the aristocratic and wealthier classes keep their own musicians, who are so highly trained, and by nature so exclusive as to shrink from cooperation with outsiders whose performances are, presumably, inferior to their own standard of excellence. It is easy to understand that, in a country where music is generally popular, there should be plenty of emulation among those who can afford the luxury of a band. There are indeed few houses of any size without their Ranats, and all the other instruments are also employed where the householder can afford to purchase them (Verney 1885: 9–10).

The first part of the above quote indicates a guild system that languished, but only because the aristocracy so strongly supported the traditional music. According to the latter part, not only the upper classes but also the common people apparently took great interest in music then. Indeed, Graham makes the rather sweeping statement that "the taste for music is so widely diffused that almost every man is more or less proficient in playing at least one instrument . . . and most girls of education play the Siamese viol (sǭ sām sāi) or the zyther (čhakhē) in private . . ." (Graham 1924: II, 195–196).

After the Thai monarchy was overthrown in 1932, the royalty and nobility were downgraded in power and ceased to exist as focal points of cultural activity. In the absence of thriving guilds, any young person who wanted to learn to play an instrument attached himself to the household of a well-known and respected player of that instrument. In return for

lessons he acted as a house-boy and servant to his teacher. Often several young people gathered around one teacher, and in this way an unofficial school was formed. Such a situation has existed in the household of the musician-composer Sǭn Silapabanleng (whose official title, bestowed on him by King Rama VI, was Luang Pradit Phai Rǫ). An editorial in the *Bangkok World* (1959), an English-language Thai newspaper, spoke of this musician as follows:

> When his services with the King ended Luang Pradit established himself with his family in the rambling old house behind which his son has now built his theater. There the gentle, almost ethereal musician received students from all over the country; young men and women who, bearing a gift of rice or fruit, came to sit at his feet and study his technique.
>
> The old man received no pay from his students, but kept up his school and his family with offerings presented at funerals, weddings, tamboons and other ceremonies at which his troupe of young people played or danced.
>
> We happened to be visiting him years ago, when a young man with no more baggage than the shorts and shirt he wore, the pakaoma in which he carried his gift of rice and the flute he carried in his hand, arrived to offer himself as a student. The old man received the gift and acknowledged the youth's obeisance absently and motioned him without a word to take his place among the other students practicing on the porch. It was understood that the boy would eat at the family kitchen and find a place to sleep somewhere on the compound with the others.

Since the death of Luang Pradit in 1954 the school, now known as the Phakavali Institute of Dance and Music, has been carried on by his son Prasidh and the Silapabanleng family.[13]

But with the rapid increase of Western influences and the desire of many of the upper-class people of Bangkok to be as Western as possible, Thai traditional music came to be considered out-of-date and inferior——an unwanted and anachronistic reminder, perhaps, of the days of absolute monarchy. During the middle 1930's the public performance of traditional music on Thai instruments was discouraged by the new government practically to the point of being officially forbidden——tolerated only if the compositions were played on Western instruments similar to the Thai instruments.[14] At this time also the new government established a Department of Fine Arts, including a national symphony orchestra that utilizes Western instruments and performs Western classical and semi-classical music. Western-style music has come to predominate in the department's outdoor live performances and in television and radio. In Bangkok young people seem attracted more by Western popular music than by their own Thai music; the newest recordings from the West can frequently be heard on the streets, blaring from radios in the open shops. Most of the records resulting from a postwar influx of American ideas and techniques are Thai imitations of Western popular songs. The nightclubs that feature Western dancing use, of course, ensembles of Western instruments, the musicians being predominantly Philippino.

A number of Thai, particularly in Bangkok, do not want their traditional arts to disappear, a situation that is presently happening in many other areas of the world under the onslaught of Western power and influence.[15] These have begun efforts to restimulate activity in the Thai arts. The Thai Department of Fine Arts, for example, has broadened its scope in several ways. It teaches Thai music and dance to young persons who wish to learn and to help preserve their cultural heritage. Outdoor concerts and television and radio programs include not only Western music but Thai classical music played by the traditional ensembles attached to the department; the ensembles sometimes go out to supply the musical portion of special temple ceremonies. Broadcasts also feature some Thai popular music, this being a curious blend of a simple Thai-style melody with a few common chords of Western harmony. Productions of Thai dramas, which include traditional music and dance, are given at the national theater each year, although the audiences for these presentations are more Western tourists than Thai nationals. Programs are presented for tourists by the department and by some of the small independent schools, such as the Phakavali Institute of Dance and Music; the programs, given several times a week, offer a group of selections and excerpts from the various types of Thai music and dance—traditional, folk, instrumental solos, and Thai "fencing." Some recordings of traditional compositions have recently become available, and some nightclubs have for several years featured traditional Thai music and dancing once or twice a week.

Nevertheless, except for these few sources the people of Thailand have little opportunity to hear their own music. And young people have little incentive to take up the profession of music, for few opportunities exist for a professional musician in Thailand. Anyone exhibiting such a desire runs the risk of being considered unrealistic and strange, and if he is lucky enough to obtain some kind of musical job, it will most likely be for small financial return. Most Thai musicians today, even many in governmental departments and at the television station, in order to make an adequate living must hold other jobs as well or perform their musical functions in addition to other tasks.

Until the present study, no comprehensive research was done in the field of Thai music by a Westerner working in Thailand—such, for example, as was done by Jaap Kunst in Java, Gironcourt and Knosp in Indochina, and Fox-Strangways in India, to mention a few. The most important Western references to Thai music of the nineteenth and twentieth centuries can be reviewed quickly.

The first specific investigation by a Westerner, and paradoxically one of the few that attempted to be objective and scientific, was the work of the Englishman Alexander J. Ellis. Ellis's reports appeared in the publications of the *Musical Association* and the *Society of Arts* in London in 1884 and 1885 and in the appendices to his translation of Helmholtz's *On the Sensations of Tone* (1895). These articles present the first tunings taken of Thai instruments and contain valuable material relating to some of the technical aspects of Thai music procured by Ellis from Thai musicians performing at the Inventions Exhibition in London in 1885.

Of the general reference works by Westerners devoted entirely to Thailand, one deserves special mention: the two-volume work *Siam* by Graham. Besides a lengthy and detailed report on both the traditional music and dance as well as information about the music of rural tribes, the book gives an excellent bibliography on Thailand containing titles of publications from the sixteenth century down to and including the early twentieth century.

In 1944 in the magazine *Contemporary Japan* appeared an article in English by Klaus Pringsheim entitled "Music of Thailand." Although still general, this is a more comprehensive treatment than Graham's because Pringsheim was a musician and was writing an article specifically on the music, not on the whole culture, as was Graham.[16] The article contains much information on the instruments, photographs of many of them, some samples of the music in Western notation, and some discussion of the simpler theoretical aspects of the music.

The largest Western work dealing with Thai music is by Carl Stumpf, published first in 1901 and revised in 1920, entitled "Tonsystem und Musik der Siamesen." The study was made in 1900 when a troupe of Thai musicians and dancers who were traveling through Europe were in Berlin and Stumpf availed himself of the opportunity to listen to many of their performances. He notated samples of the music, recorded on wax cylinders four of the compositions played by the ensemble, and later transcribed one of them —Hornbostel's analysis of this transcription was published in 1920. Stumpf's monograph is valuable as one of the first major ethnomusicological studies; that it seems somewhat naive today and is not a comprehensive technical study of all aspects of the music does not minimize its importance as a primary reference source, particularly the section dealing with the tuning system.

Mention must be made of the contributions of several Thai scholars. Vichitr-Vadakarn, one of the early Director-Generals of the Department of Fine Arts, wrote an article on the evolution of Thai music and instruments which, though in English, was unfortunately published only in Bangkok in magazines no longer available.[17] It was from Vichitr-Vadakarn that Klaus Pringsheim obtained most of his information.

Vichitr-Vadakarn acknowledged that work on the musical aspect of Thai culture was begun by two Thai princes particularly devoted to their traditional arts. Both of these men have long formal names, but are known informally as Prince Damrong (Rajanubhap) and Prince Dhani (Nivat). One of Prince Dhani's works was quoted earlier in this chapter. Prince Damrong wrote an account of Thai music, published by the Royal Institute in both Thai and English (1931),[18] which is particularly useful for its history of the evolution of Thai musical ensembles and photographs of reconstructions of these ensembles.

In 1956 appeared the fourth edition of a pamphlet in English entitled *Thai Music,* by Phra Chen Duriyanga. This is one of the few presently available works specifically on Thai music. It is limited in its scope, however, as it deals only with the

pī phāt (percussion) ensemble and a few elementary aspects of the music theory. It does include samples of music, photographs of the pi phat instruments, an excellent detailed account of the drumming techniques (some of which are quoted in Chapter III), several tables of instrumental ranges, and a discussion of the tuning system.

One of the most active contemporary writers on cultural matters is Dhanit Yupho, until recently Director-General of the Thai Department of Fine Arts. When I was in Thailand in 1958–1960, I translated into English Mr. Yupho's book on Thai musical instruments; published by the department in 1960, the English edition is now unfortunately out of print. The important material relating to the traditional instruments is included in Chapter III of this study. Mr. Yupho has also written much on Thai traditional dancing and theatrical forms.

Among the staff members of the Department of Fine Arts special mention should be made of Montri Tramote (quoted and referred to previously in this chapter), who has a great knowledge of the history of Thai music and of the background of many of the traditional compositions. In addition to composing in the traditional idiom, Mr. Tramote has written much about these aspects of Thai music in program notes for concerts, in the explanatory notes that accompany the traditional compositions published in the *Silpakọn Magazine,* a bi-monthly publication in Thai of the Department, and in a recent publication by the department of a booklet on Thai musical terms.

Although all the above articles and books are good in certain ways and add to our knowledge of the technical and theoretical aspects of Thai music as a music system, they are incomplete. General characteristics are stated, quoted, and requoted, but theoretical and organizational factors of the music itself are not touched on. Further, a large body of the musical repertoire has not until now been analyzed with the aim of showing the specific characteristics that make the music distinctly Thai, though actually it is only recently that a suitable basis for such a study became available.

Thai music was until recently learned and handed down from master to pupil by the oral or rote method (see fig. 26). As long as this was the method of transmission, comprehensive analysis was impractical if not impossible: even the exceptional musician

Figure 26. Learning by rote, the author and his teacher, Chirat Atchanarong, at the Department of Fine Arts, Bangkok. In the background to the right are stands of several Thai sets of gong-kettles; in the center background are cases for two <u>bonang</u>, part of a set of Javanese instruments sent by a Javanese sultan to the king of Thailand in the 1920's.

who by rote can learn his part of a large repertoire does not know all the parts of enough compositions to do such analysis. Moreover, such a theoretical undertaking as musical analysis has never been a part of Thai ambition. Prince Damrong had long urged that the repertoire of traditional music be notated and thus preserved, and this undertaking was finally begun shortly before World War II.[19] Before work was interrupted by the war and supporting funds were withdrawn, over four hundred compositions had been notated—some for the complete pī phāt ensemble, others the main melody only. Although the existence of the collection was known to some Westerners, it remained unavailable[20] until my stay

in Bangkok in 1958–1960, when the entire collection was microfilmed; these microfilms are now a part of the archives of the UCLA Institute of Ethnomusicology. We may be thankful for the preservation of the collection, for the notations had been done with pencil on a soft, porous paper that had begun to disintegrate in the high temperature and humidity of Bangkok. Even at the time the manuscripts were being made it was lamented that many of the traditional compositions were no longer known, and many of those that were notated seem to have been forgotten during the years since. This collection forms the basis of this study.

Chapter II

The Fundamentals of Thai Music

The first impact of a foreign music seems to be sensual and emotional rather than intellectual; it is sound alone that attracts or repels. Mantle Hood, a composer as well as a musicologist, says of his own first exposure to Javanese gamelan that "the unique orchestral color caught my immediate interest" (1954: vi). Reports by travelers, for the most part nonmusicians, indicate that laymen have the same initial reaction. Here are a few quotes concerning Thai music, the first from the seventeenth century.

> Although the Siamese seem to us to be a trifle melancholy, they like to have their entertainments. They often have barge races on the river. These races are made very entertaining by concerts of a vocal and instrumental nature, when they clap their hands in cadence. The most pleasing of these instruments is somewhat similar to that we hear here from two violins playing in perfect harmony. But there is nothing more disagreeable than the small edition of this instrument—a kind of violin with three brass wires. Their copper trumpets resemble in sound the cornets our peasants use to call up their cattle. Their flutes are scarcely any softer, and besides these, they perform a carillon with small bells, a pleasing performance if it be not mixed up with their bronze gongs which distress those not accustomed to the sound. They have also an earthenware drum which does not make so much noise. It is a hard-baked earthenware pot having a long and very narrow mouth but no bottom. They cover it with buffalo-hide and beat it with the hand in such a way that it takes the place of the bass viol in their concerts (Gervaise 1688: 53–54).

This, written during the Ayuthaya period, is valuable as one of the first references in a Western language to Thai music. Though we need not go into them here, there are several inaccuracies regarding the instruments.

Another set of comments, from the early nineteenth century, are:

> . . . The late Dr. Finlayson who accompanied Mr. Crawfurd's mission to Siam very correctly observes that the vocal music of the Siamese is plaintive and the instrumental lively, playful, soft and sweet. . . . Mr. Crawfurd I believe has observed that Siamese music is pitched on a key unknown to barbarous nations *(sic)*. . . . The music would be very pleasing were one or two of the wind instruments laid aside, especially the *pi chanai,* a harsh sort of hautboy. The Sticcado, composed of a number of metallic bowls disposed on a circular frame of bamboo which are beaten by a muffled stick, is an instrument of considerable compass (Low 1839: 333–392).

From the twentieth century, two typical accounts:

> The loud—very loud—orchestra, consisting of 57 men . . . were prepared for a display of the most disinterested self-sacrifice and effort. . . . Gongs, drums, lead pianos, flutes and fifes, wooden kettledrums and two-stringed violins combined to produce something which perhaps those well-versed in music might have enjoyed. I, who can only remember the simplest of European tunes with a great deal of trouble, sincerely admire the way in which all the different instruments managed to keep together in the most complicated "fireworks," although they evidently were played without any notes (Morganthaler 1923: 201).

> . . . The actors were really first class, and surprisingly so; the orchestra melodious, seeing that the chief instruments were drums and sweet-toned gongs; but the singing was too dreadful . . . (Foran 1935: 159–160).

The subjective nature of terms like "disagreeable," "plaintive," "playful," "sweet," "dreadful," and so forth in the reactions and descriptions quoted above is apparent. But if we are not justified in describing a music system with such terms, how may we proceed to do so more objectively? Let us try.

Thai music is nonharmonic, melodic, or linear, and as is the case with all musics of this genre, its fundamental organization is *horizontal.* There is no underlying harmonic progression in the Western sense. It is impossible to describe in a simple way the whole of Western music of the last thousand years with its great variety of styles and forms in order to have a basis for comparison and contrast between Western and Thai music, but the development of tonal harmony has characterized the evolution of Western art music from about 1600 to 1900 and popular music of the twentieth century. The romantic music of the nineteenth and twentieth centuries is probably what the average nonmusician thinks of when he thinks of "Western music." Harmonic progression—systematic movement from one chord (i.e., a group of pitches heard simultaneously) to another and, by extension, from one tonality or key to another—underlies this music and controls the development of the melody. Upon the harmonic understructure a composition proceeds by the principles of repetition and contrast: a theme is stated, sequentially varied or developed simultaneously with itself (i.e., fugally) or with another theme (i.e., contrapuntally), restated, alternated with contrasting material, harmonized in different ways, and so on. The typical impression given is of a dense music in which many pitches sound simultaneously yet form few identifiably independent strata. The movement from chord to chord furnishes the tension-relaxation complex, the motor power that drives the composition forward; the *vertical* complex characterizes Western harmonic music.

Thai music in its horizontal complex is made up of a main melody[1] played simultaneously with variants of it which progress in relatively slower and faster rhythmic units. The several strata of sound—each usually carried by but one instrument and readily discernible to the ear educated to this type of music—stating and varying the melody at the same time impress the uneducated Western ear as proceeding according to no logical organization, producing a cacophony of unrelated simultaneous sounds. Individual lines of melody and variants sound in unison or octaves only at specific structural points, and the simultaneity of different pitches does not follow the Western system of organized chord progressions. Between the structural points where the pitches coincide (unison or octaves) each individual line follows the style idiomatic for the instrument playing it. The vertical complex at any given intermediary point follows no set progression; the linear adherence to style regulates. Thus several pitches that often create a highly complex simultaneous structure may occur at any point between the structural pitches. The music "breathes" by contracting to one pitch, then expanding to a wide variety of pitches, then contracting again to another structural pitch, and so on throughout. Though these complexes of pitches between structural points may strike the Western listener as arbitrary and inconsequential, the individual lines are highly consequential and logical *linearly.* The pattern of pitches occurring at these structural points is the basis of the modal aspect of Thai music.

Not the relationship of one melody to an underlying progression of solid complexes of sound, as in Western harmonic music, but the relationship of one melody to specific variants of itself—one idea viewed simultaneously from several different viewpoints, multiplicity within unity—characterizes Thai ensemble music. The technique of combining simultaneously one main melody and its variants is often incorrectly described as heterophony; *polyphonic stratification*[2] seems a more precise description, since each of the "layers" is not just a close approximation of the main melody but has distinct characteristics and a style of its own.

A linear style of music-making is used by a majority of the world's peoples, who are understandably indifferent to the typical Western attitude that music is not "music" unless it has some kind of Western harmony connected with it.

. . . It is this absence of harmony and presence of simultaneous performance, having its own peculiar but decidedly non-harmonic character, that gives a European, so accustomed to harmony that he is apt to forget it is a comparatively recent discovery, an opportunity of appreciating what must have been the effect in early times when people heard 'the sound of the cornet, flute, harp, sackbut, psaltery, dulcimer, and all kinds of music' playing together, and relying for their effects, not on harmony, but on diversity of quality of tone for the same note, or its octave, or flashing away into labyrinths of eccentric discant, but returning duly to the original theme of which these flourishes were but the embroidery. We may thus learn to see that extensive pieces of music can be put together, with a full appreciation of the relation of parts to a whole, relying solely upon melody without harmony, and come to understand that the latter art, however indispensable to modern European music, is not essential to the existence or enjoyment of music in general (Ellis Oct. 1885: 1103).

So wrote Ellis at a time when most Westerners assumed that the rest of the world had nothing that could really be called music.

The combination of the melodic and rhythmic elements of Thai music, expressed in the tone color of the particular ensemble, might be likened to a stream whose main current flows onward in an almost hypnotically steady pulse. Various and sundry eddies and swirls flow in and around the main current, created by the simultaneous variations of the main theme. In the percussion ensemble the relatively unsustained sounds of the melodic percussion instruments — xylophones and sets of gong-kettles — are blended together by the thread of continuous and unbroken sound of the oboelike reed instrument. In the string ensembles the resinous quality and sometimes harsh sound produced by Thai bowed stringed instruments is lightened and highlighted by the relatively pure sound of the bamboo flute and the agile, fluttering line it plays. The tapestry of sound is enlivened by the rhythm of the drums and is punctuated at specific points by the chiming sounds of the little hand cymbals that hold the tempo steady and indicate the form by the pattern of strokes they play.

Finney raises the question: "Has Western music lost something by eliminating the melodic possibilities inherent in the smaller and less regular intervals which the music of other cultures still values?" (1947: 9). Asking the reader to leave aside for the moment the rhythmic aspect of music, Finney goes on to say that to a person of a culture using a linear musical system, "melody and music are virtually synonymous. . . . Melodic beauty is the measuring stick by which he judges music. From the Easterner's point of view, every limitation of material which robs melody of subtlety and variety, even though it results in added richness at another point (i.e., harmony), is a move in an inartistic direction. That part of music which to him carries the sense of the art, that part which to him really *is* the art, is being made poorer in artistic possibility" (loc. cit.). The Thai music system is one that has developed melodic possibilities rather than harmonic ones.

Before proceeding to a discussion of the characteristics of Thai melodies, the tuning system used in Thai music must be discussed.

A. THE TUNING SYSTEM

No extant written records give information on the evolution of the tuning system in Thailand, but almost all references say the system developed in a different way from that of the West. Most comments on the Thai tuning system are general ones, stating that it has seven equidistant pitches to the octave, each interval being about three-fourths or seven-eighths of a Western whole step. Daniélou, in his booklet on the music of Cambodia and Laos (1957: 2), says that equidistant tuning in Southeast Asia came from the *Gândhârâ-grâma,* a seven-pitch equidistant scale *(grama),* the third scale of ancient Indian music.[3] He does not document his opinion, however, and it is difficult to know how he arrived at this conclusion since the books on Indian music give various *shruti* divisions for this grama, such as 3-3-3-4-3-2-4 (Bake 1957: 208) and 3-2-4-3-3-3-4 (Popley 1950: 36), which are not equidistant.

In the latter part of the nineteenth and early twentieth centuries Ellis and Stumpf measured scientifically the intervallic structure of the Thai tuning system.[4] In his article of 1885 Ellis quotes the Thai ambassador ("Envoy Extraordinary and Minister Plenipotentiary for Paris, Berlin, Vienna, and the other capitals of Europe"), Prince Prisdang, who said that "the intention was to make all the intervals from note to note identically the same" (Oct., 1885: 1105); this may be the statement echoed by subsequent writers on Thai music. Ellis was tone-deaf and therefore unable to test Thai tuning with his own hearing, but to substantiate the theory that the Thai tuning system was one of seven-pitch equidistance he set up such a tuning and played it for visiting Thai musicians, who "pronounced the scale good" (ibid.). Stumpf's study was largely devoted to proving this theory, which he did to his own satisfaction. Seven-pitch equidistance is stated specifically in Montri Tramote's booklet on the terms used in Thai music (1964: 46); under the entry *"siang,"* which means basically "sound," he says: "The octave is divided into seven pitches, the intervals between which are all the same (that is, equal to one another)."

To see if this intention of seven-pitch equidistance obtains in Thai music, we shall later examine the tunings of some of the Thai instruments of fixed pitch tested recently with an electronic apparatus. For the present let us look at the Thai pitches themselves, as traditionally organized.

Ellis gives the names of the pitches as told to him by the Thai musicians in 1885 (Oct. 1885: 1105). He assigns pitch I to the bar of the xylophone tuned to 285 cycles per second, the fifth bar from the left end (lower pitches) of the instrument. The fifth step (above this) of 421 cycles per second is given the name phīang q̄ (transliterated by Ellis as phong oar), and the sixth step of 458 cycles per second is called kruat (transliterated by Ellis as kruert).⁵ Stumpf says he was also given the names for the pitches and that they differed from those of Ellis; saying that they had no bearing on his discussion (1901: 108), he unfortunately did not include them in his article.

Montri Tramote (1964: 17 ff.) gives the name for each of the pitches and the ensemble and/or theatrical form for which that pitch level is used as a "home base" or "tonic." This list is given under the main heading "thāng," which means literally "way" or "method"—not "sound," as Ellis and Verney give it. Following are the pitch names according to Tramote:

1. phīang q̄ lāng (also called by the term "nai lot," which means "one pitch lower than nai level," the next pitch higher than phīang q̄ lang).

This pitch is notated in Western notation as F. Tramote says it is the name for the pitch of the tenth gong-kettle from the left (lower-pitched end) on the khǫng wong yai, the set of gong-kettles or the gong circle. Tramote does not say why he refers it to the tenth kettle rather than to the third kettle, the lower octave.

The old name for this pitch was simply "phīang q̄," the name of the flute (khlui phīang q̄). With the advent of the mahōrī and khrȳang sāi ensembles, a division into two types was made: phīang q̄ lāng (below) and phīang q̄ bon (above), the level a fourth above (or a fifth below). (The ensembles are discussed at the end of Chapter III.)

This pitch level is considered the "home" or "tonic" level for the pī phāt mai nuam (the pī phāt ensemble using soft—that is, padded—sticks) and the short-lived theatrical form dụkdamban.

2. nai. One pitch above phīang q̄ lāng.

This pitch is notated in Western notation as G.

This is the home level for the standard pī phāt ensemble. It is used with the lakhǫn nai, lakhǫn nǫk, and khōn. (For a discussion of the forms of theater see Yupho, Bowers, and Brandon. Some of the theatrical forms are mentioned throughout this study.) The name of the pitch comes from the pī nai, the double-reed instrument used in this pī phāt ensemble.

3. klāng. One pitch above nai.

This pitch is notated in Western notation as A or A♭.⁶ This pitch level is sometimes called "lūk ōt" because many of the "ōt" or lament-type songs are performed at this level.

The name "klāng" comes from the pī klāng, the medium-sized double-reed instrument ("klāng" means "middle" or "medium").

This was the home level for the pī phāt ensemble when it used this instrument and accompanied the nāng yai (shadow plays) and khōn in the old days.

4. phīang q̄ bon (also called nǫk tam, that is, one pitch lower than the next higher pitch, nǫk). One pitch above klāng.

This pitch is notated in Western notation as B♭.

This is one of the home levels for the khlui phīang q̄.

This pitch level is used with the mahōrī and khrȳang sāi ensembles.

5. kruat (also called nǫk, after the pī nǫk; the fingering on the pī nai on the G (nai) level produces on the pi nǫk the same pattern on C). One pitch above phīang q̄ bon. "Kruat" means "pebbles" or "coarse sand"—that is, something hard or rough.

This pitch is notated in Western notation as C.

This is the pitch level for many sēphā compositions (entertainment songs). It was the home level for the pī phāt accompanying lakhǫn nǫk in the old days when the pī nǫk was the pī used.

6. klāng hāep. ("Hāep" means "harsh, grating" in describing tone quality.) One pitch above kruat.

This pitch is notated in Western notation as D.

This level is rarely, if ever, used as a home level.

7. chawā. One pitch above klāng hāep. The pitch gets its name from the pī chawā ("chawā" = Java).

This pitch is notated in Western notation as E or E♭ (see note 6).

This is the home level for the khrȳang sāi ensemble when the pī chawā is combined with it. For the *pī phāt nāng hong,* the phīang ǭ bon (lower) is used, as it better suits the melodic percussion instruments in the ensemble.

Phīang ǭ and kruat are also used as names of tunings or tuning levels of the stringed instruments. The pitches for these correspond with those of Tramote's list but not those of Ellis's; they will be discussed shortly.

Thai music never uses all seven pitches of its tuning system as principal pitches, though certain compositions are in a style that contains passages using six pitches and sometimes all seven. But the method of using the pitches establishes a hierarchy among them—some occur on the emphasized beats, others only as passing tones in secondary positions—and the result is in effect a mode or scale of five pitches (pentatonic) and an auxiliary, additional, secondary pitch (or pitches) used for decoration. In practical modes and/or scales a gapped or nonequidistant pattern occurs. Musical practice also shows that the system of "modulation" and the transference of a musical phrase or section to another pitch level demands an equidistant structure, in essence similar to the need for equidistance in Western musical practice which led to the adoption of tempered tuning.

There are a number of difficulties in trying to measure the tuning of Thai pitches. Since Thai musicians do not theorize to any great extent about

Figure 27b. Tuning a Thai instrument: comparing the same pitch on the xylophone and the set of gong-kettles.

their music, it is not easy to know exactly what "in tune" means to them. Further, the four main instruments of fixed pitch in the Thai pī phāt (percussion) ensemble—the two xylophones and two circles of gong-kettles that my measurements were focused on—are tuned by ear by the addition of lumps of a mixture of beeswax with lead shavings to the ends of the undersides of the wooden bars and inside the bosses (knobs) of the gong-kettles (figs. 27 a and b, 33, 45). As Ellis stated ". . . in attaching these tuning lumps the Siamese tuner seems to be guided solely by ear, and the peculiar intention of their scale . . . rendering this very difficult, the result obtained is by no means always perfect" (Oct. 1885: 1103). Also, as the wax lumps dry out and become brittle, small bits continually fall off under the impact of the mallets when the instruments are played or during the process of moving the instruments from place to place; or if the whole lump falls off, as often happens, some of it is invariably lost in the process of remelting and reattaching it to the instrument. Whether these four instruments are ever completely "in tune" for any length of time is doubtful; the instruments I heard in Bangkok seem to be in tune about as frequently as is the piano in the average American home and nightclub.

One of the many difficulties in determining the tuning system of a musical culture is procuring accurate readings of the pitches in practical use. Ellis, Stumpf, and other early investigators had to rely for

Figure 27a. Tuning a Thai instrument: adjusting the wax in the boss of a gong-kettle.

their readings on a tonometer, an apparatus consisting of a series of tuning forks (one for every three or four vibrations) covering the range of an octave; pitches between those of the tuning forks had to be approximated. A more accurate device is the monochord, consisting of a single metal string stretched over a wooden resonator with a movable bridge so that the vibrating length of the string can be varied; the device is adjusted by ear to sound the same pitch as the one being measured, and a reading is taken in cycles per second. But the accuracy of the monochord is directly proportionate to the ability of the ear to "hear" correctly, and the device is easily affected by climatic conditions. The monochord has a range of only slightly more than one octave; pitches lying outside this range must be raised or lowered in the operator's mind to the proper register. Further, the metal string of the monochord forces a comparison of sounds of different quality when the device is used with the instruments that produce sound with materials other than metal strings. Another difficulty often arises with instruments such as the gong-kettles, metallophones, and xylophones: the partial structure that gives the quality or tone color of the sound is a nonharmonic series.[7] Ellis realized this, for he says of the Thai gong-kettles, "The sound is bell-like, but like bells, full of inharmonic proper tones" (Oct. 1885: 1103). Sometimes the fundamental pitch is weaker than one of its overtones; sometimes there is more than one fundamental, and the two may be sounding close together.

More precise pitch readings have become possible recently with the development of the Stroboconn, an electronic apparatus that holds to 1/100 of a semitone (called a "cent") in accuracy.[8] The "cent" system, devised in about 1884 by Ellis for use in comparing intervals,[9] is based on the Western tempered tuning system of twelve equidistant intervals (semitones) and was intended for use by those familiar with Western tuning and intervals. The octave is divided into 1,200 equal parts with each of the twelve Western semitones encompassing 100 cents, each whole tone 200 cents, and so on; in a decreasing amount a tempered quarter-tone would comprise 50 cents, an eighth-tone 25 cents, and so on (the cent system applied to Thai tuning will be seen subsequently). Thus the Stroboconn provides a refined measurement of pitch. But because it is bulky

and requires a stable electric current for operation, its use in the field is usually not possible—and unfortunately most of the instruments whose pitch measurements are wanted are in the field. Until a battery-operated electronic tuner becomes available,[10] field workers must rely on a monochord.

In Thailand I used a monochord. As is the custom, to compensate for inconsistencies of hearing and climate, several readings of the pitches of the four main fixed-pitch instruments of the pī phāt ensemble—the two xylophones and two gong-kettle sets—were taken on days ranging from hot and humid, the prevalent condition in Bangkok, to relatively cool and dry. The readings of the pitches of five different groups of instruments were taken: those of the Thai Department of Fine Arts, the Publicity Department, the University of Agriculture, the national television station, and the Phakavali Institute of Dance and Music. When I returned to UCLA in 1960, I tested the monochord against the Stroboconn. It was found that pitches produced on the monochord deviated from those indicated on the Stroboconn by about 10 cents over the entire range of the monochord, not always on the same side of the pitch or consistently from one test to another. Inaccuracies near the extreme ends of the range of the monochord also occurred: between a pitch measured in the upper extremity of the monochord in the area of 450 to 500 cycles per second (the top limit of the monochord) and the next higher pitch, which had to be read an octave lower at the lower extremity of the monochord in the area of 250 to 300 cycles per second, the interval was usually noticeably larger than intervals between pitches measured in the central part of the monochord, and larger than the theoretical equidistant interval should have been. These large intervals were not found to exist in Stroboconn readings made in 1961 of two instruments of the Phakavali Institute which they brought with them when they toured the United States. Otherwise the monochord and Stroboconn readings are comparable. Since the latter are the more dependable, we shall dispense with the monochord readings; two representative sets are, however, included in the master tuning chart in Appendix B for comparative purposes.

Several Western writers have remarked on the tuning ability of the Thai. Parry said: "Their sense of

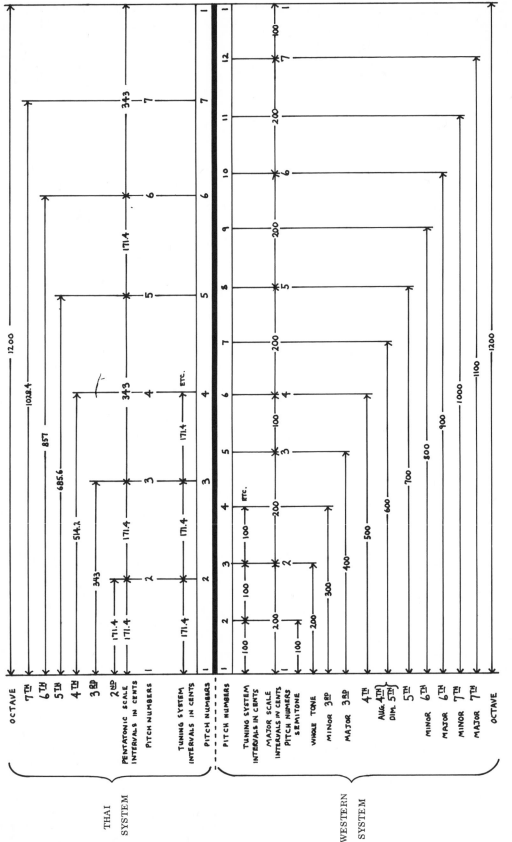

Chart 1. Comparison of Thai and Western tuning systems.

the right relations of the notes of the scale is so highly developed that their musicians can tell by ear directly a note is not true to their singular theory" (1930: 51). Bowring, speaking of women musicians who played for the dance dramas, said their ". . . perception of concord in the notes is as acute as that of an European musician, and they are equally as long in tuning their instruments" (1857: 150). But Ellis stated (previously quoted) that the result of tuning Thai percussion instruments by ear is not always perfect. And Sachs said, even more strongly: "The actual justness of these distances (that is, between the pitches of the Thai tuning system) is of course questionable, since the ear without physical and mathematical help is not capable of correctly dividing an interval" (1943: 132).

The readings I made of pitches on Thai instruments of fixed pitch support the first statements above rather than that of Sachs; they also substantiate statements that Thai tuning idealistically is equidistant and as found on instruments of fixed pitch considered "in tune" is reasonably close to equidistance. Small deviations from the theoretically correct tuning in the Thai system should probably not be attributed to any assumed inability, even impossibility, of obtaining such precise tuning by ear in a system that does not use intervals found in what some Western musicians and musicologists term the "natural scale" derived from the partials of the harmonic overtone series (see note 7). The Western twelve-pitch tuning system is founded more or less on the simpler relationships of the partials in the harmonic overtone series (1:2 representing the octave, 2:3 the fifth, 3:4 the fourth, and so on)—but no matter how "natural" this scale may seem to Westerners, it was Ellis's conclusion after taking the tunings of a variety of non-European instruments that ". . . the Musical Scale is not one, not 'natural,' nor even founded necessarily on the laws of the constitution of musical sound, so beautifully worked out by Helmholtz, but very diverse, very artificial, and very capricious" (Mar. 1885: 526).

The division of the Thai octave into seven equidistant parts results in a set of pitches with a different intervallic structure from any of the seven-pitch modal patterns in either just or tempered Western tuning, and of course very different from the twelve-part equidistant division of the Western

tempered system. If one wishes to compare the two systems, one method is to divide the octave into eighty-four parts (seven pitches of the Thai system times twelve pitches of the Western system); each system can then be shown as a different division of eighty-four, Thai pitches lying one-seventh of eighty-four or twelve units apart and Western pitches lying one-twelfth or seven units apart.

Another method of analyzing the two intervallic structures is with Ellis's cent system previously discussed. Each of the twelve Western semitone intervals is 100 cents; the intervals between the seven Thai pitches are 171.4 cents, about an eighth of a Western whole tone less than that interval (200 cents). The theoretical Thai third is about 343 cents, the Western minor third is 300 cents and the major third 400; the Thai fourth is about 514 cents and the Western fourth 500; the Thai fifth is about 686 cents, the Western fifth 700; and so on. In Chart I the structure of the two systems is shown—the Western major mode/scale with its large intervals, or whole tones, of 200 cents and its small intervals, half-tones or semitones, of 100 cents, and the Thai pentatonic gapped mode/scale with large intervals of 343 cents and small intervals of 171.4 cents. On the top and bottom of the diagram is shown the distance of each pitch in cents from an arbitrary mutual starting point.

It is often said that the pattern of the type of pentatonic scale/mode found in China and Thailand can be represented on the black keys of the piano:

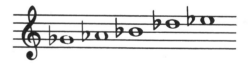

This oversimplification has perhaps done more harm than good, assuming as it does that approximation can be the same as authenticity and completely ignoring the aesthetic factors in the particular tuning of the non-Western system. Chart I shows that the Thai fourth and the Western fourth (that is, the interval between pitches 1 and 4 of the major scale/mode) and the Thai fifth and Western fifth are the intervals in the two systems which are most similar; the Thai fourth of about 514 cents is slightly larger than the Western tempered fourth of 500 cents, and the Thai fifth of about 686 cents is slightly smaller than the Western tempered fifth of 700 cents.

The other pitches and intervals in the two systems do not correspond at all. For this reason it is really impossible to duplicate the true sound of the Thai system in Western pitches.

Let us look now at the correspondence among the "same" pitches in different sets of Thai tunings and different Thai ensembles, first taking the pitch labeled "I" by Ellis. This, the fifth bar from the left end of the xylophone, has 285 cycles per second. The readings taken by Stumpf and his colleagues fifteen years later show the pitch to be a few vibrations higher, 286 to 288 cycles per second, but this is their reading for the *sixth* bar from the left end of the xylophone. Both Ellis and Stumpf are dealing with instruments with twenty-one bars. Instruments do occasionally show a "dislocation" by one or two pitches (bars or gong-kettles), but the extra bar sometimes added to the xylophone is at the top of the range. At any rate, regardless of which bars, the pitches in both Ellis's and Stumpf's readings are practically identical.

The tuning level of the instruments of the Phakavali Institute, I was told, represents an older tuning level that the Institute preferred to retain rather than change to a slightly higher tuning level as some of the other ensembles in Bangkok have been doing. In the pitch area just discussed the average pitch of the Phakavali instruments is about 277 cycles per second, though on some instruments it is as high as 281 or 282. These were monochord readings. The Stroboconn readings show 273 cycles per second for the xylophone and 278 for the gong circle. This pitch, then, is slightly lower than the comparable one in Ellis's and Stumpf's readings.

The monochord readings of the instruments of the Department of Fine Arts show this pitch to be anywhere from 281 to 288 cycles per second, about the same as that of Ellis and Stumpf.

The average of the instruments of the University of Agriculture is 289 cycles per second, while that of the instruments of the Publicity Department is 289.3 and that of the television station's instruments is 288.

I was told that the reason for the higher pitch level, as used by the ensembles other than those of the Phakavali Institute, was to raise the pitch level so that one of the pitches would be the same as one of the Western pitches. If the pitch of about 288-290 cycles per second is used, the pitch next below it in the Thai tuning is about 262 cycles per second, the pitch of middle *c* in Western tuning (actually 261.63 cycles per second, based on A = 440). Though the other pitches of the Thai system of course do not match Western pitches in cycles per second, the desire to have one pitch identical in the two systems may have been the reason for the gradual rise of the pitch level. Since the pitches taken by Ellis in 1885 and Stumpf in 1900 are very close to those of the instruments of the Department of Fine Arts, the Publicity Department, and the television station today, it may be that the pitch level of the Phakavali instruments does represent one in use prior to 1885.

We may say, then, that although there is no standard pitch level in Thailand and therefore no close agreement between corresponding pitches among different ensembles, within one properly tuned ensemble the instruments are closely in tune with one another. The tuning of Thai instruments approaches equidistance closely, although not perfectly on any instrument of fixed pitch. The intervallic structure of the pitches of the ensemble in the Institute of Ethnomusicology at UCLA (which I purchased in Thailand in 1960 and which was tuned for me before it was shipped to the university) is not exactly equidistant; the pitches for the most part lie within an area of about 10 cents above and below the theoretically correct pitch, a total distance of about 20 cents, far greater than the 8 cents allowed by Mantle Hood in his work with the tunings of Javanese gamelan.[11] The few pitches of the ensemble which deviate beyond this distance are not placed according to any pattern, nor is there any pattern to the placement of intervals smaller and larger than the theoretically equidistant one.

Since in Thai music only five of the seven pitches occur as principal pitches in the various modes, producing a widely gapped structure that allows for intervallic areas of a relatively wide range of acceptability, perhaps the need for great precision in tuning is not felt. Otherwise, the "rough and ready" approach to precise tuning could be evidence of (1) decline in the tradition, (2) the limitations of the ear, or (3) a developed aesthetic based on mild clashes as in the technique of *surupan* in the Sundanese area of Java and the "paired" tuning of Balinese instruments.[12] Of these latter possibilities the status of traditional music in Thai culture today compared to what it was until forty years ago, according to the older Thais and the written records, supports the possibility of decline; vocal practice and the playing of stringed instruments by experts is accurate enough to contradict any claim that the hearing ability of the Thai has deteriorated since Bowring and Parry commented on its precision, and that mild clashes in the tuning are a conscious part of the aesthetic has never been claimed, stated, or discussed—theoretically or otherwise—by anyone, including the Thai.

After having studied Thai music for some time—having lived in Bangkok for two and a half years and listened to the music at some length, having played it and examined numerous examples in manuscript—my feeling is that the intention in the tuning system is indeed for equidistance, the need for which grew out of the evolution of the musical practice, but that the intention is often imperfectly realized on the instruments of fixed pitch. The deviation of pitches from a theoretical standard obtains for two reasons: (1) the method of final tuning of the wooden bars of the xylophones and the gong-kettles of the gong-kettle sets is done with wax lumps whose permanence, when the instrument is moved around and used, is not dependable; (2) the pentatonic, gapped modes/scales—basic in the music system—allow a relatively wide area of acceptability of tuning of the individual pitches.

B. MELODY

The main melody in Thai music, as in Western music, may be either motivic or lyrical. A motivic melody is one capable of being separated into smaller, musically valid units that may serve as a basis for later development. A well-known instance from Western music is the first theme of the first movement of Beethoven's *Fifth Symphony,* in example 1.

Example 1.

A lyrical melody is one that is continuously spun out, not easily broken up into unified fragments, and therefore capable of only limited development. The romantic melodies of the nineteenth and twentieth centuries are of the lyrical type. A well-known instance is the melody of Schumann's piano composition *Träumerei,* in example 2.

Thai melodies in the older traditional instrumental compositions are of the motivic variety, as illustrated by the excerpt in example 3.

Example 2.

Example 3. *Rŭang Phlēng Ching Phračhan* (beginning).

Example 4. "Khamēn Sāi Yōk" (3 chan) 8 (*Silpakǫn Magazine*, 2 (May 1958), 70).

(Main melody simplified).

being rare—occurring primarily in *thao* (fill-in) motives (marked thus in example 3; the term will be explained in detail shortly) and in playing techniques idiomatic to the instrument playing the main melody

A comparison of the rhythm of these two examples will show a characteristic difference between the lyric and motivic styles: the lyric style has more rhythmic variety, the dotted rhythms and sustained pitches being typical, while the motivic style uses fewer rhythms, the dotted rhythm as such

(see pp. 49-50) — with sustained pitches rarely occurring.

Lyrical melodies are characteristic of Thai traditional music of the more recent sepha style, a well-known instance of which is "Khamēn Sāi Yōk"; the beginning is shown in example 4.

Each two measures in example 3 can be considered a motive; these motives are the "melodic species" of Thai music. Each motive occurs in many other compositions, in the combinations here or in different combinations of motives. These motives or melodic species will be discussed in further detail in Chapter IV on mode.

A few other generalities concerning Thai melodies may be observed: they tend to be conjunct and based on a pentatonic pattern indicated by the use of the numbers 123 56. Rarely does the melodic line within a motive leap more than two steps from any given step; this means that rarely does a motive

adjoining in the pentatonic pattern and therefore are not leaps). Leaps of more than a fourth occur in two contexts. First, they may appear as parts of special motives in lyrical melodies, such as in the excerpt from "Lāo Sīang Thīan" in example 5.

Usually, however, the large interval is a result of shifting part of the melody, which would otherwise be conjunct, to a different register or octave, either because of the limited range of the instrument playing the melody or perhaps to avoid having the melody cover too wide a range. The tessitura is the governing principle here. The beginning of the first section of a composition is often in the lower range

Example 5. "Lāo Sīang Thīan"(Thao) (*Silpakǭn Magazine,*
        4 (Jan. 1961) , 82).

3 chan.

contain a leap of more than the interval of a Thai fourth (about 514 cents, heard by the average Western ear as a tempered fourth of 500 cents), which occurs between pitches 2 and 5, 3 and 6, 5 and 1, and 6 and 2 of the pentatonic mode. The leap of a Thai third (about 343 cents) between pitches 1 and 3, 3 and 5, and 6 and 1 is common (it is actually a leap only between pitches 1 and 3; pitches 3-5 and 6-1 are

of the instrument, while the beginning of the second section, for contrast, is often in a high tessitura. The second section of "Khamēn Sāi Yǒk," for instance, begins as in example 6.

The part marked in the example with a bracket *could* lie an octave lower on most of the instruments, in which case the melody would be conjunct as in example 7.

Example 6.

Example 7.

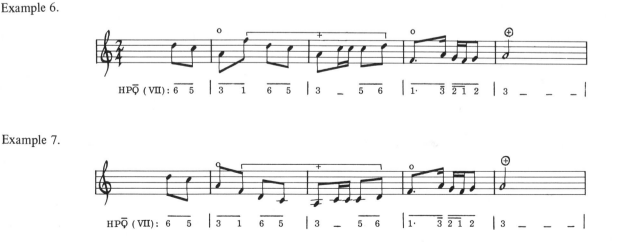

The excerpts from melodies quoted thus far are clearly pentatonic, as the cipher rendition of the melody beneath the example shows. Pitches 4 and 7 function as passing tones when they in no way suggest a change in the relative position of pitch 1, or, if we may use the Western term here for the moment, "modulation." As in Western music, these pitches

Two excerpts from "Khamēn Sāi Yōk" (ex. 8) give an instance of pitch 7 as an unaccented (*) and semi-accented (†) passing tone; the motives, one from each of the two sections, are similar in outline.

An excerpt from "Phrarām Dōēn Dong" (ex. 9), part of one of the long suites *(rŷang),* provides examples of pitch 4 as an accented (*) and semi-accented (†) passing tone.

Example 8. "Khamēn Sāi Yōk."

Section 1:

Section 2:

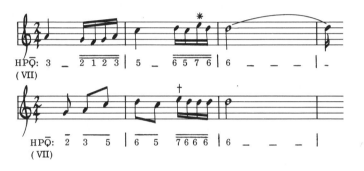

may be termed accented or unaccented passing tones accordingly as they fall on an emphasized beat of the metric structure or not. When they occur on the emphasized part of an unaccented beat, pitches 4 and 7 may be termed semi-accented passing tones.

In Thai melodies in the simple pentatonic style passing tones are rare, pitches 4 and 7 occurring for the most part in the process of "modulation," which will be dealt with subsequently. In the *mǭn*[13] or hexatonic-heptatonic style pitch 4 or 7 (sometimes

Example 9. "Phrarām Dōēn Dong."

Section 3:

both) is prominently and consistently used, particularly in running passages. Whether the pitch of the passing tone should be labeled 4 or 7 depends on which pitch level is chosen for the passage. Usually six pitches, forming a hexatonic mode, are used for compositions in mǭn style. The excerpt from the composition "Tǭi Rūp" in example 10 illustrates the

mǭn style; it may be analyzed in two different pitch levels, as the two sets of cipher notations show.

The use of all seven pitches—that is, a heptatonic scale (or mode)—in one composition, without "modulation" occurring, is rare; example 11 is an illustration.

Example 10. "Tǭi Rūp" (ms. coll. no. 359).

3 chan.

Section 3 (starting about halfway through, to the end).

(N. B. On this and successive examples the ching strokes will be indicated only above the first line.)

Example 11. "Khaēk Tȯi Mǭ" (Thao) (*Silpakǫn Magazine,*
    4 (Nov. 1960) , 49).

3 chan (main melody simplified)

Section 1:

LK (IV):   2   —   3   —   4   — | 5 6 5 4̄3̄ | 2̄1̄2 3 4   5 | 3

HPǬ (VII): 6   —   7   —   1   — | 2 3 2 1 7 | 6 5 6 7 1 2 | 7

—   —   — | ₋2̄1̄2 3   4 | 5 2̄2̄ 2   3 4 | 5 6̄5̄4̄ 5 6 7̄5̄ | 6

—   —   — | ₋6 5 6 7   1 | 2 6 6 6   7 1 | 2 3 2 1 2 3 4 2 | 3

—   —   — | 1   2   — | 4   — ₋5̄4̄3̄ | 2̄3̄2̄ 1 4   5 | 6

—   —   — | 5   6   — | 1   — ₋2 1 7 | 6 7 6 5 1   2 | 3

—   ₋2̄1̄6̄ | 5   — ₋1̄6̄5̄ | 4   — ₋5̄4̄3̄ | 2̄1̄2̄3̄ 4   3 | 2   —

      6 5 3 | 2   — ₋5 3 2 | 1   — ₋2 1 7 | 6 5 6 7 1   7 | 6   —

Again, it might be thought that the melody could be analyzed in either of two pitch levels, as the cipher notations below the example indicate, but the upper set of ciphers in the pitch level marked LK, comparable to the key of C in Western notation, indicates the proper level. The reason is that if the melody were analyzed as the line marked HPǬ, comparable to the key of F in Western notation, the first line would end on pitch 7. This is one of the principal structural points, and pitch 7 would not occur on this beat in the Thai musical system unless a "modulation" were taking place; no "modulation" is indicated here.

In examples 3, 9, and 10, part of a line is bracketed and labeled "thao." This set of letters, or this sound, can be several different words in Thai and can thus have several different meanings.[14] For the word used here the literal meaning is "equal to" or "equivalent." As a musical term it refers to certain standard patterns—usually covering a span of one, two, or four measures—used to fill in a part of the melodic line that would otherwise be a sustained pitch. It is not idiomatic of most Thai instrumental styles to sustain pitches except in the lyric melodies of the recent, more songlike styles. The "melodic" thao is felt to give a better effect than a simple reiteration of the pitch. Sustained pitches that are rolled or trilled (the *krǭ* technique, explained in the next chapter in the section on the *ranāt ēk),* are not ordinarily of two measures length; thus the thao and the *krǭ* technique are not interchangeable. The most frequent types of thao are the following:

(1) Circling around the main pitch with reiterated pitches, as illustrated in examples 3, 9, and 10. This may occur on any main pitch of the composition. Some other instances are given in example 12.

Example 12.

(a) on pitch 2:

    (1) on "F" level:

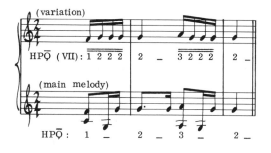

    (2) on "C" level:

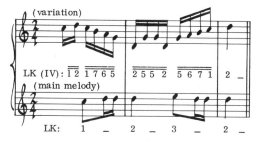

(b) on pitch 1, "C" level;
   or pitch 5, "F" level:

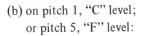

    (2) A melodic fragment, as in example 13.

Example 13.

This last example is idiomatic for the gong circle, which usually plays in octaves, broken octaves, or other intervals such as the fourth and second; the instruments playing the faster variations, such as the xylophone, use the style shown in (1).

Although there are names for the pitches which could be used as names for the pitch levels ("tonics") of compositions, after having become familiar with the main principles of Thai music it seemed to me that several factors were from a theoretical standpoint against this.

First, pitch "klāng hāep" (D) is only rarely, if ever, used as a home level or tonic. The fifth above—"klāng" (A)—is used only in the rather special case of the pī chawā with the khrụ̄ang sāi

frequency, as the instrument is not a member of any of the three main ensembles. Four pitch levels remain, by far the most used: F, G, B♭, and C. "Phīang ǭ" is used as a name for two of these levels, F and B♭. Tramote lists the pitches in ascending order, with the result that F is called the "below" position of phīang ǭ and B♭ is called the "above" position. But because of the way the pitches lie on the melodic percussion instruments and the octave technique used in playing, the B♭ a fifth below phīang ǭ lang is the usual location of pitch 1 as the finalis on that level (ex. 14).

The levels of nai (G) and kruat (C), also a fifth apart, are related in that they are levels for different sizes of pī.

Example 14.

(a) ranāt ēk range:

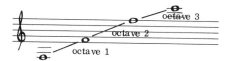

(b) phīang ǭ lāng level, as played by the ranāt ēk (trills, that is, the krǭ technique, are not indicated):

"Khamēn Sai Yōk" from the beginning.

HPǬ (VII):   5 | 3· 5 3 2 1 | 2· 3 2 1 6 | 1 6 2 1 1 1 | 1

(c) phīang ǭ bon level, as played by the ranāt ēk:

"Lāo Kham Hǭm," excerpt.

LPǬ (III): 1 _ _ 2̄   3 _ 5   _   2̄ 3 2̄ 1̄   5 _ _ _

ensemble, an instrumentation practically if not entirely obsolete. The pī chawā level itself—E—cannot be said to be used with any

Second, the tuning patterns for the stringed instruments emphasize these fifth relationships and use the names "phīang ǭ" and "kruat," although the stringed instruments are not included in the ensembles using the pī. If, however, the strings played on the kruat level (C), they would be tuned to kruat. This tuning, for the *sǭ duang* (the higher-pitched of the two bowed lutes used in the string ensembles), refers to two pitches a fifth apart, the higher about 545 cycles per second and the lower about 370:

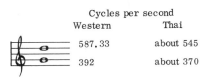

In reality the Thai pitches are closer to the Western C# = (554.37 cycles per second) and F# = (369.99 cycles per second). In notation this would involve the use of many accidentals — sharps, flats, natural signs, and so on; the notators apparently chose to use a simpler method instead of overburdening the notation with many marks and symbols.

The two strings of the *sǭ ū* (the lower-pitched two-stringed bowed lute) are tuned a fifth lower:

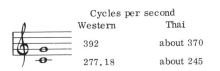

Because the G (nai) level is the home level for the pī phāt — most of the rǖang (suites), the oldest compositions in the repertoire, are played at this level—it would seem basic to the system. The pī phāt also plays many compositions at the kruat (C) level, even though the pī nai has replaced the original pī nǭk. Because of this, because the tuning for the strings is called "kruat" (the name of the "C" pitch), and because the two pitches (kruat and nai) are a fifth apart, I decided to refer to them as "high kruat" (abbreviated HK), for the G (nai) level, and "low kruat" (abbreviated LK), for the low level.

Similarly with the phīang ǭ levels: because the tessitura of compositions played in phīang ǭ bon is actually lower than in phīang ǭ lāng, I decided to call the upper level (phīang ǭ lāng) "high phīang ǭ" (abbreviated HPǬ), and the level a fifth lower (phīang ǭ bon), "low phīang ǭ" (abbreviated LPǬ).

The pitch represented by G on the Western staff has been chosen, then, as the focal, beginning point of the system of pitch or tuning levels, and the other pitches have been numbered accordingly. In referring to pitch (tuning) levels, Roman numerals and the words "pitch level" are used. When referring to pitches in a given pentatonic mode[15] at whatever pitch level of the tuning system they may lie, the word "pitch" along with an Arabic numeral is used. The notation below, for example, represents a pentatonic mode on pitch level I. The numbers of the pitches of the tuning system and the pentatonic mode, in this instance, coincide.

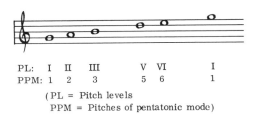

The following notation represents a pentatonic mode on pitch level IV; the two sets of numbers do not coincide.

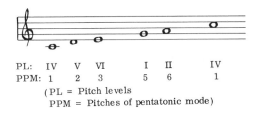

When the khlui (bamboo flute) is used, the compositions are played at the F or B♭ level and the two-stringed instruments are tuned accordingly, represented in notation as:

Numbers of the tuning system, that is, pitch levels		Cycles per second	
		Western	Thai
IV		523.25	about 493
VII	sǭ ū	349.23	about 335
III		233.08	about 225

In the process of "modulation" pentatonic modes on other pitch levels, which have no specific names, are occasionally used. When this occurs, the pitch level itself is referred to. For example, in conjunction with high kruat (HK) a mode on pitch level V, a fifth above, is sometimes used and in conjunction with low phīang ǭ (LPǬ) pitch level VI, a fifth below, is sometimes used.

The same Thai composition may be played at different pitch levels. This factor of transposability, depending on which wind instrument is used or which ensemble plays the composition, seems one of the most decisive arguments supporting the claim for equidistant tuning in the Thai system. If the tuning were not equidistant, playing the composition at one pitch level would give a set of intervallic relationships that might be equated with a certain mood, while playing the composition at a different pitch level would give another set of relationships and a different mood, perhaps something like playing a Western composition in C major or d minor. However, to my knowledge such a situation does not obtain in Thai music; the composition at whatever level played is considered to be the same essential composition with the same intervallic relationships between the pitches of the mode, the only difference being its tessitura, that is, whether the range of the melody lies high or low in relation to a particular human voice or range of an instrument.[16]

Some compositions, such as those in the rǖang (suites), as was mentioned, are played traditionally by only one ensemble—in the case of the suites, by the pī phāt ensemble whose home pitch level is pitch I of the tuning system, called here "high kruat." This does not mean, however, that among these compositions pitch levels other than the high kruat level are not used in sections of "modulation"; indeed, such a practice is common. But the suites, for instance, which contain compositions in all three tempos (to be explained presently), with the exception of one special suite, all conclude with the same "farewell" composition on the home or high kruat level (I). This composition is discussed in detail in Chapter V.

The more recent compositions in the Thao (see note 14) or variation form, as well as other types of compositions, can be played by any ensemble, theoretically at least. (Compositions are often considered to be most appropriate for a specific ensemble, played at a specific level.) If played by the pi phat, the tuning and pitch level at which the composition is played will be one of the kruat levels;

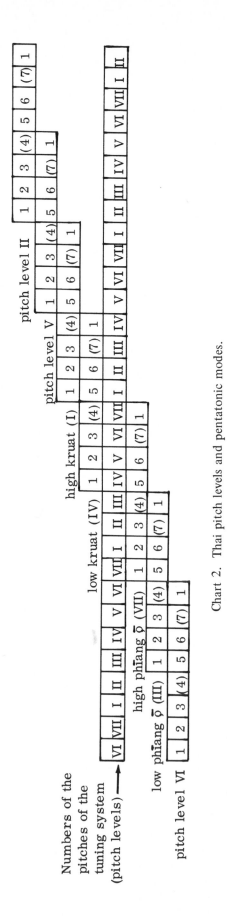

Chart 2. Thai pitch levels and pentatonic modes.

if played by either ensemble using the khlui and stringed instruments, the same composition will be on the corresponding phīang ǭ level, that is, one step lower.

Generally the pitch levels other than the four main ones occur only in sections of contrasting phrases or in "modulation" sections, not as home levels for an entire composition. Because of the equidistant tuning, the pī and khlui can of course play at any pitch level. Hence the use of pitch levels other than the two kruat levels are frequently found in the suites, many of which contain very long compositions in which contrast is obtained by the use of these other related pitch levels. In the Thao compositions—which are, in comparison to many of the compositions in the suites, much shorter—"modulation" is less used; contrast is obtained in these compositions by other means.

Movement away from one pitch level ("modulation") is usually to one a fifth above or below. From high kruat (pitch level I), for example, "modulation" will occasionally ascend to pitch level V or, more usually, descend to low kruat (pitch level IV). Occasionally a melody "modulates" to a pitch level two fifths above or below the original level by skipping the first fifth—for example, high kruat (I) to high phīang ǭ (VII). The melody would normally "modulate" to pitch level IV and then to the fifth below that, pitch level VII. The result of this elision is

to identify the pitches are shown in chart 2. It can be seen from this diagram that a pitch in the Thai tuning system may function in many ways according to its relation to other pitches in a given composition, just as in Western music. This relationship of pitches one to another and their function in "modulation" will be discussed in detail in the chapter on mode.

C. METER, RHYTHM, AND TEMPO

Meter is always duple in Thai traditional music whenever a steady tempo is observed, and it has become customary to notate it in Western notation with a 2/4 time signature regardless of the tempo of the composition. There was at least one recent experiment using triple meter in a type of Thai "operatic" style, but it did not succeed in becoming permanently established.[17]

As for rhythms, typical patterns can be seen in the examples presented throughout this book. Great complexity of rhythm in the main melody is not characteristic of Thai instrumental music; simple, straightforward, nonsyncopated divisions of the main beats is the rule, with occasional use of a dotted rhythm. Syncopation in the main melody is rare and when used is elementary, as in the following excerpt in example 15 from the composition "Sōm Sǒng Sāeng".

Example 15. "Sōm Sǒng Sāeng" (*Silpakǒn Magazine,* 2 (Nov. 1958) , 50).

3 chan.

Section 1:

LK (IV):   5   6   1   _   3   _2 1 2   3   5   6̄ 1 5   6

a conjunct or diatonic movement of the "modulation."

The various positions of pentatonic modes in relation to the tuning system and the numbers used

The most usual occurrence of syncopation in the main melodic line played by the large gong circle results from an idiomatic style of playing called *sabat,* meaning "to flutter, to shake off" (ex. 16).

Example 16.

(a)

Simple style:

Idiomatic style;
"Sabat":

(b)

Simple style:

Idiomatic style;
"Sabat":

Syncopation often occurs in the variation parts, as will be shown in the next chapter in the discussions of the individual instruments. Syncopations are sometimes the result of the interplay, in certain parts of the Thao form, of the ranāt ēk and the rest of the ensemble, as illustrated in the excerpt in example 17 from the composition *Sāo Sǭt Wāen"*.

Example 17. "Sāo Sǭt Wāen" (*Silpakǭn Magazine*, 6 (Nov. 1962) , 107).

3 chan.

Section 1:

Ensemble:

Ranāt ēk:

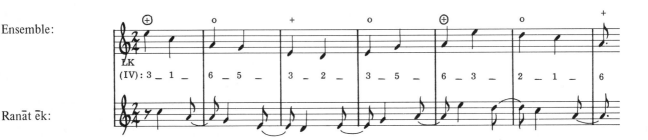

One cannot really speak of different tempos, in the Western sense, in Thai music, although two old terms would seem to indicate tempo: *phlēng chā,* literally, "slow songs," and *phlēng reo,* literally, "fast songs." Rather than tempo distinctions, Thai traditional music uses basically three different rhythmic-percussive patterns, in all of which the durational value of the quarter-note (in Western notation) remains essentially the same. A *feeling* of an increase in tempo is obtained by an increase of activity with the hand cymbals (ching) and the drum.

The term "slow tempo" might be applied to the *prop kai* pattern in which one ching stroke occurs to each measure of Western notation. Two types of ching stroke are used (as will be discussed further in the next chapter on the instruments): undamped, for which the symbol "o" is used, considered an unaccented beat or stroke; and damped, for which the symbol "+" is used, considered an accented stroke. These two types of sounds are alternated. In the prop kai pattern the fourth stroke—the second + stroke—is further reinforced with a gong stroke. The ching-gong sound is notated as ⊕. The prop kai pattern, then, is:

♩ = 50-60 $\frac{2}{4}$ |o |+ |o |⊕

This pattern is used in the first or "slow" division of the old suites (rʉ̄ang) and in the extended version *(sām chan)* of the Thao form (discussed in detail in Chapter V).

The pattern in which two ching strokes are sounded per measure is called sǭng mai, literally, "two beats":

♩ = 50-60 2/4   o |⊕   o |⊕   etc.

The gong sounds on every + beat. This pattern is used in the middle division of the suites and for the middle version of the Thao (sǭng chan).

When the sǭng mai pattern is doubled, it is called "phlēng reo":

♩ = 50-60 2/4   o ⊕ o |⊕   o ⊕ o |⊕   etc.

This pattern is used in the final phlēng reo or "fast" division of the suites and for the short version of the Thao (chan dio). [18]

In the Western pattern of metric emphasis with the strong pulse on the first beat of a measure, the three patterns for the ching appear as in chart 3.

In this method of notation the ching pattern for prop kai begins with an unaccented stroke, while the other two ching patterns begin with accented strokes. The reason for this is that, as indicated below in the last measure, each division ends with an accented ching stroke; therefore, according to this method of notation, the pattern for the next "faster" pattern must be introduced in the final measure of the preceding pattern (chart 4).

These patterns are made much clearer and become more organized and systematic if notated in the pattern of emphasis found in Southeast Asian music with the emphasis on the final beat of the group of pulses or the phrase (chart 5). [19]

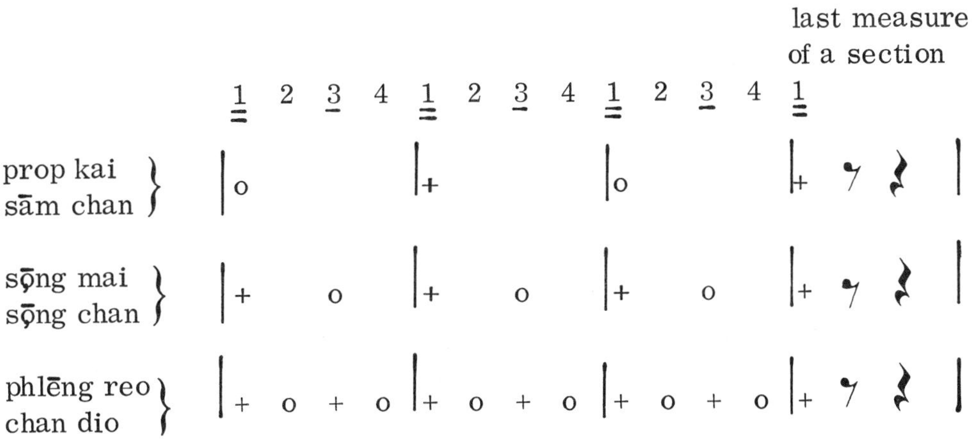

Chart 3. The three basic ching patterns; notated in Western style.

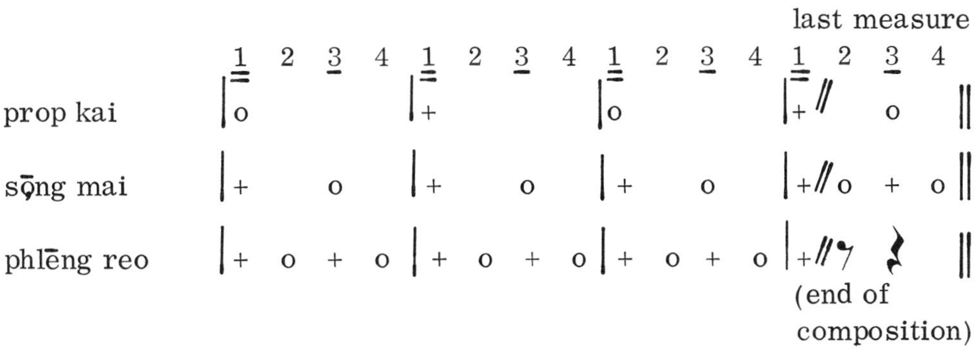

Chart 4. Ching patterns, with beginning of the following pattern.

last measure

1	2	3	4	1	2	3	4	1	2	3	4	1	2	3	4

prop kai } sām chan } | o | + | o | + ||

sǫng mai } sǫng chan } | o   + | o   + | o   + | o   + ||

phlēng reo } chan dio } | o + o + | o + o + | o + o + | o + o + ||

Chart 5. Ching patterns, notated in Southeast Asian style.

The cipher notations for the string parts made by Thai musicians are done in this way, as is illustrated in the discussion of the stringed instruments in the next chapter, further substantiating this system of emphasis. [20]

The three patterns (or "tempos") are illustrated briefly in example 18 with a typical melodic phrase from the composition "Khāek Sai" as it appears in each pattern and version. The melody is notated in Western style with the ching patterns above the staff and cipher notation beneath. The same phrase is found in both the original version in the rụ̄ang and the sǫng chan division of the Thao; it is accompanied in the original by the prop kai pattern and in the Thao by the sǫng mai pattern. This may be the reason that only two general terms exist for tempo: both prop kai and sǫng mai are perhaps considered as "phlēng chā"—that is, "slow."

The discussion of ching patterns makes it pertinent here to explain something of the notation used in this study. In order to retain the essential structure of emphasis in Thai music, yet present examples of the music in a form as easily read as possible by the Westerner, examples are given in the following format: the Western measure is retained in both the staff and cipher notations, but the four-measure, double-motive unit of Thai music (called in this study a "phrase-unit"; discussed in detail in Chapter IV) is retained in the way the lines of staff notation are printed. Thus a line of music will usually begin on beat two or three of the Western measure, as an anacrusis or "pick-up" phrase in Western style, and will end on beat one of a Western measure on an accented ching-gong stroke (⊕) in Thai style. In addition, the cipher notation will often be simplified to indicate only the main pitches, omitting decorative and/or nonessential pitches. This arrangement can be seen in example 19, the beginning of a section with the prop kai pattern.

Example 18. "Khāek Sai."

(a) sām chan (in Thao):

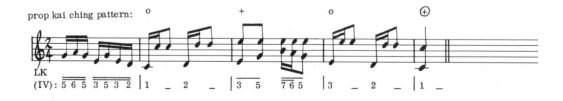

Example 18 (continued).

(b) sǭng chan (Thao) and original (Rῡang 12):

prop kai pattern
in the rῡang:

sǭng mai pattern
in the Thao:

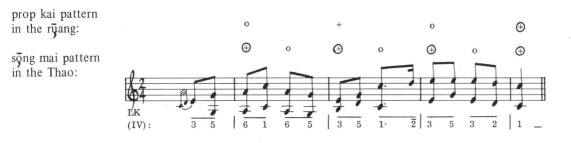

LK
(IV):   3   5 | 6   1   6   5 | 3   5   1·   2̄| 3   5   3   2 | 1   _

(c) chan dio (Thao):

phlēng reo
pattern:

LK
(IV): 2̄ 3̄ 5̄ 6̄ 5̄ 6̄ 1̄ | 5   5   1·   2̄| 3   5   3   2 | 1   _

Example 19.

LK (IV):   6   _ | 1   _   2   _ | 1   _   6̄ 1̄ | 2̄ 1̄   2   _ | 1

5̄ 1·   2̄| 3   6̄ 5̄ 3   2 | 1·   3̄ 2̄ 3̄ 1̄ 2̄ | 6̄ 1̄ 6̄ 2̄ 1̄ 2̄ 6̄ 1̄ | 5̄

Thai ensemble music is always in a definite, regular pulse except for one important rubato style called *rua*, which is used between longer divisions in a regular pulse in some of the rῡang, some ceremonial suites, and theater music. When the three divisions (i.e., the three metrical patterns) are used in a suite, an acceleration of the pulse occurs near the end of a division, heightening the tension, which is released at the change to a new ching pattern. At the end of the last part of a phlēng reo and at the end of the coda following a chan dio division of a Thao, the acceleration builds gradually to the last ching-gong stroke ( ). At the end of a composition in only a slow tempo, such as one in only sām chan, a slight ritardando is characteristic of the style.

Thai music does not make use of dynamics except in solos, and even in solos dynamic changes are much less used than in Western style. Thai instruments are not capable of a wide range in dynamics, and ensemble music is played from beginning to end without any organized dynamic changes. The string ensemble, which has no melodic percussion instruments, is softer in volume than the other two ensembles, which do include such instruments, the volume of sound depending on the size of the ensemble and the distance of the listener from it. Subjectively, the volume of sound of the string ensemble is generally mezzo-piano to mezzo-forte. In the percussion ensembles the general volume will be louder, ranging from mezzo-forte to forte.

Chapter III

Instruments, Their Idiomatic Characteristics, and Ensembles

Dhanit Yupho[1] says that from earliest times to the present the Thai have adopted musical instruments from neighboring cultures and adapted them, and have devised and developed instruments of their own (1960: 3). Because of the paucity of evidence, just when these events took place cannot in most instances be stated conclusively. Instruments used in the traditional high-art music will be described in detail in the section on instruments in this chapter; some instruments not used in the traditional music will be touched on in the following section on ensembles. For a complete account of all Thai instruments, Yupho (1960) may be consulted.

The oldest musical instruments used by the Thai were given simple, one-syllable names of onomatopoeic derivation. Characteristic examples of these are the following:

krɔ̨̄ (small "slit drum" made from a piece of bamboo with nodes at each end)

krōng (large bamboo "slit drum," several nodes in length)

krap (rhythm sticks made from pieces of bamboo, cut and polished)

ching (small metal hand cymbals)

chāp (medium-sized metal hand cymbals)

khlui (vertical bamboo flute with pegged mouthpiece)

phia (stick zither with four strings, the stick attached to a half-gourd chest resonator, which is placed against the bare chest of the performer during performance; see fig. 82)

sɔ̄ (generic term for bowed stringed instruments)

khɔ̨ng (gong or gong-kettle)

klɔ̨̄ng (drum)

From these early simple instruments more complex ones were evolved. The names given to these were altered or combined words, such as:

ranāt (xylophone—set of wooden keys on a stand)

khɔ̨̄ng wong (set or circle of gong-kettles on a stand)

A few instruments were named according to the particular ensemble in which they were used:

khɔ̨ng rabēng (gong used for the rabēng, an ancient type of vocal entertainment music)

klɔ̨ng chātrī (drum used in the southern theater)

Some Thai instruments have names describing their shape or some other characteristic feature:

čhakhe ("crocodile," a three-stringed floor zither)

sɔ̄ sām sāi (bowed, three-stringed instrument)

klɔ̨ng yāo (long drum)

sɔ̨ng nā (literally, "two-faces," that is, a two-headed drum)

A few Thai instruments whose foreign origins are well known are named according to the area from which they originally came:

klǭng khāek	("foreign" or Indian drum)
klǭng malāyū	(Malayan drum)
klǭng marigan	(American bass drum)
pī chawā	(Javanese "oboe")

For other instruments the names in the language of the culture from which they were borrowed were retained:

phīn	(stick zither with one string and a half-gourd resonator; India, from Sanskrit; see fig. 81)
sang	(end-blown shell trumpet; India. Some examples of this can be seen in the carvings at Angkor, for example in fig. 9 at the left)
pī chanai	(double-reed instrument, body with conical bore, about a foot long or less; India)
bandǫ	(small hourglass drum; India; Pali: "panawa")
krajappī	(long-necked plucked lute; origin unknown, name from Sanskrit)
thǭn	(goblet or vase drum; India, from "dhol"?)

Instruments will be classified in the following general groups: melodic percussion, rhythmic percussion, woodwinds, and strings. Specific techniques of each instrument, the characteristics of the line of music it plays, and its function in ensembles will be dealt with in some detail.

A. MELODIC PERCUSSION

1. Sets of Gong-kettles

a. Khǭng wong yai

The main melody or nuclear theme of a composition is played on a set of sixteen gong-kettles placed horizontally, left to right, in order of pitch from low to high, in a rattan frame rack in the shape of an almost complete circle which rests on the floor—the name "khǭng wong yai" means "large circle of gongs" (figs. 31, 32; 102–105, 108–111.)[2] The frame of an average instrument measures about four feet from side to side and about forty inches from front to back. The player sits in the open space inside the framework and plays on the bosses (knobs) of the gong-kettles with two mallets made of thick, disc-shaped pieces of water-buffalo hide into which handles are inserted.

The Thai adopted this instrument set from the Khmer at Angkor, the eight or nine gong-kettles of the Khmer set having been placed on a rack in the shape of a gently curved arc (figs. 3, 3c, 5, 6, 7, 15a and b). An eight-kettle set of the Khmer probably represented a set of seven pitches and the higher octave of the first kettle,[3] since a tonal supply based on the division of the octave into seven pitches is used on instruments of fixed pitch by the Thai as well as the Javanese (*pélog* tuning system), the Burmese, the present-day Cambodians, and the Laotians. Seven-pitch tuning systems have also been known in China.

Relative to this matter of the tuning system, Daniélou, in a discussion of the heptatonic tuning system found in this area, points out that it was the harp that was earlier the instrument of fixed tuning both in India and in Southeast Asia (1957: 4). The harp is prominent among the carvings of musical ensembles at Angkor (figs. 10–13). No reference to harps having been used by the Thai has been found. When I was in Bangkok in 1960, a painting on cloth in which a harp is prominently displayed was dug up at a temple site in northern Thailand (fig. 28). It had

Figure 28. Tapestry with harp, unearthed in Thailand.

been folded and placed in a clay jar probably sometime in the fifteenth, or possibly the sixteenth, century. This was at least a hundred years after Ayuthaya was founded. Since there is no record of harps in early Thai music, this tapestry was probably brought to the area from India or possibly Angkor. In India the harp was replaced with lute-type stringed instruments. Daniélou believes it was replaced in Indochina with the set of gong-kettles (loc. cit.).

An early Thai model of the gong-kettle set, also with eight kettles but on a straight rack *(khǭng rāng),* is on display in the National Museum in Bangkok (fig. 29). Its date is uncertain. This early instrument with its narrow range was subsequently expanded to a sixteen-kettle set with a range of just over two octaves, which necessitated enlarging the frame. But rather than a straight rack as has been retained for the Balinese trompong and modern réong, which have fewer gong-kettles (figs. 17, 18), the Thai model was made in the form of a nearly complete circle so that the kettles would be within easy reach of the player;

that is, the rack was "bent" around the player. Old models of the Javanese bonang were also in the shape of an arc,[4] but the contemporary model is a rectangular rack on which the gong-kettles are placed in two rows (fig. 16). The gong-kettles of the Javanese models are unattached, being set on the rope supports, while those of the Balinese and Thai models are fastened permanently in place with thongs that pass through holes in the sides of the kettles and are wound around the framework. The kettles are given their final tuning by a mixture of beeswax and lead shavings melted into the underside of the bosses (fig. 33). The Burmese also have a set of gong-kettles similar to the Thai model (Sachs 1940: 236, 241; 1917, pl. 2; Scott 1924: 232. See also fig. 116 in this book.)

The gong-kettle instrument set in its contemporary form was apparently well established by the end of the Ayuthaya period (middle of the eighteenth century). A bookcase in the National Museum at Bangkok dating from this time (one that

Figure 29. Khǭng rāng, early form of the Thai gong-circle in the form of a straight rack. This instrument is in the National Museum, Bangkok.

Figure 30. Carving of a gong-circle on a bookcase, from the Ayuthaya period. As with the presentation of the set of gong-kettles in the Khmer sculpture, the gong-circle here is also shown tipped toward the viewer; its actual playing position is flat on the floor. At the extreme left and right are players of wind instruments, and at the right are players of plucked-lute type instruments. The remaining figures are probably singers and time-keepers. The bookcase is in the National Museum, Bangkok.

Figure 31. The contemporary Thai model of the gong-circle in its playing position on the floor.

Figure 32. The gong-circle being played in the Institute of Ethnomusicology, UCLA, Los Angeles, California. In the rear can be seen some of the metallophones of the Balinese gamelan belonging to the Institute.

escaped the destruction in 1767) has carved on it an ensemble showing the gong-circle prominently placed (fig. 30). A manuscript book dated *circa* 1730 (also in the National Museum) contains an illustration of a small percussion ensemble that includes the instrument (see frontispiece). The possible origin of the sets of gong-kettles was discussed in Chapter I. Although the cultures of Indochina were Indianized, Daniélou (1957: 24) says that metal instruments of this type did not exist in India. He adds, however, that instruments conceived on the same principle—sets of tuned water bowls and drums—were known very early. He concludes that

Figure 33. The inside of a gong-kettle from a set of gong-kettles showing the tuning wax in the boss.

although India appears to have known several instruments of this genre, the Khmer may well have had the idea of constructing one with small gongs, since sets of gongs have always played an important role among the peoples of Indochina. Recent researches of Mantle Hood (1970) indicate that the sets of gong-kettles were developed by the Javanese from sets of metal drums.[5]

The sixteen gong-kettles of the khɔ̌ng wong yai cover a range of two octaves and two pitches. The general pitch level and range, as represented on the Western staff, are as follows:

(N.B. This represents the actual pitch; in notation the part is transposed down an octave.)

The typical method of playing the main melody on the khǭng wong yai is in octaves and broken octaves, as in example 20.

Example 20.

HK
(I): 1 _ 2 _ | 3̄ 5̄ 6̄ 5̄ | 3 _ 2 _ | 1 _

In passages that are too fast to render efficiently in octaves, the single line of melody is divided between the two hands as in example 21.

Example 21.

right
hand

left hand
HPǬ
(VII): 3̄ 5̄ 3̄ | 2 _ 1 _ | 6/2 6̄ 5̄ 3̄ 5̄ 3̄ 2̄ | 1 IV

Certain idiomatic passages include intervals of less than an octave, the fourth and second being particularly prominent (ex. 22).

Example 22.

LK (IV): 2̄ 3 5 | 6 6 3̄ 6̄ 5̄ | 6 2 1 _ | 2

Another idiomatic way of handling certain conjunct passages is to prolong a pitch and then treat the following two pitches as a quick embellishment of the next following pitch, a technique called sabat (ex. 23).

Example 23.

Simple method:

Idiomatic method; "sabat":

LK (IV): 7̄ 6 5 | 4̄ 3̄ 2 3 4̄ 5̄ | 6

LK (IV): 7̄ 6 5 | _ 4̄ 3̄ 2 3· 4̄ 5̄ | 6

In passages near the top range of the khǫng wong yai, where the right hand cannot complete the octave it continues to play on one of the top kettles as an ostinato until the melody descends to the point where it is again an octave or more below the top limit of the instrument (ex. 24).

every detail except smaller (figs. 84, 85; 104, 105; 109—111). This smaller model measures about forty-four inches from side to side and about thirty-eight inches from front to back. There are usually eighteen gong-kettles, of which the two to the far left are "dummies,"[6] being included only because the gong-kettles on this instrument are rather small

Example 24.

Often in the fast sections of the rǖang (suites) rapid, intricate passages occur, as in example 25.

and more than sixteen are required to fill a framework large enough to give the player adequate space in which to sit and move. The disc-shaped hide hammers are a little smaller than those for the larger

Example 25.

b. Khǫng wong lek

Yupho states that the khǫng wong lek ("small circle of gongs") was devised during the reign of King Rama III (1824—1851) by Thai musicians who decided to make an instrument like the khǫng wong yai, exact in

model. The range of the instrument is the same as that of the larger size; the pitch level is one octave higher.

This instrument, generally used only in medium-sized and large ensembles (small ensembles usually use only the khǫng wong yai), plays a rapid variation of the melody in passages of practically constant note values with the addition of a few idiomatic embellishments. One of these—also called "sabat" (see also ex. 23)—consists of replacing a single pitch, often the fourth of a group of four pitches, with two pitches, the first of which is the reiteration of the third pitch and the second its upper neighbor leading to the next pitch above it, as in example 26.

Example 26.

(main melody)

HK

(I):3 _ 1 2 | 3 5 6 5 | 3 _ 2 _ | 7 _ (6) 7 2 |

Figure 34. The khǭng wong lek, a small set of gong-kettles.

(N.B. For the meaning of the accidentals above the staff, see the explanation in note 19 to Chapter I, pp. 224-225.)

Another idiomatic embellishment (ex. 27) is the anticipatory reiteration of a pitch (a technique also much used on the ranāt thum), also called "sabat."

Example 27.

Notated:

Played:

c. Khǭng (wong) klāng

A medium-sized model of the gong-kettle type of instrument, called the *khǭng (wong) klāng* ("medium-sized circle of gongs"), or sometimes a smaller model of the regular instruments, is usually used in the string ensembles. The smaller volume of sound produced by these reduced models is considered to blend better with the volume of sound produced by the strings. The style of part of this instrument is similar to the two just described.

Figure 35. Detail of the gong-circle showing the method of fastening the gong-kettles to the rack, and the mallets.

d. Khong mọn

Another type of khong, called the khong mọn (figs. 36–38; 112), is used in certain ensembles in place of the regular model. In this mọn model the gong-kettles are also in a curved row, but the framework stand is in a vertical crescent shape with the ends extending upward rather than in a circular shape parallel to the floor or ground. The stand is of heavy wood,

hollowed out on the inside and beautifully carved and decorated with gold paint and bits of colored glass and mirrors on the outside. The end of the crescent to the player's left is carved to represent the head of a mythical creature, half bird, half human, called *kin nọn;* the other end of the crescent is carved and decorated to represent the tail. The heavy framework is supported on a wide, flat pedestal under the center of the instrument.

Although this instrument stands upright, its measurements are more or less comparable to those of the regular models. The instrument is made in two sizes to match the two sizes of floor model, but each has one less gong-kettle than the regular instrument. This makes the instrument rather difficult to play, since the number of gong-kettles between octaves will vary from place to place on it—a fourth is normally substituted for the octave that cannot be sounded at this point.

The pitch level and range of the mọn instruments are the same as those of the regular Thai models; indeed, the sound of the two is identical. The difference is one of function: the mọn instruments are traditionally used in place of the regular Thai models in ensembles playing funeral music.

An unsubstantiated theory has been voiced by some Thai historians that the Thai khong wong was evolved from this mọn model and was changed to lie flat for the convenience of women players.

Figure 36. Khong mọn yai being played.

Figure 37. Khǭng mǭn lek being played.

Figure 38. Several khǭng mǭn at a cremation ceremony.

2. Xylophones

How, where, and when the xylophone first made its appearance in Thailand is not known. No xylophones are represented among the carvings at Angkor, though this in itself does not preclude the possibility that they may have been used by the Khmer but were considered by them to be common or folk instruments not elegant enough to be included in a mural glorifying a king. On the other hand scenes of everyday life abound among the carvings on the Bayon—the building at the exact center of the old city of Angkor Thom—in which, if the xylophone had been a common instrument, it might logically be present. But other than the percussion ensembles accompanying outdoor processions (shown in Chapter I), the musical ensembles portrayed at Angkor are composed primarily of stringed and woodwind instruments with rhythmic percussion, usually accompanying dancing. Primitive xylophones are shown among the carvings on temples in central Java, the earliest being on the Borobudur of the late eighth or early ninth century.[7] Ancient stone lithophones have been unearthed on the Indochinese peninsula,[8] but whether the idea was transferred to wood is not known. Wood is highly perishable in a humid tropical climate such as that of Southeast Asia, and if ancient wooden models existed, none remains.

The first reference to a xylophone in Thailand known to me is the illustration in the manuscript dated *circa* 1730, previously mentioned on page 48 and shown in the frontispiece. Whatever its early history, apparently the instrument was well established by the latter part of the Ayuthaya period. Yupho suggests (1960: 12) that the Thai created their xylophone from a pair of *krap sēphā,* two nearly square bars of hardwood about one and a half inches wide on each side by eight inches long, which are said to have been in use by the Thai for a very long time. These krap are used in pairs, one pair in each hand (fig. 39). The two bars of a pair are rolled against each other, producing a sound something like that made by castanets. The krap were used to provide rhythmic punctuation for the sēphā, long chanted recitations of epic proportions. Yupho speculates that, sensing a pitch in the sound of the krap striking each other, someone conceived the idea of placing them on a rack and hitting them with a mallet; more

krap were added and tuned, and thus the xylophone was evolved. On the other hand, the Thai may well have adopted the xylophone either from a Khmer model—for which, it is true, no evidence exists—or from the Javanese xylophone referred to earlier.

The word *mai,* "wood," is sometimes found appended to the names of the *ranāt ēk* and *ranāt thum,* the xylophones discussed here. This was the custom for a time after the creation of the two metallophones next discussed, to distinguish the two types.

a. Ranāt ēk

The *ranāt ēk,* a xylophone with a boat-shaped resonating box supported on a small pedestal, is perhaps the most distinctive in shape of all the Thai instruments (figs. 40; 102–105; 108–112). Sets of bars are made both of bamboo, which produces a rather soft tone, and hardwood, which gives a louder sound. Instruments generally have twenty-one bars or keys covering three octaves, though sometimes on instruments built for virtuoso work a twenty-second bar that completes the highest octave may be added — that is, this extra bar has a pitch three octaves above the lowest pitch. The keys are strung on a cord that passes through the acoustical nodes and is supported on a pair of hooks at both ends of the case. The keys are cut in gradated sizes. Some of them are further shaved out underneath to tune them roughly (fig. 45), and all are given a final tuning by the application of a mixture of beeswax and lead shavings to the undersides of the ends of each bar. The instrument is played with two mallets that have either padded ends for indoor performances or hard knobs for outdoor.

The etymology of the word ranāt is of interest: it is said to come from the word *rāt,* which was expanded to two syllables by the insertion of the consonant "n" before the vowel "a," causing the first consonant to become a short syllable: *"ra."* This is not an isolated occurrence; other words have been modified similarly. Occasionally the original one-syllable word, *rāt,* is still used in some musical terminology applying to certain ensembles. This original word means "to spread out or expand in an orderly series," which seems applicable to the construction of the ranāt "keyboard." The word

Figure 39. Krāp sēpha being played.

Figure 40. Ranāt ēk being played.

ranāt is also used as the name of some of the wood beams of a certain type of river boat, and the ranāt ēk case itself resembles closely the shape of boats used on the rivers and canals in and around Bangkok (figs. 42, 43). Thai linguistic experts do not know which was the original use of the word. Daniélou suggests another origin for the name of the instrument: he indicates that several Sanskrit works (titles not given) mention a *raghunâthā-vînâ*(1957: 27). If the principle of fixed pitch was transferred from a harp to another instrument of fixed pitch, such as the xylophone, the name might have been transferred also. Similarity is found between the Sanskrit name (raghunâthā-vînâ), the Thai name (ranāt), and the Cambodian names *(rang nat, ronéat,* or *ro nad).*

Figure 41. Ranāt ēk used in the pī phāt ensemble (left) and the one used in the mahōrī ensemble (right) shown side by side.

No Western-type conductor leads a Thai ensemble; the ranāt ēk player assumes the function of leader. He generally begins the introduction and indicates changes of tempo, whether or not repeats are to be observed, and so forth. Sometimes when an ensemble is playing merely background music for a social function or before the overture proper at the theater, the repertoire is optional. When a composition is finished, the ranāt ēk player simply begins a new one of his choice and the other players enter as soon as they recognize it. The new composition can be identified almost immediately by the musicians, who know the repertoire, so this system works very well.

The range of the ranāt ēk is as follows:

(N.B. The first bar at the left is traditionally not tuned to a specific pitch, though the tendency today is to tune it to the proper pitch of the tuning system. Some instruments built for solo virtuoso work have a twenty-second bar added at the top of the range.)

Prior to the beginning of the twentieth century the ranāt ēk part consisted of a variation of the main melody played in octaves. The variation consisted of swift running passages of notes of the same duration,

while the main melody proceeded at a slower pace and had more rhythmic variety. Early in the twentieth century Luang Pradit Phai Rǫ (Sǫn Silapabanleng) began to exploit a more melodic style in which, with minor exceptions, the ranāt also played the main melody, sustaining pitches of longer duration by a technique of rolling or trilling an octave, that is, rapid alternation of the two playing sticks on bars an octave apart. This technique is called krǭ, which means "to wind, to twirl, to twine, or to twist," in contrast to the older method of playing in simultaneous octaves, called kep, which means "to keep or collect; to pick up; to put away."[9]

In normal ensemble playing the ranāt ēk part does not involve much embellishment; this is used primarily in introductions of compositions and for solo and virtuoso playing. The most characteristic idiomatic embellishment used in the krǭ method of playing, shown in example 28, is a simple decoration of a sustained pitch by preceding it with one or two pitches closely adjoining it in the pentatonic scale/mode; the interesting feature of this embellishment is that it is played on the beat, not preceding the beat as an anticipation.

Example 28.

(N.B. These are played in octaves with the two beaters.)

Figure 42. River boat, showing the similarity to the case of the <u>ranāt ēk</u>.

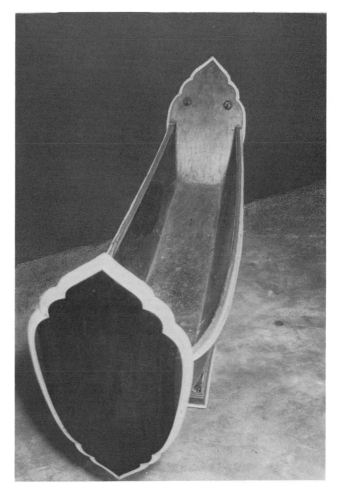

Figure 43. <u>Ranāt ēk</u> case without the keyboard.

To illustrate the two styles of ranāt ēk playing, example 29 shows two ways of playing the same music. It is from the middle section of the Thao composition "Khamēn La Ǫ Ong," one of the famous compositions by King Rama VII (1925–1935).[10] The ranāt ēk may play the melodic version (the lower line) the first time and the variation (the upper line) on the repeat or, since the melody is being played on the set of gong-kettles, may play the variation both times.

b. Ranāt thum

Yupho holds that more and more keys were gradually added to the ranāt ēk until the number became too large for one stand to hold conveniently, and another ranāt was devised to hold the lower-pitched keys.

Whether or not this is true, according to authorities, the ranāt thum (figs. 45; 103–105; 109–112) came into being during the reign of King Rama III (1824–1851). The body of the instrument is a narrow rectangular box about 50 inches long, with the two long top edges of the sides slightly curved. The tops of the two end pieces sometimes curve outward slightly, rather than being flat and straight like those of the ranāt ēk. The seventeen keys, of bamboo or hardwood, are longer and wider than those for the higher-pitched keys of the ranāt ēk and are strung on a cord that passes through the acoustical nodes, and the keyboard is suspended on hooks on the two end pieces, similarly to the ranāt ēk. The keys are tuned with the mixture of beeswax and lead shavings applied to the under sides of the ends of the keys (fig. 44). Only padded playing sticks

Example 29. "Khamēn La Q̄ Ong" (Thao)
            (as taught to the author).

2 chan.

Section 1:

are used on this instrument, the padded ends being slightly larger than those for the ranāt ēk.

The ranāt thum extends a few pitches below the ranāt ēk but is identical with that of the higher-pitched instrument for most of its range, which is in all about one octave less than that of the ranāt ēk:

The ranāt thum plays a variation of the main melody. The instrument being larger and the range being smaller than the ranāt ēk, long passages of simultaneous octaves do not occur. Intervals of the octave and fourth are, however, frequently used; other intervals are occasionally used. The part consists primarily of one pitch at a time in runs, the pitches being divided between the two hands. Usually great rhythmic variety characterizes this part, especially syncopations achieved by playing off the beat, holding pitches into the next beat, or anticipating the beat. The part is sometimes said to have a mischievous character, and one can imagine ranāt thum parts being created in somewhat the same spirit as some bassoon parts in Western symphonic literature. A typical ornamentation is a quick reiteration of a pitch in anticipation of the main beat:

Figure 44. The under side of the ranāt thum keyboard, showing the tuning waxes.

Figure 45. Ranāt thum being played.

Notated: Played:

Example 30 shows two characteristic ranāt thum parts:

Example 30.

(1) Excerpt from a rūang:

khǭng wong yai

Example 30 (continued).

(2) Section from a composition in sēphā style: "Ton Phlēng
Ching" (as taught to the author).

2 chan.

Section 1:

3. Metallophones

Since these instruments were added to Thai percussion ensembles relatively recently, it is possible that they were suggested by the *saron* and *gender* instruments of Java and Bali. The heavy metal keys of the saron are also supported on a track, in their case padded, but are further held in place by metal pins fastened into the trough resonator and extending upward through holes in the metal bar at the acoustical nodes (fig. 48). The thin metal keys of the gender are supported by a cord that runs through the nodes, the same procedure as that used with the wooden bars on the Thai ranāt (fig. 49; the Balinese gender-type instruments may be seen in the background of fig. 32). The functions of the instruments in the different cultures are not the same, however. In Java the saron are indispensable, carrying the nuclear theme or main melody, the pitches of which are usually of rather similar durational values.[11] The gender play variation parts, but of a different type from the Thai variation parts. These instruments are an essential part of a Javanese gamelan, while in Thailand the metallophones are used only in large ensembles.

The metallophones are played with beaters similar to those used with the gong-kettle instruments—discs of hide into which handles are inserted—but the discs are somewhat smaller and the handles a little smaller and longer.

Figure 47. Ranāt ēk lek and ranāt thum lek.

a. Ranāt ēk lek
(ranāt thǫng)

This instrument (figs. 46, 47; 105; 110) is said to have been originated in the reign of King Rama IV (1851—1868). At first the keys were made of brass or bronze, and the instrument was called *ranāt thǫng.* Later the keys were made of iron also. In both cases the keys are the same in number, closely resemble those of the ranāt ēk (except, of course, for the material out of which they are made), and have the same pitches, so the instrument came to be called simply the *ranāt ēk lek*—"iron ranāt ēk."[12] The body of the instrument is a long rectangular box about forty inches in length. Along the tops of the sides run narrow wooden tracks that support the metal keys at the acoustical nodes. From each side of the body extends a narrow rack that projects out under the keys, and along the edge of this is a molding that covers the ends of the keys—the top of the molding is flush with the tops of the keys. The body has four short legs, and casters are sometimes added for convenience in rolling the instrument along the floor. The keys are tuned by filing away part of the metal; the beeswax mixture is not used with the metal keys.

The range of the instrument is identical with that of the ranāt ēk, and when the instrument is used it doubles the ranāt ēk part. The range and the style of part, then, need not be illustrated separately.

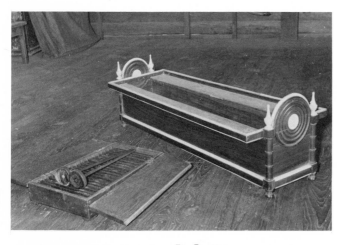

Figure 46. Ranāt ēk lek, open case and metal keys in their carrying and storage box.

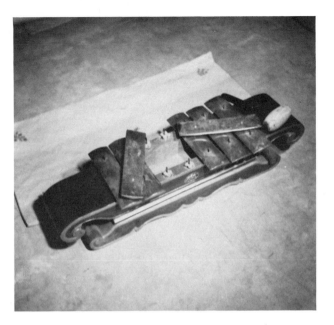

Figure 48. Javanese <u>saron</u>, with two of the metal keys removed to show the mounting pins. (Photograph from the collection of the Institute of Ethnomusicology.)

b. Ranāt thum lek

The idea for this instrument (figs. 47, 105, 110) is attributed to the brother of King Rama IV (1851–1868), who was known during that reign as the "second" king. He thought of making another

instrument of the same type as the ranāt thǫng (ranāt ēk lek), but lower in pitch to patch the ranāt thum. The instrument is similar to the ranāt ēk lek in construction except that it is a little larger, about forty-two inches long. The range of the instrument is identical with that of the ranāt thum and need not be illustrated separately.

The ranāt thum lek does not double the ranāt thum. Its part—a variation of the main melody similar in style to, but less active than, the ranāt thum part—consists mainly of broken octaves, simple fragments of scale passages, and syncopation around the principal pitches of the main melody. The ranāt thum lek has the slowest moving of the six principal parts in the polyphonic stratification of the ensemble music, not so much in the number of pitches it plays, but in the number of pitches of the main melody which occur as emphasized pitches in the part—generally the same as those of the main melody on the accented beat. The ranāt thum lek often anticipates these structural pitches, and the pitches leading up to the structural pitch are decorative. Example 31, which includes the ranāt thum part and the main melody for purposes of comparison, is a typical section from a ranāt thum lek part from a rǖang.

Example 31.

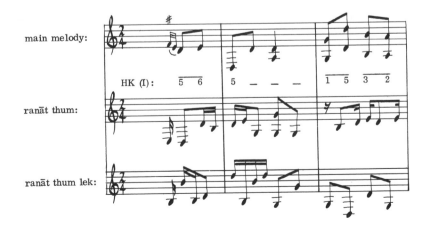

(cont. on following page)

Example 31 (continued).

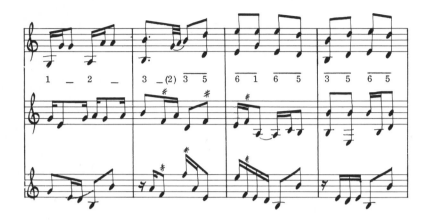

Figure 49. Javanese gender, in the Institute of Ethnomusicology, UCLA; at the rear left are two tjelempung, the Javanese slanted zither. (Photograph from the collection of the Institute of Ethnomusicology.)

B. RHYTHMIC PERCUSSION

1. Cymbals

a. Ching

The ching (figs. 50, 51) are a pair of cymbals made of thick metal and shaped like teacups or small hollow cones. Each measures about two and a half inches in diameter across the open side and at the top of the cone has a short cord attached to it, often decorated with ribbons. The ching are played by holding one cymbal cupped in the left hand and striking it with the other, held by the right hand. Two types of stroke are used. In one (fig. 51a), the cymbal in the right hand strokes the cymbal in the left hand with an outward sliding motion, and the sound is allowed to ring; this melodious, chiming sound is called *"ching,"* which is said to be onomatopoeic and gives the instrument its name. In the other (fig. 51b) the cymbal in the right hand strikes the cymbal in the left hand straight downward and the two cymbals are held together, thus damping the sound; this stroke is called *"chap,"* also onomatopoeic. The instrument is sometimes referred to by both names: ching-chap. The undamped sound is used on unaccented beats and the damped sound on accented beats. The first occurrence of the ching in a composition is usually on an unaccented beat, and the last ching stroke of a composition is an accented one.

The ching are indispensable in Thai traditional music, being used in all ensembles and with all forms except some virtuoso styles and in some sections of compositions in rubato tempo. The function of the ching in an ensemble is to beat time and hold the tempo steady. The ching part in the composition indicates the form by the number of beats per measure which it plays.

In the manuscript collection the ching part is represented on one line by the appropriate durational values (of the Western notation system):

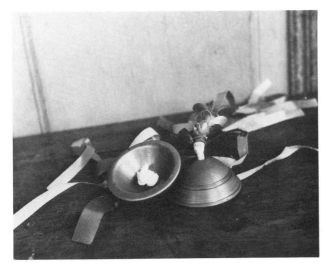

Figure 50. A pair of <u>ching</u>, small hand cymbals.

A shorthand style of notation for the ching can be used when it is desired to show the ching beats with excerpts or one-line melodic extractions. For this purpose "o" represents "ching," the ringing, unaccented beat, and "+" represents "chap", the damped, accented beat. The marks are put above both cipher and staff notation.

Figure 51<u>a</u>. The open, undamped stroke of the <u>ching</u>, called "<u>ching</u>."

Figure 51<u>b</u>. The closed, damped stroke of the <u>ching</u>, called "<u>chap</u>."

In rubato tempo the ching often play a series of fast unaccented beats produced by rocking one cymbal back and forth on the top of the other to give a steady chiming sound. This is notated as follows:

Other ching patterns are occasionally used.[13]

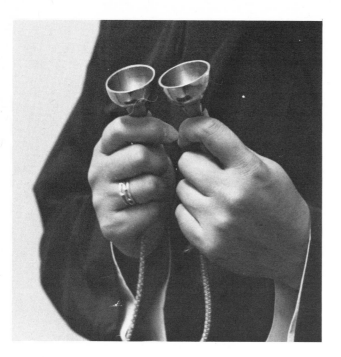

Figure 52. The Chinese shing.

b. Chāp lek

The chāp lek (figs. 53a, 54) are a pair of medium-sized cymbals of flat metal with a central rounded boss about three-quarters of an inch deep. The flange is about one inch wide, and the entire diameter of each cymbal is about five inches. Each cymbal has a cord fastened through a hole in the top of the boss, often with a tassel or fancy decoration on the end.

The chāp lek are used mainly in large ensembles. They play a line of syncopated rhythm consisting of a unit of five strokes repeated over and over:

Figure 53. Chāp lek (a) and chāp yai (b).

allowed to rattle against one another for the duration of the rhythmic value. This playing technique is not indicated in the manuscript collection, but the trill marking has been added to the above notation for accuracy and clarity.

c. Chāp yai

Occasionally in large ensembles a pair of cymbals is used of a type very much like those used in Western ensembles, though smaller (fig. 53b). The Thai models generally average about ten inches in diameter. The chāp yai play a single stroke made by striking the two cymbals together, on the same beat as the gong. The occurrence of this gong stroke varies with the musical form of a composition.

Figure 54. Chāp lek being played.

Figure 55. Khŏng rāo or khŏng hui, set of three gongs on a rack.

The first two strokes are sounded cleanly; the last three, being of twice the duration value, are not played with single sounds, but the two cymbals are

Figure 56. Mōng (on a stand).

2. Gong

a. Mōng

In Thai music of former times a gong structure of greater complexity seems to have obtained, for several gongs are described and illustrated in Yupho's book on the instruments (fig. 55). Today, however, little is known of their former use. At present one gong is used, generally only in large ensembles. This gong (figs. 56, 57) is bossed, has a lip-flange some two inches in depth, and can be from twelve to eighteen inches in diameter. The gong is suspended, by means of a cord passed through holes cut in the lip, from a tripod stand or a more modern stand made of wrought iron and is hit directly on the boss with a padded beater.

The gong stroke falls at different points depending on the musical form, but wherever it occurs it divides the music in a duple manner—that is, it may fall at the end of units of eight measures, four measures, two measures, every measure, twice per measure, and so forth. Its stroke coincides with an accented beat of the ching. In the shorthand method of ching notation, the gong is indicated by circling the ching beat with which it coincides: ⊕ .

Figure 58. Taphōn.

Figure 57. Mōng (on a tripod).

Figure 59. Taphōn mōn (left) and taphōn, showing relative sizes.

3. Drums

a. Taphōn

The barrel-shaped *taphōn* (figs. 58, 59; 102–105) is the main drum used in the pī phāt (percussion) ensemble. The spiritual leader of the ensemble, it is considered by some to be sacred. The taphōn, if it was not created indigenously by the Thai, may be derived from or related to any number of drums of neighboring cultures; for example, in the carving on Angkor Wat in which the Khmer gong-kettle instrument is pictured (figs. 3, 3c, 6) a drum much like the taphōn may be seen.

Dhanit Yupho, in his book on Thai instruments, says of the possible derivation of the taphōn:

In the old books there is mentioned an instrument called *saphōn* which was probably similar to or the same instrument as the taphōn. It has a body like the *muthing, marithang,* or *mattala* of India, that is, from the heads at either end the body tapers outward gradually to a bulge at the middle of the body. In India this type of drum is played held on the lap, or suspended from straps over the shoulders when played while standing. As for the Thai drum, it is put on a stand and played on both heads with the palms of the hands and the fingers. The marithang or mattala was widely used in ancient India. There is a legend that a Brahmin god invented it when devising the rhythm for a dance of Siva after his victory over the city of Tripura,

Figure 60. Taphōn mǫn being played
in a mǫn ensemble (see also figs. 36, 37).

and it is said that Ganesa, his divine son, was the first to play it. The reason that the drum is known as marithang or mattala is that originally the body was made of clay or earth, but now it is made of wood (1960: 35).

The body of the taphōn—nineteen to twenty inches long—is made of teak wood or the wood of the jack fruit tree, a solid block of the wood being cut and hollowed out into the proper shape. Two heads of unequal size are made, the larger being about ten inches in diameter and the smaller about eight and a half. The edge of the heads is sewed with twisted strands of cane, then leather thongs are pulled through the loops of cane on both heads alternately and pulled tight. The thongs, tied close together, cover the entire body of the drum so that the wood is invisible. Around the central bulge of the body more thongs are interwoven at right angles to the thongs running lengthwise, making a pattern about three inches wide which varies from drum to drum. A

handle is attached to the top of the bulge for convenience in carrying. The center of the heads and the rim are painted with a black mixture made from the sap of a local tree. This is done to help preserve the heads, not as a spot on which the player plays, as some have thought. A mixture of cooked rice and ashes mashed into a glutinous mass is applied to the black circle on the center of the large head to tune the drum to a more mellow tone. The thicker and heavier the paste, the slower will be the vibrations of the head and consequently the deeper the tone. Also, the paste helps to damp out certain partials with the result that the sound has a more definite pitch than would otherwise be produced by the drumhead.[14]

In his booklet on Thai music Phra Chen Duriyanga gives a comprehensive account of the eleven varieties of sound-effects or strokes used in playing the taphōn (1956: 28–30). This description, which could not be improved on, is reproduced here in full:

A. Playing with the right hand (that is, on the large head):

(1) A brisk light blow on the rim with outstretched fingers, held straight and closely together and withdrawn immediately allowing the drumhead to vibrate freely, gives the long sound of *thēng*.

(2) The same as 1, when the fingers are kept on the drumhead to damp the sound, gives the short sound of *thŏet*.

(3) The same as 1, when the fingers are withdrawn and immediately after, applied again to damp the sound, gives the short sound of *tha*.

(4) A smart blow given with open fingers and full palm of the hand and damped, gives the short sound of *pa*.

B. Playing with the left hand (that is, on the small head):

(5) The same as 1, gives the long sound of *ting*.

(6) The same as 2, gives the short sound of *tyt*.

(7) The same as 3, gives the short sound of *tup*.

C. Playing with both hands:

(8) Light blows on the rims, when that on the left is stronger than that on the right, give the long sound of *phring*.

(9) Smart blows on the rims, when the hands are immediately withdrawn, give the long sound of *phrŏeng*.

(10) The same as 8, when the sound is damped immediately, gives the short sound of *phrṳt*.

(11) The same as 9, when the sound is damped immediately after, gives the short sound of *phrŏet*.

These eleven sounds are represented in notation as follows:

Beginners on the taphōn are given short, standard basic patterns to practice. A basic pattern generally underlies one phrase or melodic unit of a given form. These patterns can be used intact in ensemble playing, or they can be used as the basis of a more complicated improvised part. Some of the basic patterns are as follows:[15]

(1) prop kai pattern (for slow tempos):

(2) sŏng mai pattern (for medium tempos):

(3) a pattern that can be used either for sŏng mai (medium tempos) or phlēng reo (fast tempos):

(4) a pattern for *krāo ram,* a dance type of medium tempo:

Following are four different versions of an eight-measure phrase from one of the rūang; the simpler versions occur at the beginning of the composition, the more complex ones as the climax is approached.

c. Sǭng nā

This name means literally "two faces," that is, two drumheads. The drum (fig. 61) is of the same general construction as the taphōn but is a little longer—twenty-two to twenty-three inches—and is more or less cylindrical rather than barrel-shaped. The large head is about nine inches in diameter and the small one about eight. The mixture of mashed cooked rice and ashes is applied to the black circle on the large head. This head is played by the left hand and the small head by the right, contrary to the playing position for the taphōn, while the drum is held in the lap of the seated player.

The drum replaces the regular taphōn in the pī phāt (percussion) ensemble when it accompanies the sēphā (chanted epics) and sēphā style compositions—such as those in the Thao or variation form—which have vocal sections. The lighter sound of the sǭng nā is more suitable for vocal accompaniment.

This drum was first used during the reign of King Rama II (1809–1824) at the time that the

b. Taphōn mǭn

This drum (figs. 59, 60; 112) is similar in construction to the Thai taphōn but much larger, and the bulge is nearer one end rather than in the middle. The body is some thirty inches long; the large head is about twenty inches in diameter and the small one about fourteen to fifteen. Two handles are put at the ends, one above each head. This drum, played in a manner similar to the regular taphōn, is used with the mǭn ensemble.

Figure 61. Sǫng nā being played in the Institute of Ethnomusicology, UCLA. In the rear can be seen some of the metallophones of the Balinese gamelan belonging to the Institute.

Figure 63a. Klǫng that: front view, with playing sticks on the floor.

The sǫng nā plays a rhythmic line very much like the taphōn, but it uses fewer different types of

Figure 62. A pair of klǫng khāek being played.

percussion ensemble began to be used to accompany the sēphā performances.

strokes. Duriyanga gives them as follows (1956: 31–32):

Figure 63b. Klǫng that: rear view,
showing the drums suspended on two poles.

A. Right-hand strokes (on the small head):
  (1) long, called *ting.*
  (2) short, called *tup.*
  (3) short, called *c̆ha.*
  (4) long, called *nang.*
B. Left-hand strokes (on the large head):
  (5) long, called *thōeng.*
  (6) short, called *thoe.*
C. Both hands:
  (7) long, called *phring.*
These seven sounds are represented in notation
as follows:

d. Klǫng khāek

The *klōng khāek* (figs. 62; 101; 103) has a long,
almost cylindrical body made of hardwood, about
two feet in length. One head is about eight inches in
diameter, the other about seven. The heads, of
calfskin or goatskin, are rolled on a hoop and lashed
down. Originally the heads were held in place with
cane or rattan split in half and tied widely apart;

today, owing to the difficulty in obtaining good
rattan and cane, leather thongs are used. The
instrument is used in pairs, with the two drums
differing in pitch and played by separate musicians.
The higher-pitched drum is referred to as the "male,"
presumably because that pitch is considered more
penetrating and authoritative; the lower-pitched one
is the "female." A complex line of rhythm is created
by the intermingling and alternating of the sounds of
the two parts.

This drum is sometimes referred to as the *klǫng
chawā,* or "Javanese drum," it being thought that it
originally came from Java; drums somewhat similar
are used in the Javanese and Balinese gamelans, often
in pairs also. The klǫng khāek has probably been in
use in Thailand for a long time—in the old laws
concerning the system of degree of dignity or rank,
the titles of the chief klǫng khāek player and his
subordinates were given with the amounts of land to
which they were entitled. In those days the drum was
probably used in royal processions when the king was
carried on an elephant or on the river in the royal
barge. Later it was added to the percussion ensemble
that accompanied the theatrical presentations of the
Thai version of the Javanese epic, *Inao.* In the latter
part of the Ayuthaya period, for example, the
ensemble accompanied the *kriss* dance performed by
the actor playing Inao. Today the klǫng khāek is
sometimes substituted for the taphōn in the
percussion ensemble and for the *thōn-rammanā*
combination in the string ensembles; it is also used
with the *pī chawā* to accompany performances of
classical fencing or Thai-style boxing. Today the
choice of drum used with an ensemble seems to be
based on formality versus informality: if the
percussion ensemble plays formally for a specific
function, the taphōn is used; if the occasion is
informal, the klōng khāek is preferred. Also in
informal situations both the taphōn and the pair of
klōng khāek might be used together, particularly if
enough musicians are present and all want to play.
Improvisation on the pair of klōng khāek is
frequently the method of playing, but formal, basic
patterns, which the beginner learns, are also used. The
following are ones that were taught to me:

(1) For slow tempos:

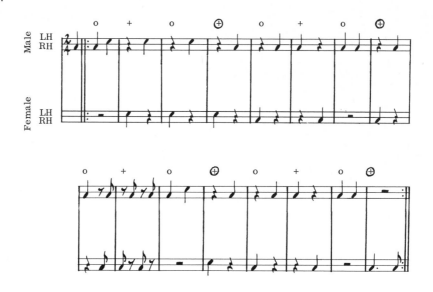

(2) For medium tempos the same pattern is used at twice the speed:

(3) For fast tempos:

e. Klɔ̄ng thát

The body of this drum (figs. 63, 65; 102, 103 [in background, not being used], 104, 105) is made from a solid block of one of the tough, strong varieties of hardwood. The outside of the barrel-shaped body, about twenty inches long, is smoothed and polished;

Figure 64. Chinese percussion instruments: t'ang ku (vertically suspended drum) front; ta ku (thin, horizontal drum) rear center; mu yu (wooden "fish"), on stand left; lo (gong), rear left; in the Institute of Ethnomusicology, UCLA.

the inside is hollowed out. The drumheads, about eighteen inches in diameter, are made of cowhide or water buffalo hide stretched tightly over the open ends of the body and fastened by means of pegs made of wood, ivory, animal bone, or metal. When the drum is played, the pasty mixture of rice and ashes is put on the black circle in the center of one of the heads, which is placed downwards, and one edge of the drum is rested on a padded ring that anchors the drum and prevents it from sliding. The drum is tilted at an angle toward the player and held by two poles about a yard in length inserted through an attached metal ring at the middle of one side of the body; the other two ends of the poles are spread apart and propped against the floor to hold the drum in playing position. Only one head is played, but two beaters are used made of pieces of bamboo about twenty inches long, with or without padded ends.

This variety of drum seems to have been in use by the Thai since ancient times. The Chinese have also used several kinds of drums with pegged heads (fig. 64), and the drums of the two cultures are probably related. Not only is this type of drum mentioned in some of the old references (Yupho: 1960: 31—34), but its use is also widespread among

the Thai in many different places and on many different occasions. It exists in various sizes, some being very large, such as those in temple compounds used for signaling. With some varieties the heads are of different sizes. In some places the drums are hung or suspended, while in others they are laid on the side on a stand so that both heads may be played. Drums of this type are often known by the activity with which they are associated, such as the klǭng khōn, used with the khōn or masked drama, and the klǭng nāng, used with the shadow plays.

The variety of this type of drum used in traditional percussion ensembles is called the klǭng that. Originally only one drum was used, but during the reign of King Rama II (1809—1824) another was added, and since that time it has been customary to use the klǭng that in pairs. The drums are not tuned to specific pitches, but as with the klǭng khaēk, one (the "male") has a higher pitch than the other (the "female"). Duriyanga reports that three of these drums can be used together (1956: 32—33), in which case they produce relatively high, medium, and low pitches.

The pair of klǭng that is generally used only in large percussion ensembles. Its function is to add another line of rhythm. This can be one of three general types:

(1) A single stroke coinciding with the mōng (gong).

(2) A short, highly syncopated pattern reiterated throughout the composition.

Ching (unaccented, open sound)

Gong

(3) In rubato tempo, a long line of gradually increasingly faster rhythmic values:

f. Thōn

The *thōn* is a single-headed drum, open at the opposite end, of a shape often referred to as "goblet" or "inverted vase." This type of drum is found throughout the Near East, where it is known by several different names.[16] Whether or not the Thai version was copied from a Near-Eastern model is not definitely known, but the thōn is mentioned by name in some of the early references (Yupho 1960: 38).

Two models of this drum are used in Thailand. One, the *thōn chātrī* (figs. 65, 105), is made of wood and is shorter and wider than the other. The head is of water buffalo hide. The drum is used in the south in pairs (one player to each drum) to accompany the southern form of theater, the *lakhōn nōrā,* and the shadow play.

Figure 66. Thōn mahōrī.

Figure 65. A pair of thōn chātrī.

The model used in traditional music, called *thōn mahōrī* after the name of the mahōrī ensemble, is a more sophisticated, refined model (figs. 66, 69; 99, 100, 106–110). The body, about fifteen inches long, is often made of some kind of ceramic or earthenware rather than wood. Often in the old days the ceramic body was made in China according to specifications sent by the Thai; the Chinese themselves, however, do not use a drum like this. The body is beautifully decorated, sometimes with intricate designs of inlaid mother-of-pearl or bits of colored glass and mirror, or applied goldleaf, silver, or lacquer. All exhibit a high

Figure 67. Two rammanā, head side (left) and underneath side (right).

Figure 68. Chinese pang ku.

degree of craftsmanship. The bowl-shaped support over which the head is stretched is larger than the southern model, and the skin used for the head—approximately nine inches diameter—is more delicate. Various kinds are used: calfskin, goatskin, or often snakeskin——usually of the python (or boa-constrictor) or the "elephant's trunk" snake.[17] The head is fastened down with split and polished rattan or strands of braided silk.

The thōn is played by striking the head with the right hand; the left hand supports the body or may be used to close the open end of the drum if a damped sound is desired.

In ensembles containing stringed instruments the thōn is usually paired with the *rammanā,* the shallow frame drum to be described next, the two being played by either the same or separate players——their light sound blends well with the volume and quality of sound produced by the strings. Their function is to accompany the ensemble with a rhythmic line similar to the drum patterns previously illustrated.

Figure 69. Thōn mahōrī (right) and rammanā (left) being played.

g. Rammanā

The rammanā (figs. 67, 69; 100, 106–110) is a shallow frame drum with one head, about the size of a Western tambourine but without the "jangles." The body of the rammanā, two to three inches deep, slopes inward from the head to the open bottom. The head, about ten inches in diameter, is stretched tightly over the wider opening in the circular frame and anchored with pegs around the edge on the sides of the frame, leaving the top of the drumhead smooth. The drumhead cannot be tightened or loosened to give higher or lower sounds, but a cord is put along the edge of the rim of the body under the head supporting it and causing a higher, more mellow sound to be produced than would be otherwise. The body is usually beautifully made of ivory or of wood inlaid with ivory or mother-of-pearl. The instrument is played with the fingers and palm of the hand.

Yupho says in his book that the name for the rammanā came from Malaya——there being a Malayan drum called *rabana* or *rĕbana* which gives a similar sound; he says that the word rĕbana came from the Portuguese (Yupho 1967: 37). A Chinese drum from which the rammanā may have been derived is shown in figure 68.

C. WOODWINDS

1. Flute Types

a. Khlui

The *khlui* (figs. 70–72; 103, 106–110) is a vertical bamboo flute. Its name is said to be onomatopoeic, from the characteristic sound produced by the instrument when it is played.

The body of the instrument is made from a long length of bamboo, cut so that a node of the bamboo is about one inch from one end——the node is pierced through, making an open shaft. After cutting and hollowing the instrument is carefully dried out over a fire, during which a process is used whereby designs are formed on the bamboo by the heat, making the instrument more attractive (special instruments occasionally made of hardwood or ivory are not decorated in this manner).

In all, fourteen holes are cut into the body of the khlui. Seven finger holes are arranged down one side. On the opposite side, near the end that is to be the mouthpiece a rectangular opening about an inch long is cut with its bottom side slanting inward from the outside surface of the body to the inside surface of the open shaft, the slant being toward the end with the mouthpiece. In Thai this device is called "the beak of the parrot," and without it the instrument will not sound (fig. 72). Below this opening there is a thumb hole. Above that, on the right side of the instrument as it is held in playing position, another round hole called the "membrane hole" is cut. Originally this hole was covered with a very thin piece of bamboo fiber, but, today it is covered with thin tissue paper or simply stopped up with a wad of paper. The thin tissue paper or bamboo fiber vibrates when the instrument is played, creating a buzzing noise and causing the total sound produced to be rougher, with more body, or acoustically speaking more complex in its partial structure. If the membrane hole is not utilized, the sound is purer, more like the tone of the Western flute. At the bottom end of the instrument two pairs of holes are made with axes at right angles—a cord or ribbon is put through the two holes with lateral axis, either for decoration or for convenience in carrying the instrument, and the other pair remains vacant.

The mouthpiece (fig. 72), a pegged or "recorder" type, consists of a piece of wood the size of the opening in the end of the bamboo. The underside of the mouthpiece is cut away diagonally on one side toward the center of the peg including a small portion of the top end—leaving, when the mouthpiece is inserted into the bamboo and fastened flush with the end, a small space through which air passes when the instrument is blown. The air is directed by this channel against the sharp edge of the rectangular hole of the "beak." In playing the instrument the lips cover the small opening of the mouthpiece, and the instrument is held vertically—in the same position as the Western clarinet and oboe (fig. 70). Great skill is required in playing the khlui, and great subtleties can be achieved. Different air pressures, positions of the lips, and angles at which the air is directed all influence the tone quality and pitch.

Besides being used as a solo instrument—often played by a person for his own enjoyment—the khlui is regularly used in ensembles that include stringed instruments (figs. 106–110), as well as with the pī phāt ensemble when the ranāt ēk uses padded sticks or for a performance indoors where a reduced

volume of sound is desired (fig. 103). Originally only one size of khlui was used, but with the evolution of ensembles three sizes were created in order to have an instrument commensurate with the general volume of sound of each of the different sizes of ensembles (fig. 71):

(1) *khlui līp,* the smallest size, about fourteen to fifteen inches long and three-quarters to seven-eighths of an inch in diameter, and the highest in pitch. This size is rarely used today, appearing only in the larger string ensembles.

(2) *khlui phīang ǭ,* of medium size, about eighteen inches long and one inch in diameter. This was the original khlui and is the size generally used.

(3) *khlui ū,* the largest size, about twenty-four inches long and one and an eighth inches in diameter. This is often used in medium- and large-sized ensembles when a pair of khlui is called for.

The khlui plays a version of the main melody characterized by constant intricate and ornate embellishment, as shown in example 32, which I transcribed from a record since no other notation for the instrument was available.

2. Reed Types

The Thai name *"pī,"* a Chinese word for "tube" or "pipe," is a basic name for several Thai instruments related to the double-reed type found throughout the Near East and Asia. [18] It is not known whether the original pī was a true Thai instrument or whether it, too, was borrowed from the Khmer. In the few references remaining from the Sukhothai period (ca. 1250–1350) the pī mentioned may or may not be a reed instrument, as other wind instruments were also called by this generic name. The string ensembles of olden times used the khlui; because of the lack of detailed delineation in most of the carvings at Angkor and the weathering that has taken place over the centuries, it is not always possible to say whether the wind instruments portrayed in them are flutes or the pī. Daniélou believes the pī is represented (1957: 28), and some of the carvings do show wind instruments with the suggestion of "bulge" and flaring at the lower end (see the illustrations in Chapter I). The instrument also appears in the percussion ensemble pictured in the 1730 manuscript pictured in the frontispiece of this book.

Example 32. Solo style for the khlui (all an octave higher).

Originally the pī may have served as leader of the percussion ensemble with which it played; this ensemble has been known as the pī phāt ensemble for a long time—it originally accompanied the shadow plays, the khōn (masked drama), and the *lakhǫn nǫk* (public theater using live actors without masks). Later, when the *lakhǫn nai* (private palace performances) were introduced using women to portray the parts (during the reign of King Rama IV, 1854–1868) and the khōn was also brought into the palace, a new pī was created to fit these new conditions: the body was made larger, and the corresponding pitch was lower and the tone mellower. This new instrument (to be described next) was called *pī nai* ("nai" means "in" or "inside"; thus the name means "pī used in performances inside the royal palace"), and the original instrument was now called *pī nǫk* ("nǫk" means "outside," thus "pī used in performances outside the royal palace"). The palace performances were usually inside a building, the public performances in an outdoor theater, a fact that gave a further distinction between "indoor pī" (pī nai) and "outdoor pī" (pī nǫk). The pī used with the ensemble accompanying the shadow plays—called pī klāng,

"medium-sized pī"—has a size and pitch halfway between the pī nai and the pī nǫk. The dimensions of the three sizes are as follows (fig. 76):

(1) pī nǫk: twelve to thirteen inches long, one and a half inches in diameter.

(2) pī klāng: about fifteen inches long, one and a half inches in diameter.

(3) pī nai: sixteen to seventeen inches long, one and three-quarters inches in diameter. Today the single name "pī" is generally used for the pī nai since the other two models are rarely used in traditional ensembles.

Three other Thai instruments of the double-reed type—the pī chawā (to be described), the pī mǫn (to be described), and the pī chanai (existent but obsolete today)—preserve the conical shape of their Near Eastern, Indian, and Chinese equivalents. The smallest of these, the pī chanai (fig. 77), was apparently widely used in early times in processions—hardly a foot long, it produced a rather high and piercing tone. The word "chanai" has no other meaning as a noun in Thai than to signify an oboelike instrument; possibly is is a modified pronunciation of the Indian word *"shahnai"* or

Figure 70. Khlui phīāng ǭ being played.

"senai" (see note 18). An Indian legend has it that the Indian model was the invention of a man named Hakeem Bu Ali Senai, after whom the instrument was named (Fyzee-Rahamin 1925: 59). Sachs attributes the name to the Sanskrit version *sanayi* of the original Persian name *surna* (1940: 230).

a. Pī nai

The *pī nai* (fig. 73), or pī, is a reed instrument whose sound is often compared to that of the Western oboe. It is usually made of one of the hardwoods, although occasionally of marble. The wooden body is turned and shaped on a lathe (by hand in the old days), flared outward at both ends and with a slight bulge at the center. The inside is hollowed out in a slightly conical shape the entire length of the body, which is sixteen to seventeen inches long. The upper end is covered by a flat hard-rubber disc, either plain or

Figure 71. Three sizes of khlui: left, khlui līp; center, khlui phīāng ǭ; right, khlui ū.

inlaid with mother-of-pearl (sometimes a convex metal disc such as that used on the pī chawa, to be discussed next, is included); the disc has a small hole in the center into which is inserted the pipe that holds the reeds (fig. 75a). At the lower end some substance such as boat-caulking material, or more often the mixture of beeswax and lead used to tune the ranāt, is applied around the circular opening to tune the instrument to the pitch level desired—lengthening the bore lowers the pitch (fig. 75b). Around the center bulge fourteen pairs of small rings are turned; they are smoothed and polished, adding to the attractiveness of the instrument. Six finger holes are bored between various pairs of these rings—four in one group on the upper end of the bulge separated by a short space from two holes on

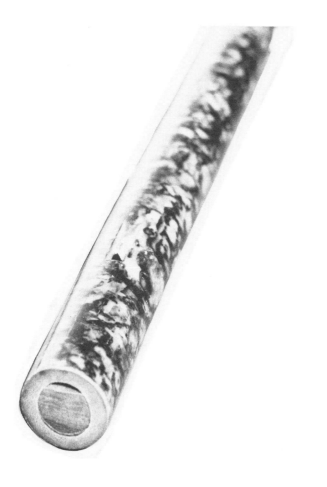

Figure 72. Detail of khlui mouthpiece, showing the "beak of the parrot" on the under side.

Figure 73. Pī nai being played.

the lower part of the bulge. Another pair of rings may be turned at each end of the group of fourteen rings, at the points where the instrument is at its minimum width; these help to give the fingers of the player support and to prevent their slipping.

Although the instrument is classified as a double reed, the reed for the pī is actually quadruple, being made of four small roundish pieces of dried palm leaf placed in two double layers and tied to a small tube usually of brass or bronze and sometimes of silver. The tube is tapered: the end that fits into the disc enclosing the top of the pī is a little larger than the end to which the reeds are fastened; this larger end is wrapped with thread to make a tight fit when it is inserted into the hole in the disc. (The process of making the reeds is shown in fig. 74a to m.). In playing, the entire reed and tube are inserted into the

mouth with the lips resting for support against the disc (fig. 73).

The instrument looks somewhat awkward and gives the impression of being difficult to play, but actually it can be made to sound very easily; intricate, complex intonation is possible on it. The musician develops a method of continuous playing—inhaling through the nose and storing the breath in the cheeks while at the same time expelling the air through the instrument with the mouth (as with the pī chawā being played in fig. 79). The result is a long, unbroken melody that helps tie together the staccato lines of the ranāt and khong.

The pī plays a variation of the main melody which, like the khlui part, is subjected to a great deal of embellishment. The beginning of the part may double the main melody fairly closely, as in example 33.

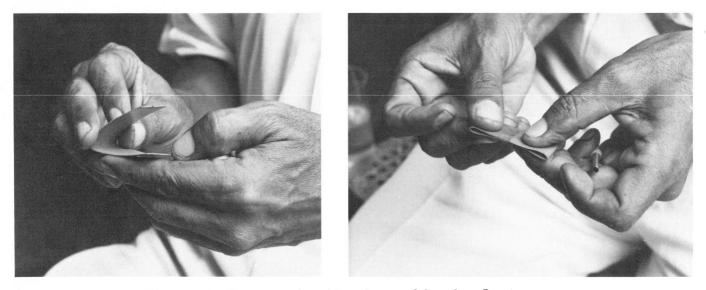

Figure 74. Process of making the reed for the pī nai:

a. left, the metal tube on which the reed is placed, wound with
   string at the bottom so that it will fit in the hole in the pī;
   center, strips of dried palm leaf; right, soaking the palm
   leaf in water prior to shaping.

b and c. bending the palm leaf into shape.

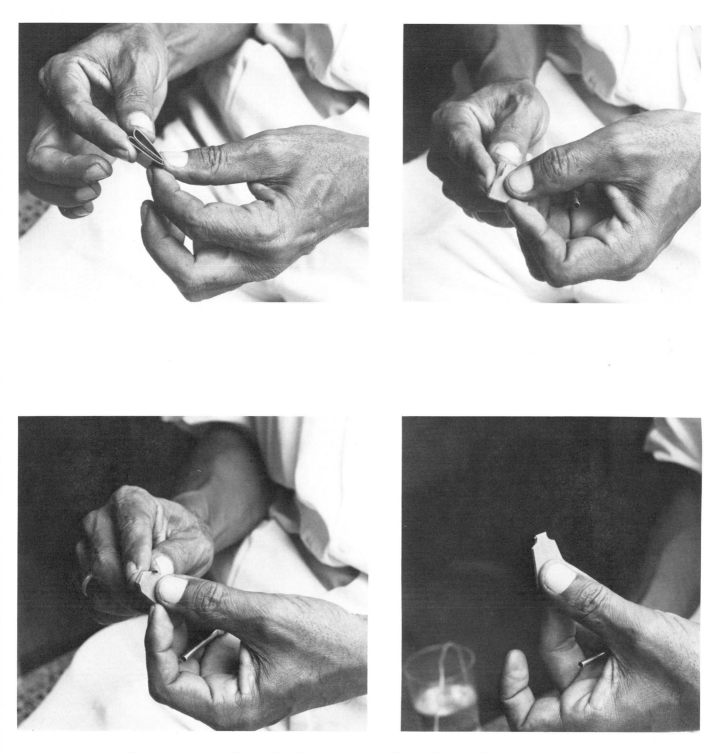

Figure 74 (continued). Process of making the reed for the pī nai:

  d. bending the palm leaf into shape.

  e. cutting the slanting sides of the reed.

  f and g. the indentations at the bottom around which the reed
     will be tied securely to the metal tube.

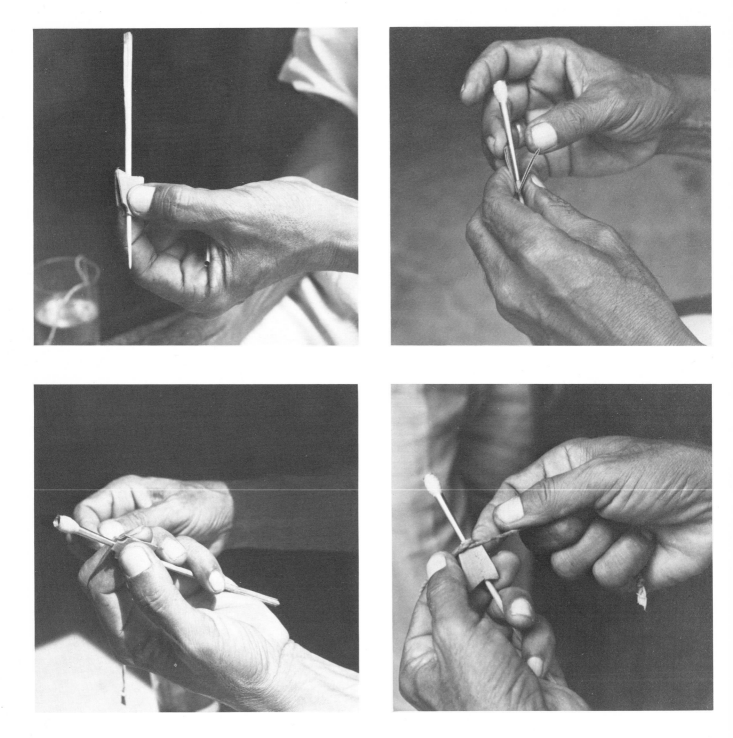

Figure 74 (continued). Process of making the reed for the pī nai:

    h, i, and j. putting the reed on the metal tube.

    k. tying the reed on the tube.

Figure 74 (continued). Process of making the reed for the pī nai:

l. rounding off the top of the reed.

m. the finished reed and tube.

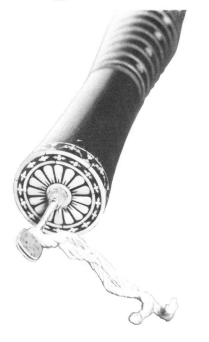

Figure 75. a. Pī nai: closed end with the reed and tube holder.

b. Pī nai: lower end, showing the tuning wax.

Example 33.

Figure 76. Different sizes of pī: a. pī nǒk; b and c. pī klāng; d and e. pī nai; a, b, c, and e are made from hardwood, d is carved from marble.

A typical instance of a highly decorated passage is example 34.

Example 34.

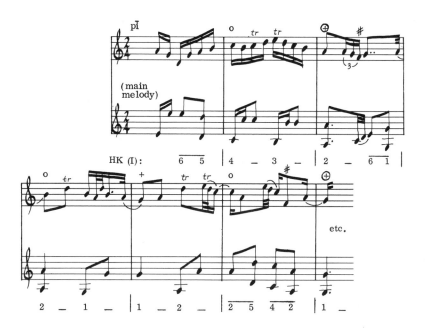

Example 35 shows a short solo section in which the pī imitates the preceding vocal section.

Example 35.

The pī sometimes has a solo introduction to a composition and very frequently plays a short solo phrase at the end of a composition. The finalis of this phrase may be the same as that of the main melody, or it may be the fourth above. This pitch, as illustrated in example 36, is also the highest pitch generally used on the instrument.

Example 36.

(a)

Glissandos or slides are idiomatic to the instrument and are often used in more rubato types of passages, as in example 37.

Example 37.

(b)

b. Pī chawā

The pī chawā (figs. 78 and 79), about sixteen inches long, is made of hardwood although special models are sometimes of ivory or of hardwood decorated with ivory. The instrument has two detachable parts—the body proper, about ten to eleven inches long, and the bell, about five to six inches long and about three in diameter at the widest part of its flare. Seven finger holes are on the top side, and a thumb hole is underneath. The reed is like that of the pī nai,

the instrument is not going to be played for very long at one time.

The type of melodic line played by the pī chawā lamenting and wailing. In former times the instrument was used in processions and for other official functions calling for martial music. Today it is mostly used with the klǫng khaēk to accompany matches of traditional Thai fencing and Thai-style boxing. It is used in the lakhǫn drama when the is the same style as that played by the pī nai. Although it would require a trained ear to distinguish the two instruments by sound only, it may be said

Figure 77. Pī chanai being played.

but there is a slight modification in mounting it: a flat disc closing off the end of the body of the instrument (like the one that usually forms the top of the pī nai and also acts as a support for the player's lips) is not present on the pī chawā because of the conical shape of the instrument—it tapers down to a rounded point at the top, so a small convex metal disc called in French a *"pirouette"* is attached to the top and is held in place by the tube on which the reed is mounted and which passes through the disc into the instrument. The pirouette is sometimes omitted if

that the pī chawā produces a tone a little more strident and penetrating. It is thus more suited for occasions such as those involving physical action or Javanese epic *Inao* is performed, to accompany the kriss dance. The pī chawā is also used in two or three small ensembles that accompany funeral ceremonies (figs. 101, 111).

The name of this instrument is self-explanatory, "chawā" being the Thai word for the name rendered in English as "Java."[19] The instrument is said to have come from Persia and the Near East to India (Sachs

Figure 78. P̄ī chawā being played, exhaled breath with the cheeks flat.

Figure 79. P̄ī chawā being played, inhaled breath, the breath stored in the cheeks.

Figure 80. P̄ī mǭn, without the reed and tube. (For p̄ī mǭn being played, see figs. 36 and 37.)

1940: 230), and it probably went from India to Java during the influx of Islam there in the fifteenth century (Kunst 1949: 238)——the Javanese model also has the conical shape of the Indian model. The name used by the Thai for their instrument suggests that they adopted it from Java rather than directly from India.[20] The instrument was adopted by the Thai perhaps during the Ayuthaya period, at the same time they took up the klǭng khāēk.

c. P̄ī mǭn

When the khǭng mǭn and the taphōn mǭn are used, a mǭn model of the p̄ī is also used (figs. 36, 37; 80; 112, 116). It is similar to the p̄ī chawā but bigger. The conical hardwood body is about twenty inches long; the metal bell is about nine inches long with an opening about four inches in diameter encircled by a flange about two and a half inches wide. The two parts of the body fit loosely together. To prevent the bell from slipping off, a cord is looped around it a few times just below a central projecting metal band

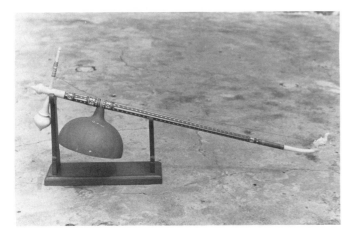

Figure 81a. Phīn nam tao, side view. This is an old instrument in the National Museum, Bangkok.

Figure 81b. Phīn nam tao, bottom view, showing the open half gourd resonator.

Figure 82. Phīn phia.

and then extended up to the top of the wooden cone, where it is wrapped between two turned wooden rings in a counter-clockwise direction. The reed and accompanying apparatus is the same as for the pī chawā, but the reed is slightly larger. The tone quality is about the same as that of the pī nai, perhaps a little mellower and less strident. The pī mǫn plays in the same general style as the other pī.

D. STRINGED INSTRUMENTS

1. Plucked

The group of plucked stringed instruments were formerly referred to in Thai by the Pali-Sanskrit generic term *"phīn,"* which has the same root as that

Figure 83. Two sizes of krajappī being played (from a color slide of the Department of Fine Arts, Bangkok).

of Indian names for a plucked lute: *vina* (south India) and *bina* (north India). This might be considered another factor to support the theory of early Indian influences on Thai music. Thai instruments that have the term "phīn" in their names are not used today in traditional ensembles and will not be discussed here.[21] Two phīn-type Thai instruments are shown in figures 81 and 82.

a. Krajappī

The *krajappī* (fig. 83) has all but disappeared from present-day ensembles in Thailand—brief mention is made of it here because it was one of the important instruments in early ensembles. The krajappī is a fretted lute-type instrument found in various sizes up to six feet long. The name "krajappī," which means "tortoise," would seem to refer to the size and shape of the sound box; this somewhat resembles a tortoise shell—oval-shaped, about sixteen inches wide, seventeen inches long, and two to three inches deep. The instrument has two double courses of strings, each attached to a peg at the top of the neck. The strings were traditionally of gut but now are usually of silk or nylon. A plectrum of bone, horn, or tortoise shell, held with the thumb and index finger of the right hand, is moved back and forth across the strings to set them in motion.

The name "krajappī" comes from the Javanese "*katchapi*," which in turn comes from the Pali-Sanskrit "katchapa." The Javanese katchapi (or kachapi), however, is a floor zither and not a lute.[22] The Dyaks of Borneo (Kalimantan) also use the name "kachapi" for a lute-type instrument (sometimes also called "sapoh"),[23] but the Dyak instrument resembles the shape of the chakhē (to be described next) more than that of the krajappī. When the Thai began to use the krajappī is unknown, but it was prominent in ensembles until the end of the nineteenth century (figs. 99, 100).

b. Chakhē[24]

The chakhē—a zither-type instrument—has been used by the Thai since at least the first part of the Ayuthaya period (fourteenth century), being mentioned in the court regulations of that time. The chakhē is thought to be a further development of the earlier phīn instruments, but like the Javanese katchapi it is a floor zither. One of the Indian phīn-type instruments from which the chakhē may have evolved is made in the form of a peacock, with the neck of the instrument being the long extended tail of the bird—the name of this instrument is *mayuri* (Sanskrit) and *taus* or *tayus* (Hindustani);[25] it is bowed, however, while the chakhē is plucked. In the old days in Thailand the front of the body of the chakhē was carved to represent the head of a crocodile, the name for which in Thai—*chǫrakhē*—became the name of the instrument until sometime later it was shortened to chakhē; models made for royalty and wealthy households were often highly decorated with inlaid ivory (fig. 84). The body of the chakhē today is very plain and smooth, resembling the body of a crocodile only in the most general way (fig. 85).

Today, for the sake of convenience, the body of the chakhē—whose total length is about fifty-two inches—is made in two parts and then fastened together. The material used is hardwood. The resonance box is an elongated oval about twenty inches long, eleven inches wide, and four inches deep—the top slopes slightly down toward the sides. The neck of the instrument is about thirty-two inches long and four and a half inches wide. The two parts are hollowed out underneath, and a flat piece of wood is fastened over the bottom to enclose the sound box; the body is smoothed and polished on the outside. The instrument has five legs, four under the resonance box and one under the neck. Three strings, one of brass wire and two of gut, pass over a bridge on the head, over the frets, over another bridge on the neck, and into the neck where they are attached inside to the pegs. The strings are tuned in a fifth and a fourth, the pitch of the highest being an octave above the lowest and the same as the lower string of the *sǭ ū* (a bowed instrument described in the next section):

N.B. Phīang ǭ tuning.

Eleven frets rise above the surface of the neck in graduated heights from three-quarters of an inch nearest the resonance chamber to one and a half inches nearest the pegs. The frets are attached securely to the neck of the instrument in such

Figure 84. Chakhē, an old ivory-inlaid case. This instrument is in the National Museum, Bangkok.

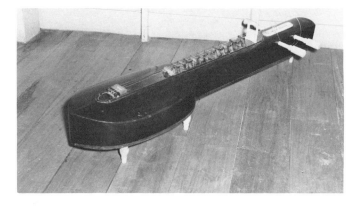

Figure 85. Chakhē, contemporary model.

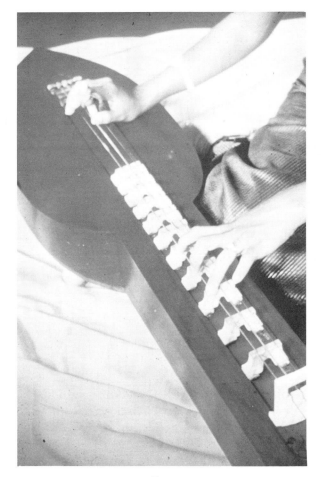

Figure 86. The chakhē being played (from a color slide of the Department of Fine Arts, Bangkok).

positions that, when the strings are pressed down on them, the pitches produced are those of the fixed tuning system. The instrument is played by fingering with the left hand, pressing the string down on the appropriate fret for the desired pitch, while the right hand strikes the string with a plectrum—a cylindrical piece of bone or ivory about two inches long and rounded at the playing end tied to the index finger of the right hand, the thumb and middle finger being braced against it to give added strength and direction. Pitches of short duration are played with one stroke of the plectrum; sustained pitches are produced by a continuous strumming of the string in a rapid horizontal shaking motion (fig. 86). The technique is comparable to the krọ technique of the ranāt, except that on the ranāt ēk octaves are

alternated and on the chakhē a single pitch is reiterated.

For some time after the fourteenth century the chakhē may have been considered more suitable for solo playing, and it is still often used in that manner. It has apparently appeared in string ensembles only since the time of King Rama I (1782–1809), the beginning of the Bangkok period; however, it has now come to be considered an important member of all string ensembles (figs. 106–110).

The chakhē plays the main melody with minor variations. The style of part ranges from a melodic treatment closely following the main melody to a more energetic style similar to the kep technique on the ranāt ēk (but single pitches rather than simultaneous octaves). This is shown in example 38, a transcription I made from a recording.

Example 38.

2. Bowed

Bowed stringed instruments are known in Thai by the generic term *"sǭ."*

a. Sǭ sām sāi

The body of the *sǭ sām sāi,* sometimes called the *sǭ thai,* is made from a special coconut shell that has grown in somewhat the shape of a triangle with three rounded bulges (fig. 87). The shell is cut in half, and the triangular section with the three bulges becomes the back of the sound box. The open part of the shell is covered with goatskin or calfskin (fig. 88). The size and length of the instrument depend on the size of shell from which the body is to be made; that plus the neck of the instrument makes the total length usually between forty and fifty inches. The neck, made of hardwood or ivory, projects through the sound box to end in a long "spike" foot (fig. 89) which is rested on the ground in playing position. Holes are made in the top and bottom of the long neck shaft, leading into hollow sections at both ends.

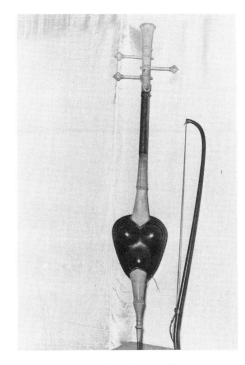

Figure 87. Sǫ sām sāī, back view, showing the sound box with three mounds on the back, with bow.

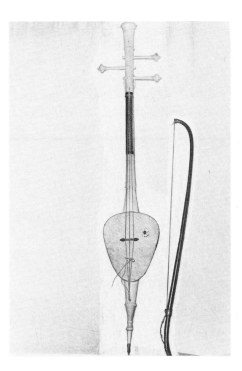

Figure 88. Sǫ sām sāī, front view, with bow.

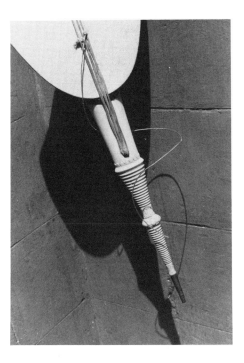

Figure 89. Detail of the spike of the sǫ sām sāī, showing the strings entering the spike.

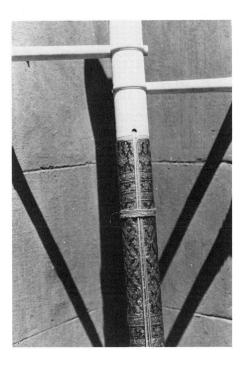

Figure 90. Detail of the front of the neck of the sǫ sām sāī, showing the strings entering the neck.

The three gut strings, tuned in fourths, are fastened inside the shaft at the lower end (fig. 89); from there they stretch over a supporting bridge on the sound box and pass over the neck, which has no frets, and through the hole at the upper end; they are fastened inside the neck shaft to the three tuning pegs, one on one side and two on the other (fig. 90). The pegs are generally rather long, up to six inches. In playing position, the side with the single peg is toward the player.

A very important part of this instrument is an object called in Thai a "head weight," which is fastened to the skin covering the sound box to the right of the bridge (as viewed from the front). This small weight is proportionate to the size and thickness of the head. It has much the same effect on the sound produced by the instrument as has the mixture of rice and ashes applied to the drumheads—it damps out certain partials, resulting in a "purer" tone quality. In the old days these weights became progressively more and more ornate as each player tried to outdo the other, until finally some were made of diamonds set in gold. Today they are usually of silver with a piece of colored glass or some type of Thai enamel or nielloware.[26]

The bow used for the sǭ sǎm sāi is large in relation to the size of the instrument; for an instrument about forty-eight inches long, a bow of about thirty-four inches is used. The wooden part of the bow is in the form of an elongated "S" curve. Some two hundred to two hundred and fifty horsetail hairs are tied between one end of the bow and the flat side of the curve at the opposite end, which serves as a handle for the right hand (fig. 87).

This instrument has been used by the Thai since at least the Sukhothai period (early fourteenth century). Prominent in the string ensembles, it is mentioned in the court regulations of the time as being an instrument difficult to play but highly esteemed for its exceptionally beautiful tone and particularly suited to accompanying singing, blending well with the human voice. During the Bangkok period the sǭ sǎm sāi was a favorite instrument of King Rama II (1809–1824), who was very musical (an excellent player of the sǭ sǎm sāi as well as a composer). The story is told that at this time, since the special coconut shell needed for the sound box of the instrument was so rare, if an owner of a coconut grove found a suitable coconut out of which a sound

box could be made, he received a license and was henceforth exempt from all taxes. The story does not say who received the coconut shell; probably it went to the royal palace.

The model for the sǭ sǎm sāi probably came from the Near East to India and then over the trade routes to Nanchao—spiked bowed lutes such as the *kemanché* and *rebab* are found in the Near East. Recent investigations by Hood (1970), however, suggest that the Javanese rebab—a two-stringed model of this type—existed in Java before the advent of Islam there.[27] The body of the Javanese rebab is also made from a somewhat triangular coconut shell, but in Java the shell is artificially pressed; the coconut is taken from the tree and cut in two, and the half that is to become the body for the rebab is put into a triangular press, oiled, and kept oiled until it is squeezed into the proper shape.[28] If Hood is right, the instrument probably came to Angkor from Java. Lute-type instruments that could easily be this one are pictured among the carvings at Angkor (see the illustrations in Chapter I), and a model practically identical with the sǭ sǎm sāi exists today in Cambodia; it is known as the *tro khmer,* "tro" being the Cambodian equivalent of "sǭ."[29] If the Khmer were using the instrument at the time the Thai conquered them, it is highly likely that the Thai in turn adopted the instrument from the Khmer. But if the original instrument did come from Java a third string was added at some time, for there is no evidence that the Javanese rebab ever had three strings or that the Thai instrument ever had two; also, since there is no record that the Thai ever used the method of artificially shaping the coconut shell, this Javanese technique of producing the body was lost along the way.

The use of this instrument has decreased sharply in contemporary Thailand—during the two years I was in Bangkok in 1958–1960 I had no opportunity to hear it played, although it was said that a few musicians who had played it privately still did upon occasion. The instrument is not a member of any ensemble, being used as a solo instrument or together with the voice (solo or with an ensemble) as a background accompanying instrument; however, it is often pictured with ensembles (figs. 98–100, 108–110). No notations of music for this instrument are available—example 39 is a transcription I made from a record of the beginning of a solo.[30]

Example 39.

b. Sǭ ū

The bowed stringed instrument with a sound box (resonating chamber or disphram) made from half an ordinary coconut shell is known as the sǭ ū (fig. 91). The back of the coconut shell is often carved in a pattern that pierces the shell, making a number of small openings that allow the sound to project better (fig. 92)—the same acoustical principle followed in putting the holes in the bodies of Western stringed instruments. The head, of goatskin or calfskin, is about five inches in diameter. The hardwood or ivory neck, which has no frets, is inserted through the sound box but extends only far enough below to hold the box securely—there is no spike "foot." The instrument is usually about thirty to thirty-two inches long.

The two strings of gut, silk, or nylon are attached to the end of the neck which protrudes through the bottom of the sound box; from there they are passed over a bridge—often made of tightly rolled cloth, sometimes of wood—placed at approximately the middle of the head; then they are fastened on the ends of two tuning pegs inserted back to front through the top of the neck. To make the strings tauter a noose is fastened around them at the neck and pulled tight, drawing them in toward the neck. This noose can be moved up or down; usually it is put at a distance above the sound box equal to the distance between the tips of the player's thumb and little finger when the hand is stretched wide. The strings are tuned in fifths; the higher pitch is the same as the lower of the two pitches of the sǭ duang (the next instrument to be discussed), and the other string is pitched a fifth below (see p. 37).

The bow is about twenty-seven inches long and in the shape of an elongated "C." The one hundred and fifty to two hundred horsehairs of the bow, after being attached to one end, pass between the strings before being attached to the other end of the bow—thus fastening it inseparably to the instrument (the same method as used with the sǭ duang, to be discussed next, as shown in fig. 95). A piece of resin is attached to the top of the body to the left of the neck (in playing position) against which the bow can be rubbed while the instrument is being played. One string is sounded by pressing the bow outward to the left against it, the other by pulling the bow in to the right against it. The instrument is held on the left thigh of the seated player, who fingers it with his left hand while bowing with the right.

The sǭ ū is one of the principal instruments of string ensembles (figs. 106–110). The musical line it plays is generally a variation of the main melody much like the kep style of the ranāt ēk except that the sǭ ū plays one pitch at a time and not octaves. An example of this style in cipher notation is shown at the end of the following discussion of the sǭ duang. The instrument can also play in a melodic style—the usual style for solos—in which glissandos and tremolos are frequent ornaments, as shown in example 39 for the sǭ sām sāi. The sǭ ū is sometimes

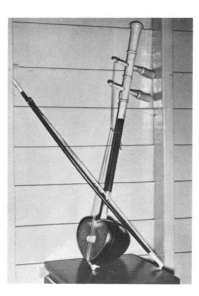

Figure 91. Sǭ ū.

Figure 92. Sǭ ū, bottom of the sound box, showing the carved hole openings.

Figure 93. The Chinese pan hu, with a piece of flat wood covering the sound box instead of leather; in the Institute of Ethnomusicology, UCLA, Los Angeles.

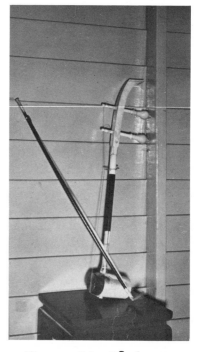

Figure 94. Sǭ duang.

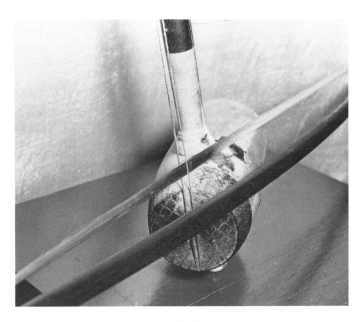

Figure 95. S$\bar{\rho}$ duang sound box, showing the hair of the bow passing between the strings.

Figure 96. S$\bar{\rho}$ duang being played.

Figure 97. The Chinese erh hu; the sound box is covered with snakeskin; in the Institute of Ethnomusicology, UCLA, Los Angeles.

added to the percussion ensemble used in the theater, perhaps to soften the sound of the percussion instruments for indoor performances. It is sometimes used with the percussion ensemble in concert performances of certain traditional compositions to which special solo sections for the s$\bar{\rho}$ $\bar{u}$ have been added.

The s$\bar{\rho}$ $\bar{u}$ is the Thai version of the Chinese *hu hu* and other similar types of stringed instruments; one difference occasionally found is that in some Chinese models the pegs are inserted from side to side rather than back to front (fig. 93). The Chinese instruments with the word "hu" as part of their name are not considered indigenous—the word "hu," meaning "barbarians," is said to refer to the people from whom the Chinese originally adopted the instrument. These "barbarians" are generally thought to have been peoples from the region of Mongolia to the north and northwest of China. The second "hu" of the name "hu hu" is said to be onomatopoeic, as is the Thai word "$\bar{u}$." Since the early Thai civilization was in close contact with the Chinese, the Thai as well have probably used this instrument for a long time. No reliable evidence exists, however, indicating that the Thai used either the sǭ ū or the sǭ duang prior to the end of the Ayuthaya period or the beginning of the Bangkok period (*ca.* 1780); they are not mentioned in any of the accounts of ensembles of pre-Bangkok times.

c. Sǭ duang

In the old days the sound box of this instrument was made from a section of bamboo about five inches long and two to three inches in diameter; now models are usually made of hardwood or ivory (figs. 94–96). Otherwise the construction of the instrument is like the sǭ ū. The usual length of the sǭ duang is about twenty-eight to twenty-nine inches. The head is usually of snakeskin (fig. 95) or an animal skin such as goatskin or calfskin; the opposite end of the resonance chamber is left open, as in the thōn drum. The bow of the instrument is permanently attached between the two strings (fig. 95). The strings are tuned in fifths with the lower pitch the same as the higher pitch of the sǭ ū (see p. 37). The sǭ duang is lighter, higher, and more penetrating in tone than that instrument.

Like the sǭ ū, the sǭ duang plays in melodic style or kep style. It doubles the sǭ ū in ensemble playing (figs. 106–110) for the most part, though occasionally, because the instruments are tuned a fifth apart, the pitches will be separated by an octave rather than be in unison. The sǭ ū and sǭ duang often play alternately in those sections that use a "statement and response" or "question and answer" style—the sǭ duang leading, comparable to the ranāt ēk, and the sǭ ū answering with the rest of the ensemble.

The sǭ duang is similar to the Chinese *hu ch'in* and *erh hu* (fig. 97) and was probably copied from these instruments. The word "duang" is also the name for a type of bamboo trap used by rural people in the northern areas of Thailand to catch edible lizards; the instrument was perhaps thought to resemble the trap and the name consequently borrowed.

3. Notation for String Parts

Two types of cipher notation have been developed for the string parts. One uses numbers corresponding to the seven fixed pitches of the tuning system, and the other uses numbers corresponding to the fingering. Both methods phrase the numbers so that the ching strokes come at the end of a unit or group of pulses rather than on the downbeat of a measure as in Western notation, as has been explained in detail in the section on rhythm, tempo, and meter in Chapter II (charts 3–5, pp. 41–42). The method of cipher notation using pitch numbers is shown in example 40; the numbers are arranged from the low-pitched string of the instrument—thus the ciphers for the sǭ ū will be a fifth above those for the sǭ duang, which is tuned a fifth higher. Since the pitches are equidistant, the intervallic pattern of 5–6–7–8 has the same sound as 1–2–3–4.

Example 40.

The method of cipher notation based on the fingering, as in example 41, also indicates the string to be used (same phrase as above).

Example 41.

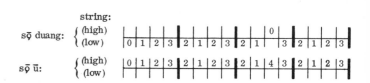

E. ENSEMBLES

In early times it is likely that rules existed for the combining of instruments into ensembles, but they were not definitely specified; Yupho says that instruments were probably brought together to give what was considered a mellifluous sound and in combinations that suited the particular performance or occasion (1960: 4). These early ensembles evolved into the three main ones now used for the performance of traditional music: (1) melodic and rhythmic percussion instruments with one type of wind instrument; (2) stringed instruments and rhythmic percussion with flutes; (3) a combination of stringed instruments, melodic and rhythmic percussion instruments, and flutes. Before dealing specifically with the contemporary groups, some of the development from early ensembles will be discussed.[31]

1. Development of String Ensembles

One of the first known Thai ensembles was called *khap mai* (fig. 98), literally "to recite or sing with a beat" or more figuratively "to perform on musical instruments." This ensemble was composed of three performers: a singer, a sǭ sām sāi, and a drum called *bandǫ* that was derived from the same type of drum found in China, Tibet, and India and is obsolete in Thailand today. The body of the drum has two bowl-shaped halves whose bottoms are placed together. The heads are held against the open part of the bowls by thongs laced back and forth between the two heads; the thongs are held in at the middle portion of the drum by another thong that encircles them. A stick, usually decorated by being turned with concentric rings, is fastened to one side of the center area where the two parts of the body are joined. A string is anchored at the end of the stick, and a small ball is attached to the string. When the drum is rolled from side to side by means of the handle, the ball bounces back and forth, striking the heads alternately and creating a line of rhythm.

Figure 98. Khap mai ensemble. Sǭ sām sāi (left), singer (center), a pair of bandǫ (right).

Figure 99. Original mah̄ōrī ensemble. Left to right: krajappī, singer
with krap phuang, sǭ sām sāī, thǭn.

Although the term *"mah̄ōrī"* now means an
ensemble composed of both stringed and percussion
instruments, it originally referred only to a string
ensemble. Prince Damrong was of the opinion that
mah̄ōrī was invented by the ancient Khmer and was
later adopted and elaborated by the Thai (1931: 3).
Originally the mah̄ōrī consisted of four members: a
krajappī, a sǭ sām sāī, a thǭn, and a singer who also
kept time with the *krap phuang* (fig. 99). The krap
phuang consists of several long thin sheets of metal
alternated with thin pieces of wood; these are put
between two heavier pieces of wood or ivory with
curving ends, and the whole is held together by a cord
put through holes at the bottom of all the pieces and
tied. The usual length is about eight and a half inches.
The krap phuang is held loosely with one hand,
usually the right, and slapped against the palm of the
other hand to mark the beats of emphasis.

The ensemble was originally played by men, but
when it became popular, men of position who had
large households caused the mah̄ōrī to be performed
by women; this apparently happened in the Ayuthaya
period, and the women's mah̄ōrī came greatly into
vogue—it continued until after the middle of the
nineteenth century.

More instruments were added from time to time.
During the Ayuthaya period the rammanā was added
to assist the thǭn with the rhythm, and the khlui was
introduced to strengthen the melody. Thus it became
an ensemble of five instrumentalists and a singer (fig.
100). After the foundation of Bangkok various other
instruments were added, mostly from the percussion
ensemble but of reduced size suitable for women; the
instruments and the reign during which they were
added are as follows:

King Rama I (1782–1809): ranāt ēk and ranāt
kāēo—a total of seven musicians. Prince Damrong
described the ranāt kāēo as a carillon but does not
further identify it, as the old books do not say clearly
what the instrument is. Yupho does not include an

Figure 100. Rubbing of a stone carving showing an early ensemble of the Sukhothai period; the instruments from left to right are: <u>thōn</u>, <u>rammanā</u>, <u>khlui</u> (in the back), <u>krajappī</u>, and <u>sō sām sāī</u>.

instrument with this name in his book, but the one he catalogs as the *khǭng rāng* is probably the same (1960: 26). The instrument, an early form of the Thai set of gong-kettles, consisted of eight kettles on a straight rack.

King Rama II (1809–1824): khǭng wong replacing the ranāt kāeo and chakhē—a total of eight musicians.

King Rama III (1824–1851): ranāt thum, khǭng wong lek, ching replacing or in addition to the krap phuang and chāp—a total of twelve musicians.

King Rama IV (1851–1868): ranāt ēk lek, ranāt thum lek—a total of fourteen musicians.

King Rama V (1868–1910): the krajappī and chāp ceased to be used regularly, leaving a total of twelve musicians.

In the Ayuthaya period women were not permitted to act on the stage outside royal service, and women of the royal households were trained only to play in the mahōrī ensemble; men played the percussion ensemble and acted on the stage. King Rama IV removed the prohibition and permitted women to be trained as actresses. The result was that the practice of employing women for the mahōrī was replaced by training them for the stage. Women players were popular on the stage and more attracted to it then to performing on the instruments, and the women's mahōrī as a result fell into decline.

Meanwhile some men musicians had been taking up the sǭ duang and sǭ ū, and they added these together with the chakhē to a small already existing ensemble called the *klǭng khāek* (fig. 101) and composed of two klǭng khāek drums, the pī chawā, and the *khǭng mēng,* a small gong held up manually by a curved wooden handle from which it is suspended and struck with a piece of wood or a padded beater; this small ensemble was probably formed when the klǭng khāek and pī chawā were borrowed from Java. The new combination with the stringed instruments became known as the large klǭng khāek ensemble. Later the klǭng khāek and the pī chawā were replaced by the rammanā-thōn combination and the khlui, and the name "string mahōrī" was given to this new ensemble. Some

Figure 101. Klǫng khāēk ensemble. Instruments reading from left
to right are: klǫng khāēk, pī chawā, klǫng khāēk, and khǫng mēng.

ensembles added the ranāt and khǫng instruments
resulting in an ensemble comparable to the other
mahōrī ensemble except played by men.

Today it is again customary for both women and
men to play the stringed instruments, often in the
same ensemble. A further distinction is made between
ensembles using stringed instruments without melodic
percussion instruments and ensembles combining
stringed and melodic percussion instruments, the
khrūang sāi and mahōrī ensembles respectively. Also,
it is common to find ensembles playing with a larger
number of some of the instruments than the standard
ensemble calls for—as many as there are instruments
available and musicians to play them; the situation is
rather like that of some folk dances: "for as many as
will." Such a situation is characteristic only of an
informal gathering, however, not of a formal
performance.

2. Development of Melodic Percussion Ensembles

The ensemble using melodic and rhythmic percussion
is called pī phāt; "pī" is the double-reed instrument,

and "phāt" means "instrumental music" in general or
"to perform music."

The pī phāt ensemble apparently was devised
originally to accompany stage performance. There
were two types of ensembles: (1) "light pī phāt,"
which accompanied the lakhǫn performances (actors
without masks), and (2) "heavy pī phāt," which
accompanied the khōn (masked drama). The "light pī
phāt" consisted of the pī, two thōn (thōn chātrī), one
or a pair of klǫng chātrī (a drum with pegged heads,
like the klǫng that but much smaller—the body
being about ten inches high, the heads about eight
inches in diameter) played by one player, and a pair
of gong-kettles called khǫng khū (kettles similar to
those used on the khǫng wong, fastened horizontally
in a small rectangular box frame). The "heavy pī
phāt" consisted of a pī, a ranāt ēk, a khǫng wong, a
taphōn, and a klǫng chātrī. When not playing the
taphōn, the musician played the ching.

Two types of ensembles were needed because in
the lakhǫn the singing and dialogue alternate with the
playing of the band, whereas in the khōn the
ensemble executes long passages necessitating more
instruments capable of playing melodies. Since the

introduction of lakhọn nai, or royal lakhọn, the heavy pī phāt of the khōn has come to be used for both; it is the main percussion ensemble of traditional music today, the light pī phāt ensemble continuing to accompany the nōrā theater in the southern provinces.

Prince Damrong proposed that the evolution of the pī phāt ensemble was in the following manner (1931: 7–8): During the Ayuthaya period, the heavy pī phāt was as outlined above. The pī was a small one that came to be known as the pī nọk after the larger pī nai was devised. The klọng with pegged heads was the small klọng chātrī size. The first modification was the devising of the pī nai and the replacing of the klọng chātrī with the larger klọng *that*. Whether this occurred during the Ayuthaya period or after the founding of Bangkok is not known. King Rama II was fond of both the lakhọn and the sēphā, the long chanted epics. Prior to his reign the sēphā was sung without accompaniment; the king introduced the pī phāt and probably also the mahōrī into the sēphā. At this time also the sọng nā was probably substituted for the taphōn as a more suitable drum for accompanying singing, and the pī nai and klọng *that* replaced the earlier models of these instruments.[32] During the reign of Rama III this sēphā style became very popular, and the ensemble was enlarged by adding a second instrument of each type. At this time also the ranāt thum, khọng wong lek, and chāp were probably devised and the second klọng *that* was added. During the reign of Rama IV the metallophones were created and added to the ensemble—perhaps also the mōng, the large single gong.

3. Standard Contemporary Ensembles

In traditional Thai music today there are three standard ensembles: pī phāt, composed of melodic and rhythmic percussion instruments and the pī; khrụang sāi, composed of stringed instruments, rhythmic percussion instruments, and the khlui; and mahōrī, a combination of the first two ensembles. There are also three standard sizes of ensembles: small, medium or "doubled," and large. These groupings are used for formal occasions (mention has already been made of their variability according to the relative informality of the occasion and the instruments and musicians available).

The instrumentation of the standard ensembles is as follows:

a. Pī Phāt

Small ensemble (*khrụang hā*, literally, "five instruments"; fig. 102):
one pī nai
one ranāt ēk
one khọng wong yai
one taphōn and/or ching
two klọng *that* (one player)
In small ensembles today a modification of this arrangement is sometimes made in order to have a richer musical texture: the klọng *that* are eliminated and a ranāt thum is used. Since the result is only one drum, the taphōn, a sixth musician is usually added to play the ching throughout. If the occasion calls for less volume of sound, especially if the performance is in a small room, a khlui is substituted for the pī (fig. 103).

Medium-sized or doubled ensemble (*khrụang khū*, literally, "a pair of instruments"; fig. 104):
two pī: pī nọk
　　　 pī nai
one taphōn
one pair of ching (chāp optional)
two xylophones: ranāt ēk
　　　　　　　 ranāt thum
two gong circles: khọng wong lek
　　　　　　　　 khọng wong yai
two klọng *that*
one mōng

Large ensemble (*khrụang yai*, literally, "large group of instruments"; fig. 105):
two pī: pī nọk
　　　 pī nai
two xylophones: ranāt ēk
　　　　　　　 ranāt thum
two metallophones: ranāt ēk lek
　　　　　　　　　 ranāt thum lek
two gong circles: khọng wong lek
　　　　　　　　 khọng wong yai
one taphōn
one pair of ching
one pair of chāp lek
one pair of chāp yai (optional)
one mōng
two klọng *that*

Figure 102. Small pī phāt ensemble. Instruments from left to right are: taphōn, pī nai, khong wong yai, ranāt ēk, klong that, and ching (photograph courtesy of Department of Fine Arts, Bangkok).

Figure 103. Small, informal indoor pī phāt ensemble with the khlui (left) substituted for the pī.

Figure 104. Medium-sized or doubled pī phāt ensemble.
Instruments from left to right are: taphōn, pī nai, (rear) khōng
wong yai, (rear center) klǫng that, (rear) khōng wong lek, pī
nōk, (extreme right) mōng, (front left) ranāt ēk, (front center) ching, (front right) ranāt thum (photograph courtesy of
Department of Fine Arts, Bangkok).

Figure 105. Large pī phāt ensemble. Instruments from left
to right are: (rear) taphōn, (to fore) pī nai, (rear) ching, (to
fore) khǫng wong yai, (rear) chāp lek, mōng, (to fore) khōng
wong lek, (rear) chāp yai, (to fore) pī nōk, (rear) klǫng that,
(front row) ranāt ēk lek, ranāt ēk, ranāt thum, ranāt thum lek
(photograph courtesy of the Department of Fine Arts, Bangkok).

Figure 106. Small khrŷang sāi ensemble. Instruments left to right are: (rear) ching, (to fore) sǫ duang, (rear) khlui phīang ǭ, (front center) čhakhē, (rear) thōn, (to fore) sǭ ū, (rear) rammanā (photograph courtesy of the Department of Fine Arts, Bangkok).

Figure 107. Medium-sized or doubled khrŷang sāi ensemble. Instruments left to right are: sō duang, (front) čhakhē, (directly behind) chāp lek, (to fore) sō duang, (rear) ching, khlui līp, mōng, khlui phīang ǭ, (to fore) sǭ ū, (front) čhakhē, (directly behind) rammanā, thōn, (extreme right) sǫ ū (photograph courtesy of the Department of Fine Arts, Bangkok).

Figure 108. Small mahōrī ensemble. Instruments left to
right are: (rear) ching, (to fore) sǭ duang, (rear) khlui phīang
ǭ, (to fore, center) sǭ sām sāi, (rear) khǭng wong yai (or:
khǭng klāng), (to fore) sǭ ū, (rear) rammanā, (rear, right)
thōn, (front, left) ranāt ēk, (front, right) čhakhē (photograph
courtesy of the Department of Fine Arts, Bangkok).

Figure 109. Medium sized or doubled māhorī ensemble.
Instruments left to right are: (rear row) ching, sǭ duang, sǭ
duang, khǭng wong yai (or: khǭng klāng), (to fore) khlui phīang
ǭ, (rear, left of center) thōn, (rear, right of center) rammanā,
(to fore) khlui ū, (rear) khǭng wong lek (or: khǭng klāng), sǭ
ū, sǭ ū, chāp lek (middle row) čhakhē, ranāt ēk, ranāt thum,
čhakhē, (front row) sǭ sām sāi, sǭ sām sāi (photograph courtesy of the Department of Fine Arts, Bangkok).

Figure 110. Large mahōrī ensemble. Instruments left to
right are: (rear row, to fore) sǫ duang, (rear) ching, (to fore)
khlui līp, (rear) chāp lek, (to fore) khǫng wong yai (or: khǫng
klāng), (rear, left of center) rammanā, (rear, right of center)
thōn, (to fore) khǫng wong lek (or: khōng klāng), (rear) mōng,
(to fore) khlui phīang ǫ, (rear) chāp yai, (to fore) sǫ ū,
(middle row) ranāt ēk lek, ranāt ēk, khlui ū, ranāt thum,
ranat thum lek, (front row) sǫ duang, čhakhē, sǫ sām sāi, sǫ
sām sāi, čhakhē, sǫ ū (photograph courtesy of the Department
of Fine Arts, Bangkok).

The pī nǫk is practically obsolete, so if two pī are used today they are usually both pī nai.

The pair of klǫng khāek can be added to the above three ensembles when certain compositions are played.

A distinction is made between ensembles in which the ranāt ēk uses playing sticks with hard knobs and those in which sticks with soft pads are needed. When the soft sticks are used, tradition allows substitution of the khlui for the pī and the addition of the sǫ ū.

The similarity between the Thai pī phāt ensemble and the Javanese gamelan is worth mention. Jaap Kunst has written an article describing this similarity (1929: 79 ff.), but since it is in Dutch and in a publication not readily available, it should perhaps be mentioned here that both ensembles use xylophones and

metallophones, sets of gong-kettles, gong, and drums. The main difference is that the Thai ensemble uses the reed aerophone, the pī, while in "loud style" the Javanese gamelan uses no wind instrument, and in "soft style" uses flutes (suling) and a two-stringed spike bowed lute, the rebab. In the Javanese gamelan the rebab—or in its absence, the drum (kendang)—functions as leader of the ensemble, while in the Thai ensemble the ranāt ēk has this function. The ching, the little hand cymbals, are not represented in the Javanese gamelan. A much larger number of gongs and a more intricate gong or colotomic structure obtains in Javanese music than is presently in use in the Thai ensembles. As has been stated, there is evidence that a greater number of gongs was formerly used in Thai ensembles (Yupho 1926: 25), perhaps similarly to those in the Javanese and

Balinese gamelan. Despite these differences, a great similarity does exist between the instruments and ensembles of the two areas.

b. Khrụ̄ang Sāi

Small ensemble (fig. 106):
one sǭ duang
one sǭ ū
one čhakhē
one khlui: khlui phīang ǭ
one thōn
one rammanā
one pair of ching
Medium-sized or doubled ensemble (fig. 107):
two sǭ duang
two sǭ ū
two čhakhē
two khlui: khlui līp
           khlui phīang ǭ
one thōn
one rammanā
one pair of ching
one pair of chāp
one mōng

No standard instrumentation is given for a large ensemble, but it might include more of the above instruments with possible additional instruments such as the low-pitched khlui (the khlui ū), the sǭ sām sāi, and so forth.

c. Mahōrī

Small ensemble (fig. 108):
one sǭ sām sāi
one sǭ duang
one sǭ ū
one čhakhē
one khlui phīang ǭ
one thōn
one rammanā
one pair of ching
one ranāt ēk
one khǭng wong   } mahōrī size
Medium-sized or doubled ensemble (fig. 109):
two sǭ sām sāi: one large
               one small
two sǭ duang
two sǭ ū

two čhakhē
two khlui: khlui līp
           khlui phīang ǭ
one thōn-rammanā
one pair of ching
one pair of chāp lek
one ranāt ēk
one ranāt thum   } mahōrī
one khǭng wong lek   } size
one khǭng wong yai
   or, khǭng klāng
Large ensemble (fig. 110):
two sǭ sām sāi: one large
               one small
two sǭ duang
two sǭ ū
two čhakhē
three khlui: khlui līp
            khlui phīang ǭ
            khlui ū
two xylophones: ranāt ēk
               ranāt thum
two metallophones: ranāt ēk lek
                ranāt thum lek   } mahōrī size
two gong circles: khǭng wong lek
                khǭng wong yai
   or, two khǭng klāng
one thōn
one rammanā
one pair of ching
one pair of chāp lek
one pair of chāp yai
one mōng

4. Special Ensembles

For the sake of completeness a few other ensembles ought to be mentioned, though they are rarely used today.

Besides the klǭng khāek, probably of Javanese origin, there is another similar drum though smaller—the klǭng malāyū—which is thought to have come from Malaya. The differences between the two drums are the size, the material with which the heads are anchored, the pattern of the lacings, and the method in which they are played. Both drums are two-headed cylindrical drums, the heads being rolled on hoops and held in position by lacings that pass back and forth between the two heads. The klǭng khāek originally retained the Javanese method of tying the heads with split cane or rattan, while the heads of the klǭng malāyū were laced with thongs. Both types are found in Java today; Solonese drums use cane, Djogyanese use hide lacings. It has been the practice for some time to use thongs on both Thai instruments. The thongs of the klǭng khāek are in a "Y" pattern created by a thong that encircles the drum near the bulge and holds the lengthwise thongs in position. The smaller klǭng malāyū has no thong encircling the drum, as the illustration in Yupho's book shows (1960: 44), and the lacings are in a "V" pattern when loose and in a "Y" pattern when tightened for playing (fig. 111).

The klǭng khāek drum is played with the hands only; the klǭng malāyū with the left hand and one curved or bent drumstick held by the right hand. Drums like the klǭng malāyū are represented in the carvings on the Borobudur in central Java (Kunst 1949: II, illus. 8 and 23).

Prince Damrong speculates that the evolution of the use of these two pairs of drums in Thai music is as follows (1931: 9):

The klǭng malāyū probably came first and was used in royal processions, such as the elephant processions, in which Malayans took part. Later it came to be used in the cremation processions of kings and royalty, and gradually its use began to be exclusively to provide music for ceremonies in connection with the dead.

The klǭng khāek was probably introduced into Thai music in connection with certain dances, such as the sword dance, the club dance, and the Javanese kriss dance. It was also employed in processions such as the tonsure (hair-shaving) procession and the royal procession of barges, in which a gong was not used. Prince Damrong supposed that originally the klǭng malāyū was employed in those processions, but when it came to be associated with ceremonies for the dead it was considered an inauspicious instrument for happy occasions and was replaced by the klǭng khāek without the gong.

The introduction of the klǭng khāek into the pī phāt ensemble probably dates from the adaptation of the Javanese epic *Inao* for the Thai stage. It is used in the pī phāt and mahōrī ensembles when they play compositions derived from Javanese compositions, replacing the taphōn and thōn-rammanā.

The original ensemble using the klǭng malāyū is called *bua lǭi*. It consists of a pī chawā, the pair of klǭng malāyū, and the khǭng mēng. The ensemble using the klǭng khāek was called simply "klǭng khāek" and used a pair of these drums with the pī chawā and khǭng mēng.

Figure 111. P̱ī p̱ẖāt ṉān̲g ẖon̲g ensemble. Instruments left to right are: (rear row) c̱ẖāp̱ ḻek̲, k̲h̲ǭn̲g w̲on̲g y̱ai, c̱ẖāp̱ y̱ai, k̲h̲ǭn̲g w̲on̲g ḻek̲, m̱ōn̲g, (front row) p̱ī c̱ẖawā, ṟaṉāṯ ēk̲, c̱ẖin̲g, ṟaṉāṯ ṯhum, and a pair of k̲l̲ǭn̲g m̲a̲l̲āy̲ū.

a. Pī phāt nāng hong

The final development of the bua lǫi ensemble using the Malayan drums, called *pī phāt nāng hong,* adds melodic percussion instruments from the regular pī phāt ensemble as well as the more contemporary models of the rhythmic percussion instruments.

Pī phāt nāng hong (fig. 111):
one ranāt ēk
one ranāt thum
one khǫng wong lek
one khǫng wong yai
one pī chawā
two klǫng malāyū
one pair of ching
one pair of chāp lek
one pair of chāp yai
one mōng

b. Pī phāt mǫn

The mǫn counterparts of several of the instruments have been described in this chapter. A formal ensemble using these instruments—which also plays

for ceremonies connected with the dead—is called pī phāt mǫn. It includes another drum that must be described briefly—actually a set of drums hung from a semicircular stand. These are of the same type of construction as the taphōn and sǫng nā but smaller, an average size being about twenty-one inches long with heads about six to seven inches in diameter. The individual drum is called the *pōeng mǎng,* and the set is called the *pōeng mǎng khǫk* (figs. 113, 114). The instrument differs from the similar Burmese model in that the framework is a semicircle, and there are only seven drums in the Thai model; they are not tuned precisely, but only in a general graduation from low to high. The Burmese model, on the other hand, has up to twenty-four carefully tuned drums suspended on a completely circular framework (fig. 116).[33]

Pī phāt mǫn (medium-sized or doubled ensemble; fig. 112):
one ranāt ēk
one ranāt thum
one khǫng mǫn lek
one khǫng mǫn yai
one pī mǫn
one taphōn mǫn
one pōeng mǎng khǫk
one pair of ching
one pair of chāp lek
one mōng

Figure 112. Pī phāt mǫn ensemble. Instruments are: (1) pī mǫn, (2) khǫng mǫn yai, (3) khǫng mǫn lek, (4) ranāt ēk, (5) ranāt thum, (8) taphōn mǫn, (9) pōeng mǎng, (10) ching, (12) chāp lek, (13) mōng (see also figs. 36, 37, 60).

Figure 113. P͞oeng m͞ang kh͞ǫk being played.

Figure 114. Back view of the p͞oeng m͞ang kh͞ǫk.

Figure 115. Burmese Anyein ensemble and ceremonial instruments (from Colston).

Figure 116. Burmese saing ensemble (from Colston).

Chapter IV

Mode

A. AN APPROACH TO MODALITY IN THAI TRADITIONAL MUSIC

In studying and analyzing Thai music with the objective of discovering the bases of the modal practice, two aspects of the musical system become immediately apparent. First, the Thai do not theorize to any great extent about their own music—there are no Thai terms for such common Western musical concepts as scale, mode, and so forth—so compositions cannot be categorized on the basis of what the culture itself says are different modal structures,[1] as is the case with such systems as the *ragas* of India and the *paṭet* system of Java. Second, examination of a representative group of compositions for details that might provide a basis for categorization shows that in relation to the highly-developed modal systems of Java and India, modal practice in Thai music is relatively simple. The music is based on a linear system that uses only seven fixed pitches in the octave and principal modes of only five or six pitches. To the Western ear much of the music may sound similar and repetitive because of these factors and the use in many compositions of standard phrases, motives, or melodic species. In fact, however, despite the relative simplicity of the musical material from which Thai compositions are built, depth analysis reveals great diversity—indeed, an astonishing variety—among them.

One hundred and thirty-six compositions were selected from the Thai traditional repertory to form a representative group for study. Most of these are from the manuscript collection and the *Silpakǫn Magazine;* a few are compositions taught to me in Bangkok. The selected compositions are of three kinds: (1) relatively short compositions in their original form (sǫng chan), (2) compositions only in the extended version (sām chan), and (3) the extended versions of compositions in the Thao (variation) form (these three forms will be discussed in detail in the next chapter).

Well over half of the compositions clearly use a five-pitch or pentatonic mode in one tonality or pitch level, or have temporary "modulations" to other pitch levels on which a similar pentatonic mode is used. Thus we may say that pentatonic modes are basic to Thai music in what will be called the simple "Thai" style. The mode is represented by a set of five consecutive pitches from the basic pattern 123 56 (1). The importance of each of these five pitches among the compositions is highly variable. No terminology for the hierarchy exists, nor does it exist as a known musical concept about which musicians verbalize—a situation, as was pointed out earlier, very different from that found in Java and India; to facilitate discussion, throughout this chapter I shall use terms that I have devised for some of these standard musical elements and practices.

Hood (1954: 228) has indicated that in the case of Javanese paṭet an attempt to formulate a modal theory primarily on the basis of the finalis of the compositions could be a dangerous and misleading procedure. However, in a linear music system with little terminology—such as the Thai music system—the finalis may possibly assume more importance than it would in a system in which harmonic progression often takes precedence over the melodic superstructure, as in Western music, or in a linear system that has much musical terminology, such as in Javanese and Indian music. Also, the following situation obtained in early Chinese music, to which Thai music is probably most closely related:

115

in pre-Han times in China (that is, before about 200 B.C.), according to Picken "each mode takes the name of the note which is *finalis,* which ends melodies in that mode" (1957: 95). Reserving judgment as to the possible importance of the finalis in Thai compositions, in those in the representative group the disposition of the finalis is as shown in chart 6.

Finalis	Number of Occurrences	Percentage
1	75	55.1%
2	19	14.0%
3	7	5.1%
4	16	11.8%
5	19	14.0%

Chart 6. Percentage of occurrences of pitches as a finalis.

Pitch 1 of the pentatonic mode is favored as the finalis in over half the compositions. Nearly all seventy-five compositions ending on pitch 1 conclude with the cadence 5321 or 321, in various rhythms, or in some variant of this, sometimes with an extension to another pitch 1 as finalis; a few have a rising cadence 561 with or without an extension.

With a tonal supply of seven pitches, it is possible to have seven starting pitches for a modal pattern; in the Thai repertory compositions are found using all seven pitches as a starting point or "tonic," but not with equal frequency. Generally speaking a Thai composition can be considered on one basic pitch level, even though it may "modulate" away from this level temporarily or even end on another pitch level. The one hundred and thirty-six compositions are distributed among the various pitch levels in the amounts shown in chart 7, further categorized according to the finalis (terms for pitch levels were explained in Chapter I).

Except for two unusual compositions, in this representative group only four pitch levels are used as basic or "home" pitch levels.

The simple dictionary definition of the word "mode" is: "manner or way in which a thing is done; style, fashion, or custom that prevails." The *Harvard Dictionary of Music* defines mode, as applied musically to pitch, as "the selection of tones, arranged in a scale, that form the basic tonal substance of a composition." Modal practices in the music of the Near Eastern and Asian cultures include a great deal more than this. The additional concepts are often implied in the term "melody types," which the *Harvard Dictionary* defines as denoting "a repertory of traditional melodies, melodic formulas, stereotyped figures, tonal progressions, ornamentations, rhythmic patterns, etc., that serve as a model for the creation of new melodies."

A seminar in ethnomusicology at the University of California at Los Angeles proposed the following tentative, but more comprehensive, definition of mode.

Mode is a traditional system applied in musical composition and/or improvisation based on a nonequidistant scale of at least three pitches, establishing a hierarchy of pitch relationships expressed in the form of characteristic melodic formulas, and may include additional refinements such as subsidiary pitches, rhythmic considerations, cadential formulas, variation, ornamentation, exchange or substitute pitches, modulation, auxiliary scales or modes, and so forth.

Pitch Level	1	2	3	5	6	Total	Percentage
high kruat (I)	9	2	0	2	1	14	10.3%
high phīang ộ̄ (VII)	18	4	0	4	4	30	22.0%
low kruat (IV)	42	10	4	10	8	74	55.0%
low phīang ộ̄ (III)	6	1	3	0	6	16	11.7%
mixed, unclear						2	1.0%

Chart 7. Classification of finalis pitches according to pitch levels.

In his recent book Mantle Hood (1971: 324–325) has refined and extended this definition as follows:

> Basic features of Mode seem to include the following: (1) a gapped scale, that is, a scale made up of both small and large intervals; (2) a hierarchy of principal pitches; (3) the usage of vocal or ornamental pitches; and (4) extramusical associations with the seasons, hours of the day or night, and so forth. In addition, modal practice might involve the usage of special registers, for example, low, middle, and high; rhythmic requirements including unmeasured "silence" following points of melodic repose (modal cadences); regulation of the *quality* of sound; special associations with language and/or text; particular requirements in connection with interrelated arts such as dance or puppetry; special practices governed by the requirements of ritual or religion; and so forth.

The essential requirements seem to be:

(1) A gapped, that is, nonequidistant tonal supply (often referred to as "scale").

(2) A hierarchy of pitch relationships.

(3) Characteristic melodic patterns, including cadential formulas.

Concerning the first requirement, the following factors may be reiterated about Thai music: the seven relatively equidistant pitches in the Thai tuning system, as represented on the instruments of fixed pitch, are never used as a scale or mode of seven pitches in any one specific, formal portion of a Thai composition. Of these available pitches five are used at any given time in the simple Thai style, forming a pentatonic tonal supply of nonequidistant intervals. In the mōn style six pitches are often prominently used, making a hexatonic tonal supply, also nonequidistant though less so because obviously in the hexatonic arrangement six adjoining (diatonic, in the Thai sense) equidistant pitches obtain—123456 or 123 567 (= 567123)—while in the pentatonic arrangement only the three equidistant pitches 123 are adjoining. But in the hexatonic pattern the sixth pitch is generally used in secondary, unaccented positions, and the hierarchy of pitches involves only five (sometimes less) principal pitches. This hierarchy, the second requirement, is based on the pitches that occur at certain points of the metrical structure, that is, at points where the ching sounds its damped stroke (already explained in Chapter II and to be illustrated shortly).

As for requirement three, some of the typical melodic patterns, formulas, and species, such as the thao fill-in motives, were illustrated in Chapter II. A few more representative formulas, used in different places on different pitch levels and in different compositions, will be shown here; others will be seen in examples presented subsequently.

1. Example 42 shows ascent from pitch 1 to pitch 3 (all notated in high phīang ǭ, HPǬ).

Example 42.

(* Idiomatic decoration style for the khǭng wong yai; see pages 49–50).

2. Example 43 shows ascent from pitch 5 to pitch 1 (all notated in high phīang ǭ, HPǬ).

3. Example 44 shows descent from pitch 2 to pitch 6 (all notated in high phīang ǭ, HPǬ).

Example 43.

Example 44.

(* This is an example of an exception to the tendency of the leap of a fourth to resolve in the direction of the first pitch. When the pitch of resolution is of a longer durational value—a quarter-note here—the first pitch is more a decoration than part of the essential melodic line, which, here, is basically diatonic: a-g-f-d.)

4. Example 45 shows the characteristic 5321 cadence occurring in "closed" position (that is, a pitch on every beat of the second half of the phrase) and some variants.

Example 45.

(a) basic form

5. Example 46 shows the cadence occurring in "open" position (that is, a pitch on each of the four main beats of the phrase) and some variants.

Example 46.

Compositions proceed according to a simple quadratic or duple structure metrically. The older style of compositions have little or no formal repetition within the section; a section is usually marked with repeat signs in the manuscript collection. The newer style of vocal-instrumental compositions often do have phrases repeated. Occasionally, particularly in the extended version, compositions have as their first phrase a standard thao (fill-in) phrase, but it is not consistently used.

Thai music, like most if not all Javanese and Chinese music, uses only a duple meter; but it does not have the well-developed colotomic structure, with its variety of gongs, which underlies Javanese music. Functionally speaking, the principal percussion instrument in Thai music is not the drum but the ching, the small hand cymbals. They are indispensable because the pattern they play indicates the form of the composition; if the gong is used, it reinforces the formal structure. The ching patterns as they indicate form have been discussed in Chapter II (pp. 40 ff.).

Thai melodies consist of a series of motives of the same length, generally grouped in pairs. In the middle version (sŏng chan) and sŏng mai ching pattern, a motive is one measure long and the pair covers two measures:

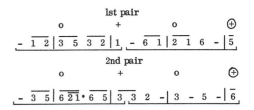

In Thai music the main melody can often be simplified into "nuclear" pitches of primarily the same rhythmic value, as in example 47. The cipher notation for examples to follow will frequently be simplified in this manner.

Example 47.

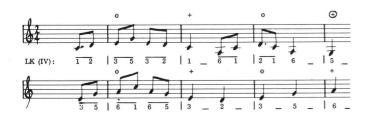

In the extended version (sām chan) and prop kai ching pattern, motives are two measures long and a pair covers four measures:

I have originated the term "phrase-unit" to designate a pair of motives because the pair contains two accented ching strokes, the second of which in prop kai is emphasized with a gong stroke, as previously explained. The four ching strokes, closing with the gong stroke, furnish a convenient unit from which, in analyzing, one can proceed inwardly into smaller units and outwardly into groups of pairs. (Since most of the compositions in the representative group are in the extended version using the prop kai ching pattern, only that pattern will be meant from this point on unless otherwise stipulated.) The smallest practical unit of four pulses in the melodic line is that group ending on either type of ching stroke:

	motive 1		motive 2	

(beats): 1 2 3 4 1 2 3 4 1 2 3 4 1 2 3 4

Each motive, then, is made up of two smaller pulse units that work together in an antecedent-succedent polarity. The motive also contains a complete pulse group of its own:

motive 1	motive 2

- 1 - 2 - 3 - 4 - 1 - 2 - 3 - 4

The phrase-unit, likewise, has its pulse grouping:

motive 1	motive 2

- - - 1 - - - 2 - - - 3 - - - 4

Two phrase-units embody a larger pulse grouping. These two phrase-units of eight ching strokes cover one cycle of the prop kai drum pattern:

```
        o    +    o    ⊕
             1         2
             3         4
```

Four phrase-units contain four ching-gong strokes and have a similar pulse emphasis:

```
        o    +    o    ⊕
                       1
                       2
                       3
                       4
```

With but few exceptions compositions in the Thai traditional repertory are made up of an even number of phrase-units, and phrase-units are always complete. The number of phrase-units is, further, usually divisible by four, and I have termed the resulting groups of four phrase-units "phrase-blocks." The number of phrase-blocks in a section is not consistent among the compositions, but two to four is the usual number. If the composition does have two or four phrase-blocks, a larger pulse grouping can be set up:

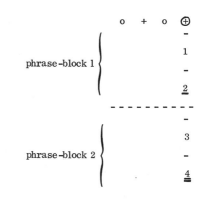

Occasionally a section has six or ten phrase-units, with the result that the section consists of one and a half or two and a half phrase-blocks; examples of this will be seen subsequently. Very rarely three phrase-units occur at the end of a section. When a partial phrase-block occurs, the extra phrase-unit or phrase-units are usually an extension melodically of the preceding complete phrase-block.

Starting with the smallest pulse grouping and proceeding from it, the phrase-block is built up and unified in the following way (this phrase-unit is a much-used one and will serve well to illustrate the principles involved here):

Pulse Group:

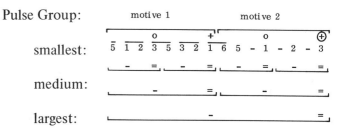

Motive one is "closed," that is, a pitch occurs on each pulse. The accented pulses of each half of the motive have the pitches 1 3 and 3 1. The pulse grouping of the complete motive, then, is 1 3̲ 3 1̲, establishing the movement from pitch 3 to pitch 1. The second motive is "open," a pitch only on the accented pulses, pitch 6 being a passing tone. The pulse emphasis establishes the movement from pitch 1 back to pitch 3: 5 1̲ 2 3̲. The pulse grouping of the phrase-unit is a larger movement from pitch 1 to

pitch 3:   3 1 1 3   (medium pulse group in the diagram above). The two halves of motive one each begin with pitch 5; the antecedent group starts on low pitch 5 and rises to pitch 3; the succedent group starts on high pitch 5 and descends to pitch 1. The first accented pulse in motive two is low pitch 5 again, and the open motive ascends at half the speed of the pulse groups in motive one from low pitch 5 to pitch 3, echoing the beginning pulse group. Pitch 5, then, is used as a secondary pitch of emphasis.

In the main melodic line in Thai music, several pulses operate simultaneously on several different levels—wheels within wheels within wheels. The drive in each separate unit is toward the final pitch of that pulse grouping, and each succeedingly larger pulse grouping in the phrase-unit leads to the final pitch in the phrase-unit. The process is then started anew in the next phrase-unit, and as phrase-units accumulate, larger pulse groupings are set up. In Thai music, then, the superstructure or skeleton of the pitch content of a composition can be indicated by extracting the pitches that occur on the ching strokes and putting them into a diagram. This "pitch outline" will indicate the principal pitches used in a composition, their hierarchy, and their interrelationships. An example of an extended version of a composition outlined in this way is in chart 8.

```
                       o    +    o    ⊕
   Section 1:     LK (IV) :‖5    5    1    5
                          1    6    5    1
                          6    2    2    6
                          3    6    3    2
                        - - - - - - - - - -
                          2    2    5    2
                          1    3    3    1
                          6    2    2    6
                          6    3    6    5:‖
                        - - - - - - - - - -
                  coda   5    5    1    5   (same as 1st phrase-unit)

   Section 2:            5    5    1    5   (same as 1st phrase-unit and coda
                      ‖:3    6    1    5              of Section 1)
                         3    6    6    3
                         1    3    3    1
                        - - - - - - - - - -
                         5    5    1    5
                         3    6    1    5
                         3    6    6    3
                         1    3    3    1   (cadence: 5321)
                        - - - - - - - - - -
   1st ending:           1    1    2    1:‖  (replaces 1st phrase-unit for the repeat)
   2nd ending:           1    1   (thao)
```

Section 1

(N.B. The thao at the end occurs after the final cadence and overlaps with the beginning of the next vocal section, which is the beginning of the sǫng chan section. Since the phrase unit in the middle version is half as long as in the extended version, the thao is half the length of a sām chan thao and is complete as it appears here.)

Chart 8. Pitch outline—"Khāek Sai" (Thao), 3 chan, ms. coll. no. 329.

The four phrase-units in a phrase-block are generally found to have this inner organization:

Phrase-unit one: though unemphasized, it introduces the composition, section, or phrase-block; thus its pitches set the scene musically for what is to follow.

Phrase-unit two: brings to a close the first large pulse group, and therefore its final ⊕ pitch is significant.

Phrase-unit three: an unaccented position in relation to the phrase-block as a whole; the main contrast in the phrase-block is usually found here.

Phrase-unit four: brings the phrase-block to a close and has a relationship to phrase-unit two.

Let us now examine the pitch outline of "Khaēk Sai," in particular those pitches on the + and ⊕ strokes:

Section One:

Phrase-block one:

Phrase-unit one: establishes pitch 5.

Phrase-unit two: pitch 1, the fifth below, closes the first half of the phrase-block.

Phrase-unit three: introduces pitch 2, the fifth above pitch 5, and pitch 6, the fifth above pitch 2, for contrast.

Phrase-unit four: pitch 6 is reemphasized, and the phrase-unit ends by returning to pitch 2.

The phrase-block is built on two intervals of a fifth, 5—1 and 6—2. The pitches on the ⊕ strokes are 1, 2, 5, and 6—all a fifth apart:

```
6 ↕ }
2     } 5th
  ↕ }
5     } 5th
  ↕ }
1     } 5th
```

Phrase-block two:

Phrase-unit one: A technique frequently used to give contrast to successive phrase-blocks or sections is illustrated here: corresponding pitches between phrase-blocks or sections are a fifth apart. In phrase-block two, the thao 5-5-1-5 of phrase-block one is inverted to 2-2-5-2; pitch 2 is the fifth above pitch 5, and pitch 5 is the fifth above pitch 1.

Phrase-unit two: consists of the much-used phrase-unit outlined by 1-3-3-1. Pitch 1 is the ending

pitch of the first half of the phrase-block, as it was in phrase-block one.

Phrase-unit three: repeats the outline of phrase-unit three in phrase-block one: pitches 2-6 are emphasized.

Phrase-unit four: consists of the fifths of the pitches in the corresponding phrase-unit in phrase-block one: 3-6-3-2 (in phrase-block one), 6-3-6-5 (in phrase-block two).

The same pitches are retained on the ⊕ strokes as in phrase-block one: 1, 2, 5, and 6; the first and last are reversed, however, so that phrase-block two has the effect of being a mirror of phrase-block one:

```
phrase-block 1:   5 - 1 - 6 - 2
                  ↕           ↕
phrase-block 2:   2 - 1 - 6 - 5
```

The strongly emphasized fifth 1-5 (or 5-1) of the first half of phrase-block one becomes the emphasized interval of the ⊕ pulse group (that is, the pitches falling on the ⊕ strokes) in phrase-block two:

The final pitches of the two phrase-blocks, 2 and 5, are a fifth apart.

Section Two:

Phrase-block one:

Phrase-unit one: the same thao as in Section One.

Phrase-unit two: retains the secondary emphasis of pitch 1 but reverses the positions of pitches 1 and 5 (of the corresponding phrase-unit in Section One, phrase-block one)—the phrase-unit ending on pitch 5, doubly emphasizing that pitch.

Phrase-unit three: uses the fifths of the corresponding pitches of the corresponding phrase-unit of Section One:

```
Section One:   6 - 2 - 2 - 6
               ↕   ↕   ↕   ↕
Section Two:   3 - 6 - 6 - 3
```

Phrase-unit four: anticipates the outline 1-3-3-1 of the final phrase-unit of the section but closes with pitch 5 instead of pitch 1, giving the effect of a "half-cadence" on the "dominant."

Phrase-block two:

The second phrase-block is a repeat of the first phrase-block except for the final pitch, which is pitch 1. The last phrase-unit is the standard phrase-unit 1-3-3-1. The final cadence of the section (and ultimately of the composition) is 5-3-2-1.

In the ⊕ pulse group, final pitch 2 of phrase-block one of Section One is replaced in Section Two by pitch 5, its fifth. Contrast pitch 6 of Section One (end of phrase-block three) is mirrored in Section Two by its fifth, pitch 3. Pitch 5 is retained for the ends of the first phrase-unit of each phrase-block of Section Two, as in the first phrase-block of Section 1. The final pitch of Section One is pitch 5; in Section Two its fifth, pitch 1, closes

the section (and the extended version, and ultimately the composition).

The movement in Section One outlines a fifth, pitch 2 to pitch 5; in Section Two another fifth, pitch 5 to pitch 1, occurs. The movement of the entire composition may be said, then, to be centered around 5-1 as the principal fifth, with 2-5 as a secondary fifth. Pitches 6 and 3 (also a fifth) are used in secondary positions as contrast.

The complete main melody is in example 48, with comments interspersed.

Example 48. "Khaēk Sai."

Section 1:

Phrase-block one:

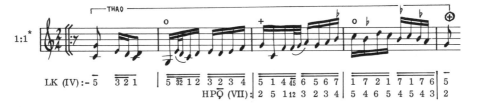

LK (IV): - 5   3 2 1 | 5 32 1 2 3 2 3 4 | 5 1 4 45 6 5 6 7 | 1 7 2 1 7 1 7 6 | 5
HPƠ̄ (VII): 2 5 112 3 2 3 4 | 5 4 6 5 4 5 4 3 | 2

(* The numbers at the head of the line indicate the phrase-block and phrase-unit.)

The word "khaēk" in the title of a Thai composition usually indicates that it may be in mǭn style; in fact, the phrase "khaēk mǭn" is used in the title of three Thai compositions. In this composition the two thao at the beginning of each phrase-block are in mǭn style, in which passing tone 4 (or 7, depending on the pitch level designated) is used prominently in running passages such as occur here. The second half of the thao is a brief "modulation"

to pitch level VII—high phīang ǭ. The notators of the manuscripts indicated this by putting a flat above the b to show that it has momentarily become a pitch 4 (in high phīang ǭ) rather than a pitch 7 (in low kruat, which would be indicated by a b-natural). After this mǭn-style introductory phrase-unit, the rest of the phrase-block proceeds in a purely pentatonic style:

(LK)   _ 1 _ | 1 3 2 1 5 | 6 _ 1 2 | 5 3 (5) 6 | 1

(N.B. The syncopation in the third full measure was explained in Chapter II, pp. 39-40, 50. A simplified version of the cipher notation will be used. The idiomatic style of playing for the khǭng wong yai includes certain ornamentations, such as in the third full measure, and various pick-up or anacrusis pitches that need not be included in the cipher notation.)

1:3 $\overline{6}$ 5   — | 6   —   1   — | $\overline{2 \quad 3}$ $\overline{5 \quad 3}$ | 2   —   1   — | $\overline{6}$

1:4 $\overline{2\ 1}\ \overline{6\ 1\ 6\ 5}$ | $\overline{3\quad 2}\ \ \overline{3\ 6\ 5}$ | 6· $\overline{1\ 6\ 1\ 6\ 5}$ | $\overline{3\ 5\ 3\ 6}\ \overline{5\ 6\ 3\ 5}$ | $\overline{2}$

Phrase-block two:

2:1 $\overline{2\ 3}\ \overline{2\ 5\ 4\ 3}$ | $\overline{2\ 5\ 2\ 3}\ \overline{2\ 5\ 4\ 3}$ | 2 $\overline{1\ 2}\ \overline{3\ 2\ 3\ 4}$ | $\overline{5\ 4\ 6\ 5}\ \overline{4\ 5\ 4\ 3}$ | $\overline{2}$·

    This is another mǭn-style thao. Here it is on the principal pitch level—low kruat—with no suggestion of "modulation," and the passing pitch is 4 in low kruat (IV).

2:2 $\overline{3\ 5\ 3\ 2}$ | $\overline{1} \quad 5 \quad \overline{1} \quad \overline{1\ 2}$ | $\overline{3\ 2\ 3\ 5}\ \overline{6\ 1\ 6\ 5}$ | $\overline{3\ 5\ 6\ 5}\ \overline{3\ 5\ 3\ 2}$ | $\overline{1}$

2:3 $\overline{3}$ 5   — | 6   —   1   — | $\overline{2 \quad 3}$ $\overline{5 \quad 3}$ | 2   —   1   — | 6

    This phrase-unit is identical to phrase-unit three in phrase-block one.

2:4 $\overline{1}\ \overline{2}\ \overline{1}$ | 6   —   5   — | $\overline{3}$ (2) $\overline{3} \quad 5$ | $\overline{6} \quad 2 \quad \overline{1} \quad 6$ | $\overline{5}$

Section 2:

Phrase-block one:

1:1   A mǭn thao, the same as in Section One,
      phrase-unit one.

1:2

$\bar{3}$ 2 _ | 3 _ 5 _ | 6 _ 2 _ | 1 _ 6 _ | 5

(In motive one, the octaves of pitches 2 and 3 are replaced
by the pitch a fourth below the main pitch. This is idiomatic
for the khǭng wong yai; it obviates the player having to
twist around to reach the lower pitch of the octave at the
far left and back of the instrument. When a fourth appears
in this context, the main pitch is the higher of the two.)

1:3

$\overline{12}$ $\overline{3\,2\,5\,2}$ | $\overline{3\,2\,1\,2}$ $\overline{3\,2\,3\,5}$ | $\overline{6\,5\,6\,7}$ $\overline{1\,2\,1\,7}$ | $\overline{6\,7\,6\,5}$ $\overline{1\,7\,6\,5}$ | $\bar{\bar{3}}$

This phrase-unit, the third—where contrast is
most likely to occur—shows mǭn style in the second
motive with the use of pitch 7 as a passing tone.

1:4

$\overline{5\,6\,5\,3}$ $\overline{5\,3\,2}$ | $\overline{1}$ $\overline{5}$ 1 $\overline{1\,2}$ | $\overline{3\,2\,3\,4}$ $\overline{5\,6\,5\,4}$ | $\overline{3\,2\,1\,2}$ $\overline{3\,2\,3\,4}$ | $\bar{\bar{5}}$

The second half of the phrase-unit is a mǭn-style
run.

Phrase-block two:

2:1

$\overline{2\,3\,4\,5}$ $\overline{4\,3\,4}$ | $\overline{5\,4\,3\,6}$ $\overline{5\,4\,3\,4}$ | $\bar{\bar{5}}$ (same as Section 1 - - - - - - - - - -)

The principal pitches of the thao are the same as
in phrase-block one, but here the first half is also
changed to mǭn style by using passing tone 4.

2:2 The same as 2:2 in phrase-block one.
2:3 The same as 2:3 in phrase-block one.

(for the repeat;
replaces the original
thao: 5-5-1-5)

The final phrase-unit returns to clear pentatonic style, with perhaps a fleeting hint of mǫn style in the use of pitch 7 as a decorating passing tone in the last motive at the beginning of the final cadence. The first motive begins with an announcement of the 5-3-2-1 cadence, here in a fast running passage, which is extended in open style to pitch 3. The section ends on a strong, open-style 5-3-2-1 cadence, reaffirming the pitch level.

A detailed examination of the main melody will give more insight into decorative and secondary pitches but will also reveal that they in no way contradict the hierarchy indicated in the pitch outline.

To summarize:

1. The composition is on one basic pitch level.

2. There are no lengthy "modulations," if any at all, despite the brief suggestion of another pitch level at the end of the initial thao. (What is to be considered a "modulation" in Thai music will be discussed shortly.)

3. The movement of the melody is toward an emphasized beat at the end of a pulse group, and the interrelationship of the emphasized pitches of the largest pulse groups is by fifths.

4. All five pitches of the mode are used in the composition on the ⊕ strokes, but on the primary ⊕ strokes only pitches 1, 2, and 5 occur; pitches 3 and 6 occur on secondary ⊕ strokes.

B. CLASSIFICATION OF MODAL TYPES

Compositions, then, may be classified on the basis of the relative lack or occurrence in them of pitches 4 and/or 7 on beats of the colotomic structure (+ and ⊕ strokes). Each composition in the group of one hundred and thirty-six representative compositions was outlined in the manner of chart 8, page 121, and as a result numerous categories or styles were shown to exist:

A. Basic 123 56 pentatonic style, without pitches 4 and/or 7 occurring on + and ⊕ strokes.

1. Without pitches 4 and 7 occurring as passing tones on unaccented ching strokes (indicated by "o" in the charts of the pitch outlines):

Cadence on 1: 33 (compositions)
Cadence on 2: 1
Cadence on 3: 3
Cadence on 5: 7
Cadence on 6: 5

Total: 49, about 36% of the total number of compositions in the representative group.

2. With pitches 4 and 7 as passing tones (on "o" strokes):

   a. With 4 as a passing tone:

      Cadence on 1: 2
      Cadence on 5: 2
      Cadence on 6: <u>1</u>

         Total: 5

   b. With 7 as a passing tone:

      Cadence on 1: 2
      Cadence on 2: 2
      Cadence on 3: 1
      Cadence on 6: <u>2</u>

         Total: 7

Total number of compositions in group A.2.: 12, about 9% of the total number in the representative group.

Total number of compositions in group A: 61, about 45% of the total number in the representative group.

B. Basic 123 56 pentatonic style, with pitches 4 and/or 7 on "o" strokes, involving a temporary change of basic pitch level, or the mǭn style:

1. Pitch 4 on "o" strokes:

   Cadence on 1: 1

2. Pitch 7 on "o" strokes:

   Cadence on 1: 2
   Cadence on 5: 1
   Cadence on 6: <u>1</u>

      Total: 4

3. Pitches 4 and 7 on "o" strokes:

   Cadence on 1: 2
   Cadence on 2: 1
   Cadence on 6: <u>1</u>

      Total: 4

Total number of compositions in group B:

9, about 7% of the total number in the representative group.

C. Hexatonic and heptatonic styles, involving pitch 4 and/or 7 on "o", +, and ⊕ strokes, with definite "modulatory" sections, and including compositions partly or entirely in mǭn style:

1. 123456 on + strokes:
   a. With pitch 4 also on "o" strokes:

      Cadence on 1: 11
      Cadence on 2:   4
      Cadence on 5:   <u>2</u>

         Total: 17

   b. With both pitches 4 and 7 on "o" strokes:

      Cadence on 1: 4

Total number of compositions in group C.1.: 21, about 15% of the total number in the representative group.

2. 123567 on + strokes:
   a. 12356 (all or less) on "o" strokes:

      Cadence on 1: 2
      Cadence on 6: <u>1</u>

         Total: 3

   b. Pitch 7 on "o" strokes:

      Cadence on 1: 3
      Cadence on 2: 1
      Cadence on 3: 2
      Cadence on 6: <u>2</u>

         Total: 8

   c. Both pitches 4 and 7 on "o" strokes:

      Cadence on 1: 7
      Cadence on 2: 3
      Cadence on 5: 2
      Cadence on 6: <u>3</u>

         Total: 15

Total number of compositions in group C.2.: 26, about 19% of the total number in the representative group.

3. 1234567 on + strokes:
   a. Pitch 4 on "o" strokes:

      Cadence on 1: 1

   b. Both pitches 4 and 7 on "o" strokes:

      Cadence on 1: 5
      Cadence on 2: 7
      Cadence on 3: 1
      Cadence on 5: 2
      Cadence on 6: <u>3</u>

          Total: 18

Total number of compositions in group C.3.: 19, about 14% of the total number in the representative group.
Total number of compositions in group C: 66, about 48% of the total number in the representative group.

These figures show that a little more than a third (36%) of the compositions in the representative group are in a simple pentatonic style. An additional 16 percent have some use of the other two available pitches but not to the extent that the basic pentatonic nature of the composition is seriously affected, thus making a total of a little more than half (52%) of the compositions in the relatively simple style. The remainder (48%) are in a more complex style involving "modulation" to different pitch levels and/or more or less extended hexatonic and heptatonic passages in mǭn style. The large percentage of compositions in this second group is conclusive proof that a great number of Thai compositions are far more varied and complicated than the simple pentatonic examples of Thai music available until now would indicate.

C. METABOLE

Before giving examples in the various styles classified above, the word "modulation" and what it implies in Thai music should be discussed. In his recent study of Vietnamese music Trần Văn Khê (1962: 225) followed the lead of Brailoiu (1955) in suggesting that "modulation" is a Western term specifically associated with and applied to a change of key area or tonality in a harmonic system and that it should not, therefore, be used to describe a change of basic pitch level in a nonharmonic, linear system. Since it would appear from an examination of the examples shown in Tran Van Khe's study that essentially the same procedure occurs in Thai music as in Vietnamese music in this respect, *"metabole"*—the term used by Brailoiu and Tran Van Khe to describe this musical technique—will be used hereafter in this study in reference to this practice in Thai music. (Such similarity of metabolic process in these two areas may indicate a wider range of mutual influence in Southeast Asia than has hitherto been thought to exist.) The term is borrowed from ancient Greek music where, it is presumed, much the same procedure was used. In the interests of evolving a more precise terminology it does not seem out of place to enlarge the musical vocabulary with this term, although the Western ear will undoubtedly interpret the occurrence of metabole in Thai music (as well as in other related Southeast Asian musics) harmonically as a modulation, rather than a "dislocation" or "relocation" generally by a fifth, of the same mode in a linear process.

It is not always clear in some Thai compositions whether a passage is merely one involving passing tones or whether a true metabole exists. Sometimes a short melodic fragment of two or three measures (in the prop kai pattern) seems to lie in a pitch area a fifth away from the basic pitch level of the section or composition; this fragment seems to be used in much the same way that in Western music a secondary dominant is used, or a momentary digression to the area of the dominant or subdominant occurs which prepares the way for a fresh start in the basic tonality. In Thai compositions such fragments sometimes occur at what might be considered cadential points and would seem to serve much the same purpose as half-cadences in Western music. The fragments usually involve a substitution of pitch 7 for pitch 1, the melody thus seeming to move to a new pitch level a fourth below or a fifth above the original, as shown in example 49.

Example 49. "Līlā Krathum" (Rฺuang 13; 4th composition of 5
          in prop kai section) (ms. coll. no. 93).

Section 2, beginning:

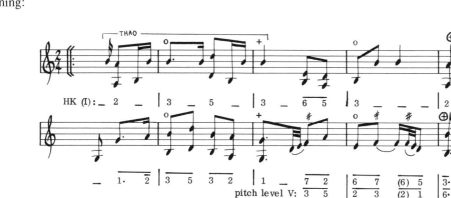

In measures 6, 7, and 8 (with the bracket underneath) the pitches used could be construed as forming a new 123 56 mode on pitch level V. Though pitch 7 (of HK) is introduced in measure 6, it does not occur on the ching strokes; the pitches that do fall there are pitches of the original mode; the outline of pitches, such as was given for "Khāēk Sai" (chart 8, p. 121), will not show this momentary use of the passing tone.

Much the same type of temporary movement away from the basic mode, or the extended use of passing tones, can also occur with pitch 4 being substituted for pitch 3, giving a feeling of a temporary metabole to the area a fourth above or a fifth below the original pitch level, as shown in example 50.

Example 50. "Phuang Rฺŏi" (Rฺuang 11; 2nd composition of 3
          in prop kai section) (ms. coll. no. 81).

Section 1, beginning:

In the second phrase-unit passing tone 7 is used on the unaccented beats. The first motive embodies the fifth 3-6. The second motive, instead of continuing the movement and emphasizing the fifth 6-2, as shown in the following notation, substitutes pitch 7 for pitch 1 and the resulting emphasized pitches are 6-1 instead of 6-2.

In the third phrase-unit the first motive is a variation of a thao that would usually be played as follows.

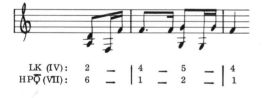

The rest of the composition is pentatonic. Perhaps the brief use of pitch 4 is to give a hint of mǭn style. Motive two in this third phrase-unit seems to mirror motive two in the preceding phrase-unit: movement in phrase-unit two is ascending from pitch 6 to pitch 1 via the passing tone pitch 7, while in phrase-unit three it is descending from pitch 5 to pitch 3 via the passing tone pitch 4. The final pitch of phrase-unit three is pitch 3 of the basic pitch level, low kruat; therefore, though a metabole has been hinted at, it has not been fully established and a change of pitch level has not taken place. Pitches 4 and 7 have functioned only as passing tones.

These two examples have been picked from the rǖang (suites) rather than from the compositions in the test group because the rǖang are nonvocal, instrumental compositions that show more diversity. Such patterns as illustrated in these two examples tend to occur more rarely in the compositions of the representative group as these are the sēphā, vocal-instrumental forms, and in relation to the compositions in the rǖang exhibit more regularity and uniformity. Also, the rǖang being the oldest compositions in the Thai repertoire, dating back to the nineteenth century or even earlier, this type of variation and diversity may be representative of an older practice.

Because there are no known rules, verbalized or otherwise, in Thai music governing what is or what is not a metabole, I decided to make an arbitrary decision in the matter for purposes of analysis and theoretical discussion. The phrase-unit is considered the unit of measurement: if the passage in question is minimally the length of one phrase-unit and uses prominently the pitch—usually 4 or 7—that distinguishes a pentatonic mode on one pitch level from the same or another mode on another level and omits the distinguishing pitch of the mode on the original level, a metabole has taken place. The metabole will usually be further established by the ending of the phrase-unit having a motive and final pitch clearly on the new pitch level, and the metabole will often continue on the new pitch level into the next phrase-unit. A metabole is generally established in the final motive of a phrase-unit, or occasionally at the midpoint of the phrase-unit. It continues through at least one more full phrase-unit, and the pitches falling on the ching strokes of the new phrase-unit on the new pitch level will usually be one of the standard patterns, such as 1-3-3-1, 2-6-6-2, or the like. If, however, the passage in question clearly returns to a principal pitch or pitches of the mode on the original pitch level before the end of the passage, or if the new level suggested in the passage is not the basis of the melody in the new phrase-unit, then the passage does not involve a metabole but uses passing tones, prominently or otherwise. Example 51 and chart 9 illustrate a short composition that contains passages involving metabole according to my analytical method.

Example 51. "Tuang Phra Thāt" (Thao) (ms. coll. no. 370).

3 chan (extended version).

Section 1:

Chart 9. Pitch outline——"Tuang Phra Thāt" (Thao), 3 chan, Section 1.

Whichever pitch outline is used, either that for low kruat or that for high phīang ǭ, pitch 4 or 7 occurs on ching strokes, indicating that a metabole probably exists.

Section One:

Phrase-block one (one phrase-block only):

Phrase-unit one: a standard thao, centering around *d* of the staff notation. The initial thao of a composition is frequently on a pitch level a fifth above that of the second phrase-unit, giving the feeling, as in Western music, of moving from the dominant to the tonic areas. But with the thao, passing tones are used, as in this example, so that the phrase has an ambiguity, a "double meaning," musically. Thai tuning has only seven pitches (to the octave), and a pitch can be interpreted according to several different pitch levels: the *d* of the notation here can be read as pitch 5 of high kruat (pitch level I), pitch 2 of low kruat (IV), and pitch 6 of high phīang ǭ (VII). These three pitch levels are a fifth apart: level I descending a fifth to level IV,

descending another fifth to level VII.

In this section, if the initial thao is considered to be on the high kruat level, three pitch levels are represented.

Phrase-unit two: after the ambiguity of the initial thao, low kruat is established; the phrase-unit ends with a 5321 cadence.

Phrase-unit three: begins with a mǭn-style run that includes pitch 4 of low kruat as a passing tone. The second motive can be analyzed in either low kruat or high phīang ǭ, for it avoids the pitch of difference in each pitch level—pitch 3 in low kruat and pitch 1 in high phīang ǭ.

Phrase-unit four: continues on the high phīang ǭ level. The phrase-unit is one of the standard ones indicated by the pitch outline 3-1-1-3. It might be considered that the 5321 cadence falls in the middle of the phrase-unit and is extended to pitch 3 as another type of "half-cadence."

Section Two, illustrated in example 52 and chart 10, continues on the high phīang ǭ level for its entirety and is also a single phrase-block.

Example 52.

```
               o   +   o   ⊕
     HPO̱:  1   1   2   1
            3   1   5   1
            1   3   5   2
            1   3   3   1
```

Chart 10. Pitch outline—"Tuang Phra Thāt" (Thao), 3 chan, Section 2.

Section Two (one phrase-block only):

Phrase-unit one: another standard thao (used as the initial thao in many compositions) with the pitch outline 1-1-2-1.

Phrase-unit two: emphasizes pitch 1.

Phrase-unit three: The second motive is the mǭn passage found as part of the first thao in "Khāēk Sai." Its presence here in the third phrase-unit of contrast is not unusual.

Phrase-unit four: the cadential unit. Here the order of the same two motives used in phrase-unit four of Section One is reversed: the pattern 3-1-1-3 now becomes 1-3-3-1. The phrase-unit begins with a one-measure statement of the 5321 cadence, extends it in open position to pitch 3, then restates the cadence in open position.

The pulse grouping of the ⊕ strokes 1-1-2-1 is anticipated in this section by the structural pitches of the first thao, but this technique is not consistently used.

The section centers around pitches 1 and 3 with secondary use of pitches 5 and 2. Pitch 6 is avoided on structural beats.

Considering Section One from the standpoint of the pitch levels used at any given time, pitches 1 and 3 are also the prominent pitches: after the initial ambiguous thao, phrase-unit two—marking the first half of the section—ends on pitch 1 (of low kruat). Phrase-unit three also ends on pitch 1 of low kruat, which may also function as pitch 5 in high phīang ǭ in this transitional motive. Section One ends on pitch 3.

The entire composition, then, swings around pitches 1 and 3, with pitch 5, supported by pitch 2, used secondarily. Pitch 6, though occurring in the melody, is avoided on structural pitches.

D. ANALYSIS OF REPRESENTATIVE COMPOSITIONS OF THE CLASSIFIED TYPES

Basic style A.1., pentatonic without pitches 4 and 7 occurring on unaccented ching strokes, is the only group containing compositions in which all five pitches of the pentatonic mode occur as the finalis. Thirty-three compositions have a cadence on pitch 1, by far the largest number in any one subdivision of the group of representative compositions. This style may be considered, then, the core of the simple Thai style whether or not it has occasional motives in mǭn style, as was illustrated earlier in "Khāēk Sai." The melody of "Khāēk Sai" is motivic. Example 53 and chart 11 show a composition in this category of the newer style in which the melody is lyrical and strictly pentatonic.

Example 53. "Lāō Sīang Thǐan" (Thao) (*Silpakǭn Magazine,*
        4 (Jan. 1961), 82).

3 chan (main melody simplified).

Section 1:
Phrase-block one:

Phrase-block two:

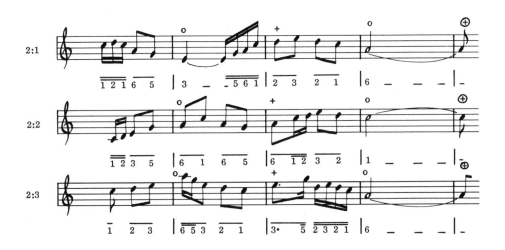

Example 53 (continued).

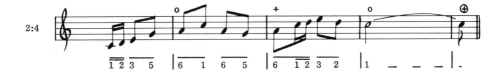

Section 2:
Phrase-block one:

Example 53 (continued).

Phrase-block two:

Section 1:

		o	+	o	⊕
	LK (IV):	6	6	5	(5)
		3	3	5	(5)
		6	6	5	(5)
		3	3	5	(5)
		3	2	6	(6)
x		6	6	1	(1)
		6	3	6	(6)
x		6	6	1	(1) (cadence: 321)

Section 2:

		6	3	5	(5)
		6	3	2	(2)
		2	5	5	5
		5	2	2	2
		3	(1)	6	(6)
x		6	6	1	(1)
		6	3	6	(6)
x		6	6	1	(1)

(N.B. Structural pitches in parentheses in the pitch outlines indicate pitches that are held over from a previous measure. Underlined pitches signify repeated motives; brackets or crosses to the side indicate repeated phrase-units within a section or between sections.)

Chart 11. Pitch outline—"Lāo Sīang Thīan" (Thao), 3 chan.

In this lyric melody the phrase-units do not consist of two clear-cut motives of two measures each, but rather one elongated motive.

Section One:

Phrase-block one:

Phrase-units three and four are a repetition of phrase-units one and two. Pitch 5 is the principal pitch in phrase-block one, supported by the fifth 6-3.

Phrase-block two:

This phrase-block follows a somewhat similar pattern—phrase-units two and four are identical. The ends of phrase-units one and two are similar, but the 3216 cadence in phrase-unit one is slower than in phrase-unit three.

The basic pitches of the first section are 5-1. The presence of pitch 6 may indicate a hinting at mode 6 for contrast. The section ends with a 321 cadence, a variation of the 5321 cadence caused by the rise of the melody to high pitch 1 rather than the usual descent from pitch 5 to pitch 1.

Section Two:

Phrase-block one: emphasizes pitches 5 and 2.

Phrase-units one and two: the first half of each is the same; the last half of phrase-unit one ascends to pitch 5, the last half of phrase-unit two descends to pitch 2.

Phrase-unit three: the first half mirrors the beginning of phrase-units one and two by ascending instead of descending, and the second half is the same as in phrase-unit one.

Phrase-unit four: the "question-answer" or "call and response" style between the ranāt ēk and the rest of the ensemble; pitches 5 and 2 are the concluding pitches of each motive, but the question-answer phrase-unit is anticipated by starting at the end of the preceding phrase-unit (three) and ending on the third measure of phrase-unit four on pitch 2, which is repeated on the ⊕ stroke in the next measure. The pulse grouping in phrase-unit three is 2-5-5-5, which, because of the way the melody is laid out, is reversed to 5-2-2-2 in phrase-unit four.

In phrase-block one of this section the 6-3 support of phrase-block one in Section One is now confined to the beginnings of phrase-units one and two. The rest of the phrase-block is centered around an exploitation of the fifth 5-2. Pitch 2 occurs on the strong pulses of the large ⊕ pulse group, balancing the use in Section One (phrase-block one) of pitch 5 only.

Phrase-block two of Section Two is an almost identical repetition of phrase-block two of Section One. The first part of phrase-unit one is different from the corresponding phrase-unit in Section One, but the phrase-unit as a whole is a variation of the phrase-unit in Section One. The repetition of the last phrase-block from a preceding section is often found in these Thao compositions.

The pitch emphasis in Section Two is primarily the same as in Section One, with the addition of pitch 2 as a primary pitch in the first phrase-block.

In the composition as a whole pitches 1, 2, 5, and 6 are used extensively; they all appear on ⊕ strokes. Pitch 3 is used secondarily, occurring only on "o" and + strokes. Pitch 3 is not used in connection with pitch 1; pitch 6 is used to support pitch 1. Thus the composition has a different atmosphere and mood from compositions such as "Tuang Phra Thāt"

in which pitch 3 figures prominently and in support of pitch 1.

FIFTH POLARITIES

The analyses of these few compositions show that fifths occur as pivotal pitches around which a phrase-unit, phrase-block, section, or entire Thai composition can be built. It would seem appropriate to call these fifths "polarities," as they work together as two ends of a functional interval. The various polarities that can occur in the 123 56 pattern are 1-5, 2-6, 5-2, and 6-3 (and, of course, their reverse positions 5-1, 6-2, 2-5, and 3-6). The fifth above pitch 3 is pitch 7 and the fifth below pitch 1 is pitch 4. Pitches 4 and 7 do not occur in the pentatonic pattern. Because of the prevalence of the 3-1 and 1-3 combinations in Thai music, it is my speculation that pitch 1 has been substituted for pitch 7 in the ascending polarity,[2] and pitch 3 has been substituted for pitch 4 in the descending polarity. The complete matching polarities may be represented as follows:

$$6 \longleftrightarrow 3$$
$$5 \longleftarrow 2$$
$$1$$
$$3 \nearrow$$
$$2 \longleftrightarrow 6$$
$$1 \longleftrightarrow 5$$

In group A.1. of thirty-three compositions with pitch 1 as a finalis, five compositions besides "Khāek Sai" have the 5321 cadence in open position. All five use all five pitches of the pentatonic mode on ⊕ strokes as well as many of the same motives and phrase-units, such as those indicated by the structural pitch groupings 1331, 6331, 1653, 3113, and 6226. Besides the same final cadence, all compositions but one have 1331 on the ching strokes of the final phrase-unit. The composition that does not has four sections—the third has this pulse group, while the fourth uses 3631 and varies the final cadence $\overline{5}\,\overline{65}|3\text{-}2\text{-}|$ 1 to $\overline{2}\,\overline{165}|3\text{-}2\text{-}|1$. Some of the compositions have but one long section with some internal development; others are short with several sections. Within the compositions different pitch polarities are prominent in different parts of the compositions. In other words they are similar but different. On the basis of their similarities, they are alike in general style and in their final cadence and finalis. Variety occurs within the larger framework of this similarity in style.

Eight compositions end with the 5321 cadence in closed position: $\overline{532}$|1. The same characteristics and variety obtain among these compositions as discussed above.

One composition has the 5321 cadence in rapid note values, $\overline{532}$|1, at the end of an extended run. The final phrase-unit, however, is 1331 on the ching strokes. Otherwise the composition is similar to those above.

Six compositions have a variation of the 5321 cadence:

1. One composition ends on the 5321 cadence in open position, but on phrase-unit three instead of four. For the first ending before the repeat of the section the fourth phrase-unit is a 1-1-2-1 thao, an extension of pitch 1. The thao is not indicated at the end of the second playing of the section. This may or may not be a mistake in the notation; incomplete phrase-blocks in otherwise regular compositions are rare.

2. One composition in sŏng chan ends with a 5321 cadence extended by a thao on pitch 1.

3. Three compositions, two of which are in sŏng chan, end with a 321 cadence; the high pitch $\bar{5}$ is lacking.

4. One sŏng chan composition has a $\frac{5321}{}$ cadence with some interpolated decoration: 5|3-$\overline{2121}$| 1.

Several compositions end on pitch 1 with cadences other than the descending 5321 or its variants:

1. Seven compositions have a cadence ascending to pitch 1, 2561, sometimes preceded in the phrase-unit by 3216 but not always at the same place or in the same way. One of these compositions has the cadence extended to another pitch 1, $\overline{356}$|$\overline{161}$-|1.

2. Five compositions have what may be a 3216 cadence extended to pitch 1:

(a) Two compositions have the simple version $\overline{321}$|$\overline{612}$-|1. One composition has this cadence at double the tempo, $\overline{321612}$|1.

(b) One composition has $\overline{632}$|$\overline{161}$-|1. This occurs in Section Five at the end of the ninth phrase-unit (an extra phrase-unit beyond phrase-block two) and may be an extension of the last phrase-unit in phrase-block

two, which cadences in open position, 1-7-|6-5-|1; this in turn may be an extension of the real cadence at the end of phrase-unit three, $\overline{23}$|$\overline{53(5)6}$|1. None of these is a regular cadence, however. The cadences in previous sections of the composition are more regular: Sections One and Two, $\overline{532}$| 1-$\overline{61}$| $\overline{21}$2-| 1; Section Three, an extended run, $\overline{532}$| $\overline{13123235}$| $\overline{2321612}$| 1; Section Four, the same as the last part of the cadence of Section Three. The cadences of all sections resolve to pitch 1.

(c) The other composition has more decoration in the final cadence, $\overline{3216}$|$\overline{665612}$|1.

There is nothing in the body of these compositions to distinguish them from the previous ones; they show the same general characteristics and variety.

Only one composition in the basic pentatonic style (A.1.) cadences on pitch 2—"Lāo Khruan." This composition is the shortest of all those in the representative group and the shortest complete traditional Thai composition in the manuscript collection, being only eight measures long. (There are a few others also eight measures long.) Though it may be played separately, it is also the last of seven compositions grouped together in a type of suite known as *Tap*, to be discussed in the next chapter on forms. (The word will be capitalized here to avoid confusion with the English word "tap.") It is also one of the few compositions in sŏng chan or middle version form included in the representative group. Two versions are given in example 54. The first, from the manuscript collection, is the main melody for the khŏng wong yai and is notated at the low kruat level; the second, slightly different as taught to me, is in the ranāt ēk style — more elaborate and decorated — notated at the high phīang ǫ level. These two versions illustrate how a composition may be played on more than one pitch level — but of course not simultaneously.

Example 54. "Lāo Khruan" (2 chan) (Tap Phralǭ, no. 30,
ms. coll. no. 215, 7th composition of 7).

The pitch outline for the two versions is in chart 12.

```
   o  ⊕  o  ⊕
3  3 (3) 2
2  2  5  5
5  1 (1) (1)
3  2 (2) (2) (cadence: 5321 2)
```

Chart 12. Pitch outline—"Lāo Khruan" (2 chan).

An examination of the two versions shows that they coincide in pitches on the accented ching strokes and on most of the unaccented ching strokes; the elaborations occur around these stable pitches.

The composition centers around the fifth polarity, 5-2. In the first half, pitch 5 is preceded by a strong emphasis on pitch 2. In the second half in phrase-unit three pitch 1, the fifth of pitch 5, is emphasized, and in phrase-unit four emphasis returns to pitch 2. Pitch 6 is avoided, occurring only as a passing tone.

It is questionable whether this composition is in a mode on 2, for the fifth of this pitch—pitch 6—is slighted. A case might be made for a mode on 5, 56

123 (5), with the ending on the "dominant," pitch 2, a fifth above pitch 5, and using pitch 1, the pitch a fifth below the "tonic" (pitch 5), as the secondary fifth interval.

Three compositions in the simple pentatonic style end on pitch 3 but differ in their hierarchical pitch emphasis.

One composition has one section composed of two and a half phrase-blocks (ten phrase-units). The second phrase-block ends on pitch 3, as do the last two phrase-units of the composition; these are probably an extension, since the last phrase-unit in the second phrase-block is 3-1-1-3, as is the last phrase-unit of the composition. Pitches 1 and 3 are emphasized, supported somewhat by pitches 6 and 2, with pitch 5 slighted. The final phrase-unit is:

$$\underline{5}\ \overline{1\ 2}\ |\overset{o}{\underline{3}}\ \overline{5}\ \overline{3\ 2}\ |\overset{+}{\overline{1\ 6}}\ 5\ \_\ |\overset{o}{1}\ \_\ 2\ \_|\overset{\oplus}{3}$$

The last motive might be considered either as a cadence on pitch 3 or an extension of the 5321 cadence to pitch 3.

Another composition having one section of two

phrase-blocks is built on the 6-3 polarity with secondary use of pitches 2 and 5. Pitch 1 is slighted, being entirely avoided on the ⊕ strokes. The final cadence is: $\overline{3\ 5}\,|\,\overline{6}\ \overline{1}\ \overline{6}\ \overline{5}\,|\,1\ \_\ 2\ \_\,|\,3$

The third composition has two sections. In Section One, four phrase-blocks, all five pitches are freely used. The first two phrase-blocks use the 6-3 polarity but end on pitch 2 supported by pitch 5; the last two phrase-blocks make more use of the 5-2 polarity and less of the 3-6, and the composition ends on pitch 5. Of the four phrase-blocks the third is the usual contrasting one in the large overall pattern. The first two phrase-blocks end on pitch 2 and the last on pitch 5, stressing this polarity. Section Two has two and a half phrase-blocks, the last two phrase-units probably being an extension—phrase-block three and the composition both ending on pitch 3. The first half of the section stresses pitch 5, on which the first six phrase-units end. The last four phrase-units use all five pitches freely, with pitch 3 the most used. The final cadence is:

$$\overline{5\ 6}\,|\,5\ \_\ 5\ \_\,|\,\overline{1\ 5}\ \overline{3\ 2}\,|\,1\ \_\ 2\ \_\,|\,3$$

—again, possibly the 5321 cadence with an extension.

These three compositions are like the others in the simple pentatonic style, except for the final cadence.

Group A.1. contains seven compositions that cadence on pitch 5. The usual cadence, 2165, is used in five of the compositions. One sŏng chan composition is from a Tap suite; it is the penultimate composition, preceding the final one, "Lāo Khruan," discussed previously. These sŏng chan compositions in the Tap suites are less regular than the Thao compositions. (Some of the Tap suites may be as old as the rŭang repertoire.) The odd measures at the end of the regular quadratic structure in this composition may be an integral part of the composition or a bridge into the next composition—the manuscript does not indicate. This composition is also very short. The cipher notation and pitch outline are in chart 13.

The cadence here may end on pitch 2, with an extension to pitch 5. The first two phrase-units are identical, with a basic movement 5-1. The third and last phrase-unit uses the 1-3 polarity at the beginning, but after the first regular motive, 5123, proceeds immediately to the 5321 cadence, on the third ⊕ stroke, which is then extended to pitch 2 on the fourth ⊕ stroke. A somewhat similar treatment occurs at the cadence of "Lāo Khruan," and both compositions are in the same style, centered around pitches 1-5-2. The two measures at the end of this composition may well be a bridge to the next composition, which begins on pitch 5. On the other hand, this motive is not marked as a second ending only but is apparently played both before the repeat and at the end.

Another Thao composition is in the regular pentatonic mode except for one phrase-unit (occurring twice and marked with an "x" in the pitch outline in chart 14). The composition has two sections, each of which has two phrase-blocks. In both phrase-blocks of both sections, phrase-units two and four are the same. Also, the second phrase-blocks of the two sections are identical.

The second and last phrase-units of phrase-block two, which are the same, use pitch 7 in a way that gives this final cadence a feeling of moving temporarily to the level of the "dominant." Since it is used as the cadence for both sections, however, the composition ends on this cadence and does not return to a strong reiteration of pitch 1. One possible explanation for this cadence is that pitch 7 is substituted for pitch 1, resulting in a 2765 rather than the standard 2165. This treatment of the cadence has not been found in any other Thai composition, however. The finalis, then, is pitch 5, or

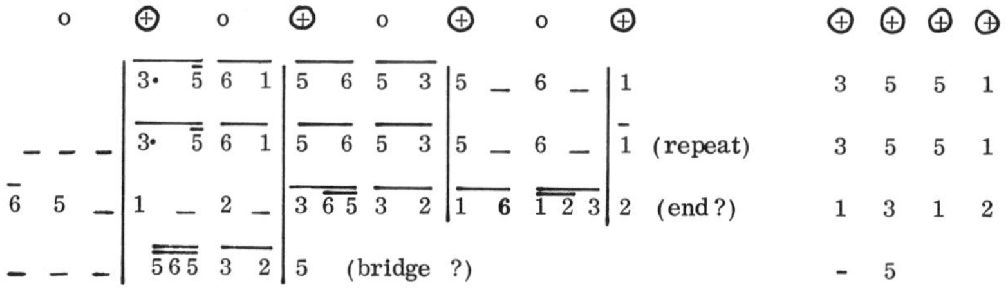

Chart 13. Cipher notation and pitch outline—"Lāo Chīang Tat Sǒi" (2 chan), ms. coll. no. 214.

```
               o   +   o   ⊕
LK (IV):       6   5   6
        (6)    1   6   3
        (3)    3   3   1
         5     1   6   3
             ┌ 3   3   3   6 ⎫
             ⎢(6)  6   6   5 x⎬
             ⎢(5)  3   3   6 ⎬
             ⎣(6)  6   6   5 x⎭
             ┌ 6   6   3   6
             ⎢ 1   1   1   3
             ⎢ 6   6   3   6
             ⎣ 1   1   1   3
             ┌ 3   3   3   6 ⎫
             ⎢(6)  6   6   5 x⎬
             ⎢(5)  3   3   6 ⎬
             ⎣(6)  6   6   5 x⎭
```

Chart 14. Pitch outline—"Nok Khao Khamāe" (Thao), 3 chan, ms. coll. no. 381.

if the cadence is considered to have moved momentarily to pitch level I, it becomes 5321 on that level and the finalis is pitch 1. This short motive, however, does not qualify as a metabole according to the previously given definition. The entire composition revolves around the 3-6 polarity, supported by pitch 1 in the first phrase-block and pitch 5 in the second in both sections. Pitch 2 is entirely avoided at all points of emphasis.

The remaining composition in this group, "Khamāe Thom," introduces several more techniques of Thai music. Based on a composition from one of the rɥang (suites), it has four sections of two phrase-blocks each. Section Three has an added phrase-unit as an introduction, a technique that is sometimes used. The pitch outline is in chart 15.

```
                               o   +   o   ⊕
Section 1:    HP Q̄ (VII):      5   1   1
                         6     3   3   5
                         1     2   5  (5)
                         6     3  (3)  2
                        ------------------
                        (2)    6   6   5
                         2     5   5   6
                        (6)    3   3   2
                         5     2  (6)  1    (cadence: 5321)

Section 2:               1     6   5   1
                         5     1   1   3
                        (3)    6  (5)  3
                         5     3  (2)  1
                        ------------------
                         6    (1)  3   5
                         3    (5)  5   2
                        (2)    5   5   2
                         3     1  (2)  1    (cadence: 5321)

Section 3:               1    (1)  3   1    (introduction, not repeated)
                       ‖:6     6   6   3
                        (3)    6   3   3
                         3     3  (2)  6
                         3     2   1   6
                        ------------------
                         6     6   6   3
                        (3)    3  (2)  6
                        (6)    6   6   5    (cadence: 2165)
                         5     5   6   5‖   (extension, same cadence repeated)
```

Chart 15. Pitch outline—"Khamāe Thom" (3 chan), ms. coll. no. 382.

Section 4:   (in HPọ)   (in LPọ)
(introduction not used)

o	+	o	⊕		o	+	o	⊕
---	---	---	---		---	---	---	---
2	2	2	6		6	6	6	3
(6)	5	6	6		(3)	2	3	3
6	6	(5)	2		3	3	(2)	6
(2)	2	(2)	2		(6)	6	(6)	6
(2)	2	(2)	6		(6)	6	(6)	3
(6)	6	(2)	2		(3)	3	(2)	6
(2)	2	2	1		(6)	6	6	5
1	1	2	1 (cadence: 5421)		5	5	6	5 (cadence: 2165)

Chart 15 (continued).

Section Four is an almost exact repetition of Section Three as far as the pitches on the ching strokes are concerned, but on the low phīang ọ̄ level, a fifth below the pitch level for the rest of the composition. The composition ends on the low phīang ọ̄ level, cadencing with a standard 2165 cadence in both Sections Three and Four. Pitch 5 in low phīang ọ̄, the finalis, is also pitch 1 of high phīang ọ̄, the pitch level for the rest of the composition—which helps to unify the two sections. When Section Four is analyzed in high phīang ọ̄ the ching-stroke pitches, though different from those in Section Three, are all part of the pentatonic mode on low phīang ọ̄, which also helps to unify the

composition. The music of the two sections (see ex. 55) is the same except for some variations, mostly caused by the range of the khǭng wong yai and the pitches available at each pitch level. Sections One and Two are alike in mood and style. They both revolve around the 1-5-2 polarities, with the polarity 3-6 used in support. Pitch 6 is used more in Section One, pitch 3 in Section Two. Section Three (and Four) emphasizes the 3-6 polarity, with pitch 2 in secondary support, except for the final cadence on pitch 5, which gives this pitch more emphasis at the cadential point. Pitch 1 is generally avoided in Section Three (and Four).

Example 55. "Khamāe Thom" (3 chan).

(Main melody simplified).

Phrase-block one:

Example 55 (continued).

Phrase-block two:

Example 55 (continued).

Five compositions in group A.1. end on pitch 6. The cadence 3216, which has been met with as an internal cadence in other compositions, may be considered the standard cadence for the finalis on pitch 6. However, it is not used in its pure form in any of these five compositions.

One composition varies this cadence only slightly. The composition has one section with a variation for the second playing rather than a strict repeat. The cadence for the first playing is:

$$\overline{1\ 6\ 5} \mid \overset{o}{3} \_ 2 \_ \mid \overset{+}{\overline{3\ 2}}\ \overline{1\ 2} \mid \overset{o}{6} \_\_\_ \mid \_ \overset{\oplus}{} \ ,$$

which is the 3216 cadence with the insertion of another pitch 2 for decoration. The cadence is also anticipated, and the final pitch 6 is held to the final ⊕ stroke. For the second version the phrase-unit has

more variety: the first motive is preceded by an ascending passage, and the cadence appears in its usual position in the last measures:

$$\overline{3\ 5} \mid \overset{o}{\overline{6}}\ \overline{21}\ \overline{6\ 5} \mid \overset{+}{3} \_ 2 \_ \mid \overset{o}{\overline{3532}}\ \overline{1\ 2} \mid \overset{\oplus}{6}$$

again with the inserted pitch 2. In the second version the entire last part of the composition is a continual reiteration of the pitches 3216, spread over one or two phrase-units and highly decorated. The body of the composition revolves around the 3-6 polarity, supported by pitch 2. Pitches 1 and 5 are used, but in secondary positions.

Another composition uses the cadence phrase:

$$\_ \mid \overset{+}{\overline{3532}}\ \overline{12}\ \overline{3} \mid \overset{o}{\overline{2321}}\ \overline{61}\ \overline{5} \mid \overset{\oplus}{6}$$

in the extended version, which is an elaboration of the middle version cadence:

$$\overline{2}\;|\;\overset{\oplus}{3}\;1\;\overset{o}{2}\;3\;|\;\overset{\oplus}{2}\;1\;6\;\overset{o}{5}\;|\;\overset{\oplus}{6}$$

The body of this composition also revolves around 3-6, with secondary use of 5-1 and less use of pitch 2.

Another composition shows an interesting deviation in the extended version from the original material. Given in the manuscript collection only in the extended version, it is based on a composition from a rŷang that uses a very conventional pentatonic mode with a 5321 cadence in both sections. In the notation for the extended version the last phrase-unit is the penultimate phrase-unit of the rŷang composition, which ends on pitch 6. Possibly a mistake was made in the notation and the final phrase-unit and cadence on pitch 1 was omitted. Section Two is long, having four phrase-blocks—to match the original it should have five phrase-blocks, but perhaps the composer felt this was too long.

The extended version cadences $2 \;\_ \;| \;\overset{o}{3} \;\_ \;5 \;\_ \;| \;\overset{\oplus}{6},$ an ascent in open position to pitch 6. The body of the composition revolves around pitches 1, 2, 3, and 5. Except for the final cadence, pitch 6 appears only in subordinate, unaccented positions.

The other two compositions are in sŷng chan form. They are short and in their general style not different from other compositions in group A.1. Because they occur in the body of a Tap suite, the usual lack of clarity exists at the final cadence, probably caused by the omission of a clear cadence in order to preserve a continuity and flow in the suite. One composition uses a 2-6 polarity supported by 1-5, with pitch 3 mostly on secondary beats and unaccented ching strokes. The other composition has two sections, the first of which cadences 321. Section Two seems to be irregular; either it starts in the middle of a phrase-unit or it ends with a short extension. Of the compositions in the manuscript collection, only the rŷang are completely notated; for all other compositions only the main melody was notated, with no indication of the ching strokes. Since most compositions follow the regular quadratic pattern, it is not difficult to know where the ching strokes fall. But this composition is an exception. Probably it begins at an irregular point and ends regularly. If so, it cadences on pitch 5 with an

irregular cadence. This last motive, however, is approached by the suggestion of a 2356 motive in the preceding phrase-unit:

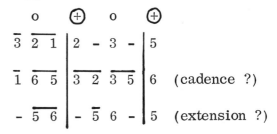

The body of the composition uses all five pitches freely. No one polarity is emphasized over another.

Group A.2 includes those compositions whose structure is clearly a 123 56 mode with pitches 4 and 7 used as passing tones on unaccented ching strokes. Since the passages in question in the twelve compositions in this group are essentially not dissimilar from the illustrations previously given of passages with passing tones, representative compositions from this group need not be discussed.

Group B includes those compositions in which a distinct change of basic pitch level exists for a full phrase-unit after the change has been introduced, that is, a metabole takes place. The compositions in this group exhibit either metabole or such an extended use of mŷn-type passages that a clear 123 56 mode on one pitch level no longer obtains. A metabole may be any length from one phrase-unit to a whole section, though a complete section on another pitch level is a rather special form of the metabole. Actually this group, which contains only nine compositions or 7 percent of the total of the representative compositions, is rather a "no man's land" musically speaking, lying between group A—compositions in the simple style—and group C—compositions with sections of definite, clear-cut metabole and compositions with a definite mŷn flavor, that is, characterized by passages with more than a passing use of pitches 4 and 7.

The first composition used to illustrate group B has pitch 4 on an "o" ching stroke and cadences on pitch 1, as in chart 16 and example 56.

Between the pentatonic mode 123 56 on pitch levels a fifth apart, four of the five pitches are the same (in sound, that is, not of course in their position in the mode). Each position of the mode will have

	o	+	o	⊕			o	+	o	⊕
Section 1 LPQ̄ (IV):	6	3	3	6	} = HPQ̄		2	6	6	2
	6	3	3	6			2	6	6	2
	2	1	6	2						
	3	1	1	3						
	6	2	2	6						
	3	6	6	3						
	3	1	1	3						
	[4]	6	5	3	= HPQ̄:	7	2	1	6	
					(LK:	3	5)			
Section 2:	2	5	3	2						
	1	3	3	1						
	1	6	6	3						
	3	3	6	3						
	2	5	3	2						
	1	3	3	1						
	5	2	6	1						
	1	1	2	1						

Chart 16. Pitch outline—"Līlā K(r)athum" (3 chan), ms.
coll. no. 405.

Example 56. "Līlā K(r)athum" (3 chan).

Section 1:
Phrase-block one:

Example 56 (continued).

Phrase-block two:

one pitch the other position of the mode does not have, as the following diagram of two positions of the 123 56 mode shows:

HPŌ: 1   2   3   (4)   5   6

LPŌ: 5   6   (7)   1   2   3

The sound that is pitch 3 on high phīang ǭ does not occur as a principal pitch in the low phīang ǭ position, and conversely the sound that is pitch 1 in low phīang ǭ does not occur as a principal pitch in high phīang ǭ. When the ching-stroke pitches are outlined as in the above example, if the pitch of difference does not fall on a ching stroke it will not be clear which pitch level is being used. The first two phrase-units and the last phrase-unit in Section One of the composition outlined above seem more clearly on the high phīang ǭ level, while the middle part of the section is on the lower phīang ǭ level, as is the entire second section. If the first two phrase-units are analyzed on the same pitch level as the rest of the section an undue use of pitch 7 results, and not in the way the pitch is generally used as a passing tone. The first section is given in notation in example 56. The last phrase-unit begins two fifths away on the low kruat level before shifting back to the high phīang ǭ level. The cipher notation gives a clue to the tonal orientation of a phrase: the cipher notation for the pitch level resulting in as few passing tones as possible indicates the pitch level of the passage. Here, if the first motive of the last phrase-unit is given cipher notation in low kruat, only one unaccented passing tone—pitch 4—results, occurring in a normal passage. Analyzing the passage on other pitch levels produces more passing tones occurring in noncharacteristic ways.

Two characteristics frequently found in the use of môn style are illustrated in this composition: (1) beginning and/or ending a section on a pitch level a fifth above or below that of the main body of the section; (2) dividing one phrase-unit between related pitch areas.

The other compositions in this transition group do not present any new characteristics. We may proceed, then, to basic group C and a more detailed analysis of the metabole technique.

The possibilities for metabole may be outlined as follows:

1. Beginning on an auxiliary pitch level (usually a fifth above or below the main pitch level), then moving to the basic pitch level and remaining there for the rest of the section or composition.

2. Beginning on the basic pitch level, remaining there, and shifting to an auxiliary level (usually a fifth above or below) only in the last phrase-unit or two.

3. Beginning and ending on the basic pitch level with metabole to an auxiliary level (usually a fifth above or below) in the central portion of the section.

4. Short metaboles interspersed at different points in a section:

    a. All metaboles to the same auxiliary level.

    b. Metaboles to different auxiliary levels.

    c. Returning to the basic pitch level after a metabole.

    d. Metabole to a second auxiliary level, then returning to the first auxiliary level or the basic level; that is, two consecutive metaboles.

5. A whole section on a different pitch level as has already been illustrated in example 55.

All the above types of metabole are found in Thai traditional compositions. In a metabole the process of moving from the first pitch level to the next may be done in either of two ways: (1) by means of a pivot pitch, when a principal pitch of the mode on one pitch level becomes a different principal pitch in the mode on another pitch level—this was illustrated in example 56; (2) by means of a passing tone, when auxiliary pitch 4 or 7 in the mode on one level becomes a principal pitch in the mode on a new pitch level.

Metabole usually involves a movement from the original pitch level to a new pitch level either a fifth above or a fifth below (or, by inversion, its octave counterpart a fourth below or above). Occasionally the metabole involves a movement to the pitch level one step (in the tuning system) above or below the original pitch level, a conjunct movement—the melody shifts to a new pitch level two fifths away, transposed down an octave, skipping the intermediary fifth. For example, if the original pitch level is low phīang ǭ (pitch level III), the metabole might involve a shift to low kruat (pitch level IV), the fifth above high phīang ǭ (pitch level VII, the intermediary fifth between them). This is clearer in diagram form:

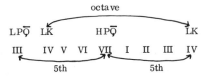

The most common interchange of principal pitches in the pivot-pitch technique is again the interval of the fifth (or fourth), that is, pitch 1 or 2

becomes pitch 5 (on the new pitch level), pitch 2 or 3 becomes pitch 6, or vice versa, and so forth. In the passing-tone technique the most common occurrence is that pitch 1 in the original mode becomes passing tone pitch 4 in the mode on the new pitch level.

With these basic characteristics of metabole in mind, let us examine representative compositions to see how the techniques are used in the music itself. All the compositions in group C have six or seven pitches occurring on the ching strokes. In the outline pattern of the ching-stroke pitches in these compositions, the metabole is clear because one of the two nonprincipal pitches, 4 or 7, will become prominent in the outline, indicating a shift of the pentatonic mode to a new pitch level.

The initial pitch level of the composition is indicated to the left of the first phrase-unit. Metabole is indicated in the pitch outline by two numbers being divided by a slash line and also by the abbreviation for the new pitch level appearing to the right of the phrase-unit in which the metabole occurs and to the left of the next phrase-unit. For example:

		o	+	o	⊕	
(a)	HPǬ:	1	3	3	1/5 LPǬ	
	LPǬ:	6	2	2	6	
(b)	HK:	2	5/2	1	6	LK
	LK:	5	2	2	5	

Chart 17 is a pitch outline of a composition illustrating the use of metabole in the central part of a section that begins and ends in the same pitch level.

		o	+	o	⊕	
(One section	HPǬ (VII):	1	1	2	1	
only; two		6	3	3	6	
phrase-blocks)		6	3	3	6	
		1	6/3	3	1	LPǬ
	LPǬ (IV):	3	1	1	6/2	HPǬ
	HPǬ:	2	6	6	2	
		3	6	6	5	
		1	3	3	1	(cadence: 5321)

Chart 17. Pitch outline—"Sām Mai Nai" (Thao), 3 chan, ms. coll. no. 3372.

The change of pitch level that is the metabole will usually be found to start at the end of the first motive of a phrase-unit and then continue for the second motive and another full phrase-unit, as illustrated here. This metabole—beginning in the middle of the fourth phrase-unit—involves movement to the auxiliary level low phīang ọ̄, a fifth below, accomplished by the pivot-pitch method with pitch 6 on the original pitch level becoming pitch 3 on the new pitch level; for the return at the end of the following phrase-unit, pitch 6 on the auxiliary level becomes pitch 2 on the original level. In Western and cipher notation the middle portion of the composition—in which the metabole occurs—appears in example 57, beginning with the last half of phrase-unit three.

In the Thai pentatonic mode the first three pitches are adjoining in the tuning system, and the two intervals involved are equidistant. As all intervals between adjoining pitches in the tuning system are equidistant, theoretically any pitch may serve as pitch 1, which means that any pitch may also serve as a passing tone. In this metabole pitch 3 of the mode on the original level becomes a passing tone in the mode on a new pitch level, while pitch 4—auxiliary pitch of the original mode—becomes one of the principal pitches in the mode on the new pitch level; pitch 7, a passing tone in the original mode, remains a passing tone (now pitch 4 in the new mode). In other words pitch 4 of the mode on the first pitch level becomes pitch 1 on the new level, pitch 5 becomes pitch 2, pitch 6 becomes pitch 3, and so on. Passing tone

Example 57. "Sām Mai Nai" (Thao).

Section 1:

Phrase-block one:

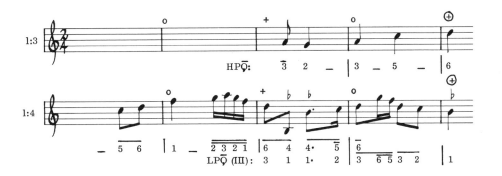

Phrase-block two:

pitch 7 is now passing pitch 4 in the mode on the new pitch level, while pitch 3 is now passing tone pitch 7. This is shown in diagram form in chart 18.

The next composition, "Hong Thǭng," illustrates both the metabole at the beginning of a composition and the mǭn style. Each section begins on an

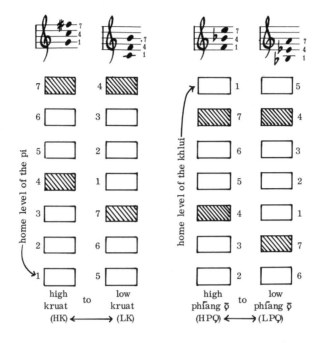

Chart 18. Pitch-exchange process for metabole.

It should not, therefore, be argued that pitch 4 is simply substituted for pitch 3. True, pitch 4—a passing tone—becomes a member of the mode on a new pitch level, while pitch 3 becomes a passing tone; but pitches 3 and 4 exchange functions, as it were—one is not simply substituted for the other.

Nor should one speak here of a change in mode, although in some musics that do not use equidistant intervals the result of such a functional exchange is a new mode with a different intervallic structure. In the present case the intervallic structure of the mode on the new level is exactly the same as that of the mode on the original level. Rather than a change in mode, then, there is a shift of the same mode to a new pitch level. Pitch 4 of the original modal level now functions as the "tonic" of the mode on the new pitch level and is demonstratively so employed. See, for instance, example 55 (pp. 142 ff.), where the music for Section Four in the low phīang ǭ level is almost identically the same as in Section Three in high phīang ǭ.

auxiliary pitch level before shifting to the basic pitch level used in the greater portion of the composition. Both sections also have passages of runs using passing tones in the mǭn style which are chameleon-like and cannot be unequivocally assigned to any one pitch level.

Section One, given in example 58, begins in high kruat with a motive ending in a 5321 cadence; the second motive of the phrase-unit involves a transition to low kruat, in which the section ends with a 5321 cadence.

Section Two (ex. 59) starts a fifth lower (or a fourth higher) than the basic low kruat level—in high phīang ǭ—before shifting back to the basic level. This section, too, ends with a clear 5321 cadence.

Example 58. "Hong Thŏng" (Thao) (*Silpakŏn Magazine,*
               6 (Jan. 1963), 64).

3 chan (main melody simplified).

Section 1 (one phrase-block only):

Example 59. "Hong Thŏng" (Thao).

3 chan

Section 2:

Phrase-block one:

Example 59 (continued).

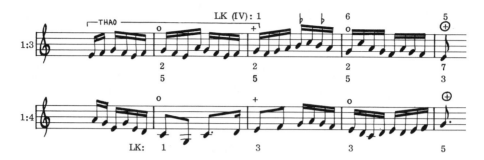

Phrase-block two:

The pitch outline for both sections is in chart 19.

The next short composition in middle version (sŏng chan) with one section only is from a Tap suite, the second of six compositions each of which has a name that begins with "Khāēk"—as was explained, compositions with this name in their title are generally in mŏn style. The metabole illustrated here (ex. 60 and chart 20) is of the conjunct type: the pitch level shifts to pitch 7 relative to the starting pitch level—high kruat (I) to high phīang ŏ (VII)—with a return to the original level at the end. Mŏn flavor prevails throughout.

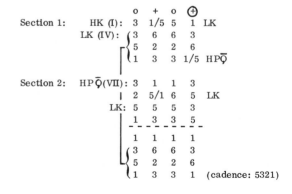

Chart 19. Pitch outline—"Hong Thŏng" (Thao).

Example 60. "Khāek Thǭn Sāi Bua" (2 chan) (Tap Ābūhāsan; no. 33, ms. coll. no. 235, 2nd composition of 6).

(One section only).

Chart 20. Pitch outline—"Khāek Thǭn Sāi Bua" (2 chan).

"Phrayā Khruan" (ex. 61 and chart 21), another composition consisting of only one section, is primarily in Thai style with a mere suggestion of mǭn style in a few runs. The composition begins with a motive on the pitch level a fifth below (a fourth above) the pitch level of the main body of the composition—pitches 1, 2, 3, and 5 being more likely than pitches 1, 4, 5, and 6. The second motive of the first phrase-unit is on the basic pitch level, high kruat. The composition is composed of three phrase-blocks, the first two of which are identical except for the final phrase-unit and a variation of the opening motive in low kruat. Phrase-block three ends in the same way as phrase-block one with a metabole to the pitch level a fifth above the basic level—pitch level V (for which there is no special name). Since this is the final part, the composition ends on an auxiliary pitch level with a run, the last pitches of which are 5321 of pitch level V. In moving from this final phrase-unit to the first phrase-unit of the repeat (which is a variation of the original first phrase-unit and the same as the first phrase-unit in phrase-block two), there is a conjunct metabole from pitch level V to low kruat (pitch level IV).

In the composition "Yǭng NGit," also of only one section, two examples of the abrupt metabole occur involving no pivot pitch that is a principal pitch in both pitch levels. Phrase-units eight and thirteen

Example 61. "Phrayā Khruan" (3 chan) (ms. coll. no. 341).

(One section only).
Phrase-block one:

Phrase-block two:

Example 61 (continued).

Phrase-block three:

Chart 21. Pitch outline——"Phrayā Khruan" (3 chan).

end on pitch 1 of low kruat; phrase-units nine and fourteen begin immediately in the new pitch level, high kruat; the final pitch on the original pitch level (LK) is pitch 4 on the new pitch level (HK). The return to the original pitch level in phrase-unit ten is also abrupt, but by the pivot-pitch method. Phrase-unit fifteen is enigmatic—it may be analyzed

equally well in either pitch level, thus forming a phrase-unit of transition between pitch levels. The composition ends with the relatively rare final cadence on pitch 3; since that is preceded by the regular 5321 cadence, it may be an extension of this cadence to pitch 3. (See ex. 62 and chart 22.)

Example 62. "Yŏng NGit" (Thao) (ms. coll. no. 325).

3 chan (one section only).

Phrase-block one:

Phrase-block two:

Example 62 (continued).

Phrase-block three:

Phrase-block four:

```
     o   +   o   ⊕
LK:  5   1   1   3
     3   6   6   3
     3   3   3   2
     3   1   1   3
   - - - - - - - -
     3   6   6   3
     1   3   3   1
     5   1   1   3
     6   3   3   1/4 HK
HK:  1   3   3   1/5 LK
LK:  3   5   5   1
     5   1   1   3
     6   3   3   1
   - - - - - - - -
     2   6   5   1/4 HK
HK:  5   2   2   6
     ⎡6   6   2   6⎤ same line
LK:  ⎣3   3   6   3⎦
LK:  3   1   1   3   (cadence: 5321 5123)
```

Chart 22. Pitch outline—"Yǭng NGit" (Thao), 3 chan.

Chart 23 contains the pitch outline of another composition in which metabole occurs.

Section One of this composition is in the simple Thai style with one run containing pitch 4. The fourth phrase-units of the first phrase-block and the following second phrase-blocks in the two sections of the composition are identical. The running passage containing the passing tone pitch 4 occurs in both sections in phrase-block two, phrase-unit two (marked with an "x" in the pitch outline and shown in notation in ex. 63); the run is a thao extending pitch 2, which occurs at the end of the preceding phrase-unit.

Example 63.

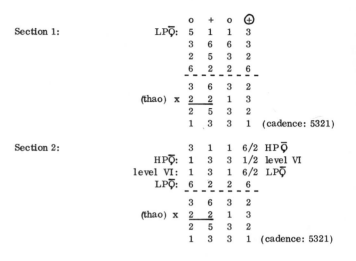

```
                    o   +   o   ⊕
Section 1:    LPQ̄:  5   1   1   3
                    3   6   6   3
                    2   5   3   2
                    6   2   2   6
                  - - - - - - - -
                    3   6   3   2
            (thao) x 2   2   1   3
                    2   5   3   2
                    1   3   3   1   (cadence: 5321)

Section 2:          3   1   1   6/2 HPQ̄
              HPQ̄:  1   3   3   1/2 level VI
          level VI: 1   3   1   6/2 LPQ̄
              LPQ̄:  6   2   2   6
                  - - - - - - - -
                    3   6   3   2
            (thao) x 2   2   1   3
                    2   5   3   2
                    1   3   3   1   (cadence: 5321)
```

Chart 23. Pitch outline—"Phat Chā" (3 chan), ms. coll. no. 414.

In the first phrase-block of the second section (ex. 64), two metaboles in succession occur before a return to the original pitch level. Each is one phrase-unit long. The first—to high phīang ǭ, the fifth above—occurs in phrase-unit two. In phrase-unit three the occurrence of pitch 4 (of high phīang ǭ) indicates movement to the pitch level a fifth below the original—pitch level VI. All the metaboles here are accomplished by the pivot-pitch method.

Example 64.

Section 2:

Phrase-block one:

In the next composition (chart 24 is the pitch outline) Section One presents no new characteristics, but a series of metaboles occurs in Section Two:

		o	+	o	⊕	
Section 1:	HK:	3	1	1	4/1	LK
	LK:	2	6	6	2	
		3	1	1	3	
		3	3	3	2	
		3	1	1	3	
		2	6	6	2	
		3	5	4	2	
		1	3	3	1/4	HK (cadence: 5321)
Section 2:	HK:	3	1/5	5	1/2	LK to LPŌ
	LPŌ:	1	3	3	1	
		6	1	1	7/3	HPŌ
	HPŌ:	3	3	3	5/2	LPŌ
	LPŌ:	3	1	1	6/5	LK
	LK:	5	3	3	5	
		3	5/6	1	3/6	LPŌ to HPŌ
	HPŌ:	5	5	5	5/2	LPŌ
	LPŌ:	3	1	1	3/2	LK
	LK:	3	1	1	3	
		3	5	4	2	(4=accented passing
		1	3	3	1	(cadence: 5321) tone)

Chart 24. Pitch outline—"Dǫk Mai Sai" (3 chan), ms. coll. no. 326.

This second section illustrates several metaboles within a relatively short space and the use of passing tones in such a way that the basic pitch level is clouded, vague, and capable of more than one interpretation. The second begins with the same phrase-unit as Section One and uses a technique previously illustrated: the first motive is in the auxiliary level a fifth above. The second motive of the phrase-unit moves to the basic pitch level of low kruat and ends on pitch 1. The section and composition are designated as being on the low kruat level because the first and final phrase-units are clearly on this level, and both sections end with the common 5321 cadence. The second phrase-unit in Section Two moves immediately to low phīang ǭ, an illustration of metabole to an area two fifths away, resulting in conjunct movement: pitch level IV to pitch level III skipping high phīang ǭ (pitch level VII), intermediary to both. Pitch 1 of low kruat becomes pitch 2 in low phīang ǭ. The first two phrase-units are shown in notation in example 65.

Example 65.

Section 2:

Phrase-block one:

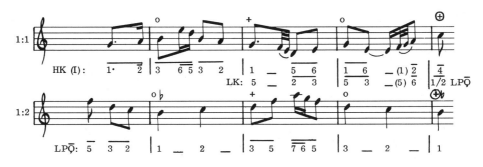

Beginning with phrase-unit three and continuing through phrase-unit nine, greater use of all seven pitches occurs with a consequent loss of a distinct and clear feeling of one tonal center of gravity. Each phrase-unit may be analyzed in either low or high phīang ō̱ with passing tones, or even in low kruat in some places, as indicated in the pitch outline. Phrase-units three through eight are shown in example 66.

Example 66.

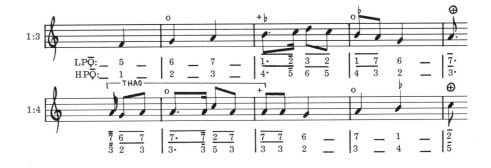

(N.B. This line is in high phīang ō̱, since a thao on pitch 7 is never used. A thao on pitch 3 is very common.)

Phrase-block two:

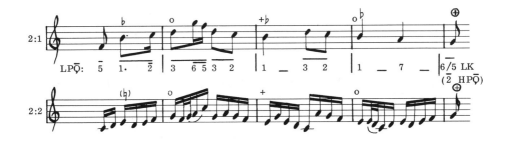

Example 66 (continued).

(N.B. In the last phrase-unit above, at the point indicated by the accidental and question mark above the staff, the flat in the first motive of the thao appears in the manuscript collection. This four-measure thao appears in other compositions, and the first motive, further, often occurs by itself. Elsewhere it gives the impression of being on an auxiliary level a fifth higher than that of the main melody, on a pitch level a fifth below.)

Phrase-block three:

(N.B. At this point the melody shifts abruptly back to low kruat, where it remains for the remainder of the section. Pitch 4 is used in one running passage.)

An illustration of a composition with three sections each of which is on a different pitch level is "Khāek Mǭn Bāng Chāng" (ex. 67 and chart 25).

Example 67. "Khāēk Mǭn Bāng Chāng" (3 chan) (ms. coll. no. 417).

3 chan.

Section 1 (one phrase-block only):

Section 2 (one phrase-block only):

Example 67 (continued).

Section 3:

Phrase-block one:

Phrase-block two (two phrase-units only):

The pitch outline is in chart 25.

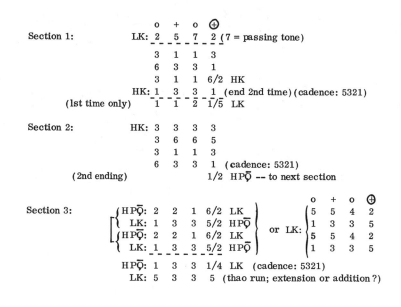

```
                                o    +    o   ⊕
Section 1:            LK:  2    5    7    2  (7 = passing tone)
                          3    1    1    3
                          6    3    3    1
                          3    1    1    6/2  HK
                     HK:  1    3    3    1  (end 2nd time)(cadence: 5321)
     (1st time only)      1    1    2    1/5  LK

Section 2:           HK:  3    3    3    3
                          3    6    6    5
                          3    1    1    3
                          6    3    3    1  (cadence: 5321)
          (2nd ending)                   1/2  HPǬ -- to next section

                                                        o    +    o   ⊕
Section 3:    ⎧ HPǬ:  2    2    1    6/2  LK ⎫         5    5    4    2
              ⎢  LK:  1    3    3    5/2  HPǬ ⎢         1    3    3    5
              ⎢ HPǬ:  2    2    1    6/2  LK ⎢ or LK:  5    5    4    2
              ⎩  LK:  1    3    3    5/2  HPǬ ⎭         1    3    3    5
              HPǬ:  1    3    3    1/4  LK  (cadence: 5321)
               LK:  5    3    3    5  (thao run; extension or addition?)
```

Chart 25. Pitch outline—"Khāek Mǒn Bāng Chǎng" (3 chan).

Section One is in a relatively simple style. The first and last phrase-units appear to be additions or extensions and the phrase-block of the section to consist of the central four phrase-units. The first phrase-unit, which uses pitch 7 as a passing tone, appears as the introductory phrase-unit in other compositions also. The last phrase-unit is used as the first ending only and serves as a transition back to the beginning; it continues on the high kruat level to which the melody has moved at the end of phrase-unit three. The metabole is accomplished by the pivot-pitch method. The cadence is 5321. Section Two is short—one phrase-block—and is entirely on the high kruat level, ending also with a 5321 cadence.

The basic pitch level of Section Three is less clear, and the mood corresponds more than that of Sections One and Two to the title, which indicates a mǒn style. The section consists of two phrase-units and their repetition. The first phrase-block may be analyzed on low kruat, in which case the initial thao (phrase-units one and three) has passing tone 4 on a ching stroke, or these two phrase-units may be considered as a temporary metabole to high phīang ǫ. If phrase-units one and three are considered to be on low kruat it would indicate that in mǒn style pitch 4

may be substituted for pitch 3, for this kind of run in simple Thai style would be:

```
        o                    +
LK:  3       5    6        5
```

The 5321 cadence occurs at the end of the penultimate phrase-unit, and the last phrase-unit is a thao. The composition may actually end on pitch 1 in high phīang ǫ with a thao extension to pitch 2, or the composition may end on pitch 2 of a 123 56 pentatonic mode on high phīang ǫ. Or, if the final thao is considered to be a temporary metabole to low kruat, then the composition ends on pitch 5 of low kruat.

The motive at the end of phrase-units two and six is similar to the motive in the thao in the preceding composition, "Dǫk Mai Sai," where it appears on the high phīang ǫ level.

A few more examples will be given of the abrupt metabole in which a principal pitch of one mode is not a principal pitch of the mode on the new level (generally pitch 1 becoming pitch 4).

The first, "Nārai Phlāeng Rūp," is analyzed in low phīang $\bar{\varrho}$ because the first phrase-unit and the final cadence are on that level—though the body of the composition, which consists of only one section, is in the typical mǒn style. In the middle of the composition the passage shown in example 68 occurs.

Example 68. "Nārai Phlāeng Rūp" (3 chan) (ms. coll. no. 412).

Attention is drawn to the occurrence again of the thao motive mentioned in the last two examples, which in this composition is syncopated.

The final cadence is varied also with a syncopation (ex. 69), one of the rare occurrences of that type in this part of a composition.

Example 69.

In cataloguing the one hundred and thirty-six compositions in the representative group according to the finalis — as was done in charts 6 and 7 on page 116 — each composition was considered to be on one basic pitch level except the two designated in chart 7 as "mixed, unclear"; in these two several metaboles occur, and they therefore cannot be said to have a firm basic pitch level. If the finalis of each of these compositions is analyzed according to the pitch level of the last phrase-unit, regardless of the other pitch levels used, then two more compositions cadencing on pitch 1 exist than the number given in chart 6 indicates. One of the compositions, "Sǒi Mayurā," is short (one section only) and is given in its

entirety in example 70 and chart 26; it illustrates the use of several metaboles—the abrupt, passing-tone type as well as the pivot-pitch type.

The same variety found in the compositions without metabole is also found in those with metabole; that is, within the general format of a quadratic structure, the general style of a conjunct melody, and the generous use of certain melodic species on any pitch level, the music in the section of metabole is not different from the music on the basic pitch level. No specific formulas are used as a bridge between one pitch level and another; one melodic motive or phrase-unit may proceed directly into another pitch level by either of the two methods. If the composition is basically in the pentatonic style, the metabole will use for the pulse grouping of the phrase-unit the pitches that establish the new pitch level. The pulse groupings 3-1-1-3 and 1-3-3-1, which securely establish the pitch level, are frequently found as the first pulse grouping of a metabole; a metabole to a pitch level a fifth below (or a fourth above) is shown by the outline 6-4-4-6 or 4-6-6-4 (in the original pitch level), representing 3-1-1-3 and 1-3-3-1 on the new level. Likewise, a metabole to a pitch level a fifth above (or a fourth below) is shown in the pitch outline by 5-7-7-5 or 7-5-5-7 (in the original pitch level), representing 3-1-1-3 and 1-3-3-1 on the new level. If the mǒn style is used in the metabole, it is more likely that pitches 2, 3, and 6 will be emphasized in the metabolic pulse grouping. A few more examples will be given showing musical elements not specifically illustrated previously—different aspects of metabole and cadences.

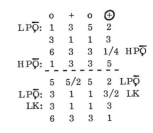

Chart 26. Pitch outline—"Sǒi Mayurā" (Thao), 3 chan.

Example 70. "Sǫi Mayurā" (Thao) (ms. coll. no. 397).

3 chan (one section only).

Phrase-block one:

Phrase-block two:

Chart 27 shows the cadence on pitch 5.

```
            o   +   o   ⊕
   ? {HPǬ:  5   5   5   5}
     {LPǬ:  2   2   2   2}
     LPǬ:  3   1   1   3/6  HPǬ
     HPǬ:  5   5   5   1
           2   6   6   3
           - - - - - - - -
           3   1   1   3
           3   5   5   3
           3   3   3   3
           6   3   3   6
           - - - - - - - -
           6   1   1   6
           2   6   6   3
           2   6   6   2
           3   6   1   5   (cadence: 2165)
```

Chart 27. Pitch outline—"Rasam Rasāi" (3 chan, one section only), (ms. coll. no. 330).

As can be seen, pitch 1 occurs on a ⊕ stroke only in the first phrase-block, so no possibility exists of a cadence on pitch 1 on another ching stroke with an extension to another pitch on a later ching stroke. The composition starts with the customary thao for the first phrase-unit, which in this composition as in many may be analyzed on more than one pitch level—here, on the basic level of high phīang ǭ or the auxiliary level of low phīang ǭ. The second phrase-unit is on the low phīang ǭ level, after which the melody returns to the basic level of high phīang ǭ.

where it remains for the rest of the composition. In the second phrase-block pitch 4 is used as a passing tone, as in example 71.

Example 72 gives the last two phrase-units of the composition, including the final cadence.

The use of passing tones and runs with passing tones gives the whole composition a delicate touch of mǭn flavor.

Though all five pitches of the pentatonic mode are used on the ⊕ strokes, pitches 3 and 6 predominate. The phrase-units are not different from those used in other compositions—3-1-1-3 and 6-3-3-6, for example, being found in many compositions. Except for the final cadence, no features of this composition support unequivocally its being classified as representative of a theoretical mode 5.

The composition "Chāng Prasān NGā" has a cadence section (ex. 73 and chart 28) that can be analyzed in either of two pitch levels. It is classified as ending on pitch 5 according to the pitch level in which the composition begins, but it can also be analyzed as ending on pitch 2 on the pitch level a fifth below. According to the first method the cadence is 2165; according to the second, 6532.

Example 71.

Example 72.

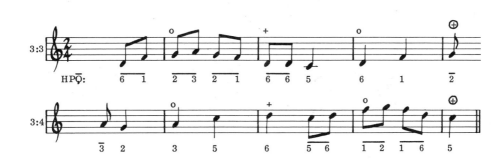

Example 73. "Chāng Prasān NGā" (Thao) (ms. coll. no. 364).

3 chan (one section only).

Phrase-block one:

Phrase-block two:

```
        o   +   o   ⊕
HK:  1   3   3   1
     2   6   6   2
     7   2   2   4/1   LK (7 is a passing tone)
LK:  1   3   5   2/5   HK

HK:  3   1   1   4/5   HPǬ
HPǬ: 1   3   3   1
     2   7   2   1/4   LK (7 is a passing tone)
LK:  5   3   5   2     (cadence: 6532)
or:  5  3/6  1   5     HK (cadence: 2165)
```

Chart 28. Pitch outline—"Chāng Prasān NGā" (Thao), 3 chan (one section only).

A cadence may have an ascending or descending form leading to the final pitch—for instance, 5321 or 3561. The descending form is more prominent than the ascending for all pitches except pitch 3, for which the typical cadence is 5123. Cadences on pitch 2 have occurred in some of the compositions already given, but a few more typical ones may be cited:

1. Ascending, open position, as in example 74.

Example 74. "Ton Nāng Nāk" (3 chan) (ms. coll. no. 430).

Two sections, both ending with the same phrase-unit (and cadence):

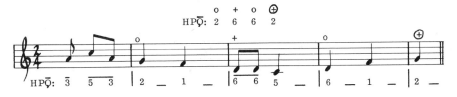

All five pitches are used on the ⊕ strokes.

Example 75 illustrates another 5612 cadence, highly ornamented.

Example 75. "Ton Phlēng Ching" (3 chan) (ms. coll. no. 358).

Two sections, the last phrase-unit:

The pitch outline for the last phrase-unit is the same as in the previous composition. In this composition, also, all five pitches are used on the ⊕ strokes.

2. Descending, closed position as in example 76; this is the most usual form of the descending cadence on pitch 2.

Example 76. "Mulong" (Thao) (ms. coll. no. 355).

3 chan (one section only; last phrase-unit):

Cadences on pitch 6 also have ascending and descending forms in open and closed positions:
1. Ascending, open position, as in example 77.

Example 77. "Pae" (3 chan) (ms. coll. no. 409).

Simple Thai pentatonic style; last phrase-unit:

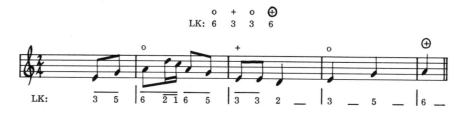

Pitches 1, 2, 3, and 5 occur on the ⊕ strokes with the exception of the last one, on which pitch 6 occurs, as illustrated above. Other compositions, however, with the same final phrase-unit use pitch 6 more frequently on the ⊕ strokes.
2. Descending, closed position; in the group of representative compositions this cadence (3216) does not occur as a final cadence without ornaments or

extension—it does occur nine times in various arrangements of 32176 in mǭn style.

An instance of the open position is example 78, the final phrase-unit of a composition having one section only, which consists of two phrase-blocks (only pitches 3 and 6 are used on the ⊕ strokes).

Example 78. "Wiwēk Wēhā" (3 chan) (ms. coll. no. 413).

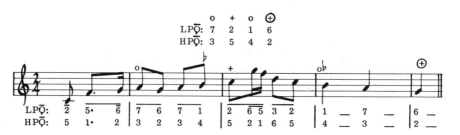

Most of the compositions with this final cadence also have the same final phrase-unit, LPǬ 7-2-1-6 (or HPǬ 3-5-4-2). The suggestions of the auxiliary pitch level in the first motive of the phrase-unit and the passing tone in the second motive in the mǭn style are not unusual.

A final cadence of this type which concludes a final phrase-unit other than the above is shown in example 79.

Example 79. "Hok Bot" (Thao) (ms. coll. no. 336).

3 chan.
One section only, final phrase-unit:

Example 80. "Khaēk Mǭn Bāng Khun Phrom" (Thao) (ms. coll. no. 393).

3 chan.

Three sections, the final cadence the same in all:

Example 81. "Nāk Phan" (2 chan) (ms. coll. no. 331).

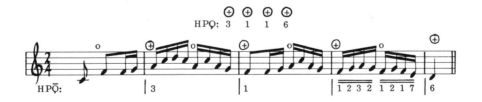

3. Ascending, closed position; this cadence, though theoretically possible, does not occur as a final cadence in any of the compositions in the representative group.

4. Descending, closed position; substantiating the tendency in Thai music for descending patterns, several forms of the 3216 cadence occur:

(a) The simple, closed form incorporating pitch 7 as a passing tone, as in example 80.

(b) In a fast run, as in example 81, the final measures of a long composition in the middle version only, with four sections.

(c) The 3216 cadence with interpolated pitches, ornaments, or extensions, as in example 82.

Example 82. (a) "Khamēn La Ǭ Ong" (Thao) (ms. coll. no.
                   375).

3 chan

Two sections, the same final cadence:

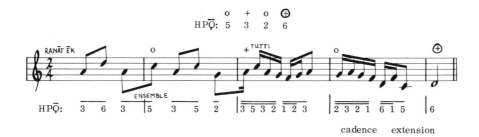

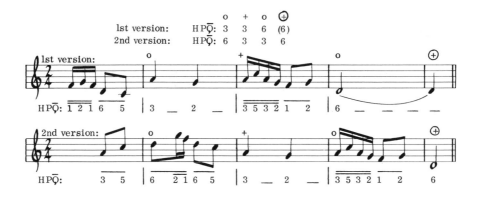

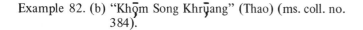

Example 82. (b) "Khǭm Song Khrұang" (Thao) (ms. coll. no.
                   384).

3 chan, one section only:

E. CODA

Before closing this chapter, one more matter should be discussed—that of the coda. The rұang compositions do not have codas for the individual compositions; the rұang itself has a coda, which will be discussed in the next chapter. Of the newer vocal-instrumental compositions in the manuscript collection only the complete Thao compositions have codas; no codas are given for sām chan compositions.

With one exception all the codas in the manuscript collection end on the pitch notated as *d* in Western notation:

The one exception, which may be a mistake in notation, ends on *g*:

This pitch is not pitch 1 of the mode of that composition, however.

During my studies in Bangkok I could discover no explanation for this characteristic of the codas. Because of this feature the final pitch will be numbered differently depending on the basic pitch level of the composition or the pitch level on which it ends. If a composition is on pitch level V, the coda ends on pitch 1 of the mode (mode 1, that is); if on low kruat (IV), on pitch 2; if on low phīang ǭ (III), then pitch 3; if on high phīang ō (VII), then pitch 6, and so on. Or often the coda will contain a metabole, in which case the final pitch does not bear the relationship to the body of the composition that it would otherwise have. Sometimes a coda is short, without a metabole, and written for a specific pitch

level, such as high kruat. If the composition is lowered to high phīang ǭ, a shift must be made in the middle of the coda so that the last phrase will be on the proper pitch level. This causes a peculiar sense of dislocation to the Western ear but apparently causes the Thai listener no distress. An example of this is found in the coda to "Khamēn La Ǭ Ong," a composition in the Thao variation form. The second and final section of the chan dio or short version is shown in example 83 as it occurs on the high kruat level (I) when played by the pī phāt ensemble, and on the high phīang ǭ level (VII) as played by the string ensembles, followed by the coda. This example also illustrates a short coda—here, of only six measures.

Example 83. "Khamēn La Ǭ Ong" (Thao) (*Silpakǭn Magazine*, 1 (Mar. 1958), 56; and as taught to the author).

chan dio.

Section 2:

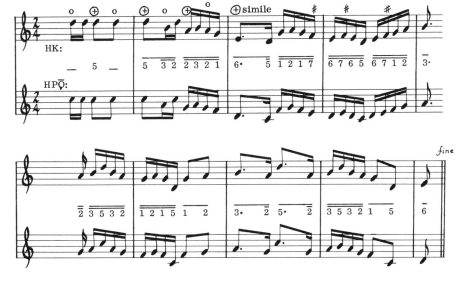

Example 84 is an instance of an even shorter coda—four measures. The composition is basically in high kruat, though the last phrase (also shown in the example) involves a metabole to pitch level V.

A coda for a composition in low phīang $\bar{\varphi}$ is shown in example 85.

passages in the "question-answer" technique followed by short climactic passages before the final coda is reached. Without the original middle version to which this extended version might be compared, it is not really possible to say where the composition actually ends—probably at the point indicated on pitch 2,

Example 84. "Phayā Ram Phụng" (3 chan) (ms. coll. no. 432).

Example 85. "Mǭn Chom Chan" (Thao) (ms. coll. no. 441).

chan dio.

Example 86 illustrates a somewhat more elaborate handling of the final section of the composition itself. The composition is in the extended version (3 chan) only; Section Two involves

the composition being on the low kruat level. The first half of the coda ends with the standard 5321 cadence and the second part on the usual coda finalis, pitch 2 in low kruat.

Example 86. "Chom Suan Sawan" (3 chan) (ms. coll. no. 360).

End of Section 2:

Example 87 illustrates a slightly longer coda of a composition in high phīang ǭ. Codas are usually of a certain number of complete phrase-units though not always an even number—in this example the coda is of three phrase-units. This coda also contains a metabole. The last two phrase-units seem to lie more on the auxiliary low kruat level than on high phīang ǭ, in which the body of the composition is written.

Example 87. "Bai Khlang" (3 chan) (ms. coll. no. 410).

End of Section 4

Some other typical characteristics of codas are illustrated in the next two examples. In the short coda in example 88, in the last four measures is found a rhythmic figure often used in codas; as here, it is frequently combined with a descending and then ascending melodic pattern.

Example 88. "Nāng Khruan" (Thao) (*Silpakǭn Magazine,* 5 (July 1961), 66).

In this example and in example 89 is illustrated the stretto often found in the coda. The ranāt ēk leads off, anticipating, and finishes before the rest of the ensemble.

Example 89. "Khāēk Lopburī" (*Silpakǭn Magazine*, 4 (Sept. 1960), 83).

Coda for the 3 chan version:

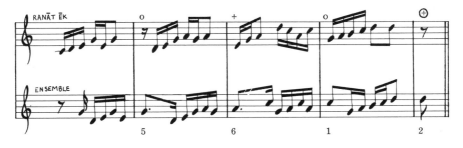

An examination of the above example will show that several pitch levels are hinted at. Most codas for compositions on high kruat (I) and high phīang ō̦ (VII) have a metabole to low kruat (IV), and the finalis is pitch 2 of the mode on low kruat (IV). Codas for compositions on low phīang ō̦ (III) generally remain on that pitch level, and the finalis of the coda is pitch 3 of the mode on that level. Compositions on high kruat (I) may remain on that level, and some codas—such as the one above on low kruat (IV)—may have a suggestion of high kruat (I) in the final phrase through the use of the passing tone. Although it is theoretically quite possible, compositions on high phīang ō̦ (VII) generally do not have codas that stay unequivocally on that level, ending on pitch 6; they usually contain a metabole to the fourth below (fifth above)—low kruat (IV)—and end on pitch 2 of the mode on that level. A composition on high phīang ō̦ (VII) having a coda ending on pitch 6 of the mode on that level is shown in the next chapter, example 94 (pp. 199-204).

A coda may be as short as one phrase-unit or a phrase-unit and a half (six measures), as has been illustrated, or may be many phrase-units long—generally two, four, six, or eight, though occasionally an odd number, such as three, may be used.

F. SUMMARY

Lack of terminology in Thai defining musical concepts in the Thai music system—such as "mode," the concept under consideration here—used by Thai themselves in verbalizing about the theoretical aspects of their music makes the formulation and codifying of such musical concepts difficult. The high degree of organization shown to exist in Thai music, however, indicates that such a concept as "mode" does exist, though either not so highly developed as in the music of some of Thailand's neighbors or, if it once was highly developed, having "devolved" as a result of other concepts having assumed more importance.

A modal practice obtains in Thai music because the music exhibits the several factors considered necessary for a modal system to exist:

1. A nonequidistant pitch supply (sometimes referred to as a "gapped scale")—represented by the ciphers 123 56, which indicate five of the seven pitches in the tuning system—is the basis of compositions. More or less use is made of the other two pitches (4 and 7) as passing tones and to shift the mode to a new pitch level, called "metabole."

2. A hierarchy of pitches is established in the pentatonic mode(s) by the coincidence of certain of the pitches with strokes of the ching and by specific cadences. Some compositions exhibit a greater degree of hierarchical arrangement than others by not using all five pitches of the mode at the structural points of emphasis. No modal system can be unequivocally stated to exist based on the finalis of compositions, similar to what has been reported to have been or to be the basis of modal practice in Chinese music. Thai traditional compositions do, however, have a quadratic structure, and compositions are "composed" by combining a number of more or less standard melodic species, called here "phrase-units," of equal length, in turn made up of two equal halves, called here "motives." Phrase-units are further shown to be organized in groups of four, called here "phrase-blocks." Each motive, phrase-unit, and phrase-block has an underlying pulse of 1 2 3 4, with the strongest emphasis on the final pulse. This pulse emphasis underlies the two motives of a phrase-unit

and therefore may be called a "pulse couplet":

$$1 \; \underset{\underbrace{}_{1}}{2} \; 3 \; \underset{\underbrace{}_{2}}{4}.$$

Because all pulses drive toward the final pulse of the group, the finalis of the composition represents the culmination of all the subgroups of pulses and therefore may be of no little importance as one of the prime indicators of mode in Thai music—if not of mode, certainly of mood.

In Thai music pitch 1 of the 123 56 mode and the 5321 cadence, on whatever pitch level, is the finalis in over half the compositions in the representative group of compositions used as the basis of this study. Many other compositions in the same style as those with a finalis on pitch 1 contain the 5321 cadence in the final phrase-unit of the composition with an extension to another pitch. If this is considered an aspect of "mode 1," then the incidence of the use of mode 1 is much higher.

3. Secondary characteristics of the proposed definition of mode also exist in Thai music:

(a) Specific melodic species and cadences are used.

(b) A technique of metabole—shifting of pitch level—is utilized, bringing into play auxiliary pitch levels (modes, scales, and so forth).

4. Of seemingly greater importance than modal variety demonstrated by a fairly equal number of compositions having a finalis on each of the five pitches of the pentatonic structure or pitch supply is an aspect of Thai music that is called here "polarity." The pitches at the end of each half of a majority of the "couplets" of pulse groupings are a fifth apart (or a sixth in the case of 1-3 and 3-1, as was explained earlier). The most highly integrated compositions in the Thai traditional repertory are based on and unified by the use of specific fifth polarities, as has been pointed out in some of the examples in this chapter. A composition exploiting the polarity 3-6 (or 6-3) supported by the polarity 6-2 (2-6) with a finalis on pitch 6 has an entirely different mood and atmosphere than a composition exploiting the polarity 1-3 (3-1) supported by 1-5 (5-1) with a finalis on pitch 1. Although not so dramatically different as these two hypothetical cases, a different mood from the first example above (polarities 3-6/6-2 would be obtained by using the same polarities, but reversed—2-6, supported by 6-3—with a finalis on pitch 2.

Often different polarities are exploited in different sections of a composition, giving variety—and frequently, no matter what polarities have been used in the different sections, the final phrase-block or even the last two phrase-units will converge to the 1-3 or 1-5 polarity, and the composition will end on pitch 1.

Although the mōn style involves more use of pitches 4 and 7, the fifth polarities are still prominent. The two main differences between simple pentatonic Thai style and mōn style are in the internal structure of the melody—the greater use of passing tones in mōn style and in the finalis, which in a composition entirely in mōn style is not pitch 1 but pitch 2 or 6, as will be illustrated in the next chapter. The finalis is not the deciding factor in mōn style, however, for we have seen in this chapter compositions in simple pentatonic Thai style with a finalis on pitches 2 and 6.

The principal identifying features of Thai traditional music are:

1. The tuning system of seven equidistant pitches to the octave, a tuning characteristic of no other known music system;

2. Pentatonic modes with more or less use of the other two pitches of the tuning system depending on which of the two basic styles is being used;

3. Pitch 1 of the pentatonic structure as a finalis in a majority of compositions;

4. The quadratic structure of the compositions, which are made up of groups of melodic units of equal length;

5. The occurrence of pitches a fifth apart—fifth polarities—at the ends of the two halves of a majority of the melodic units, coinciding with the structural beats or pulses of the quadratic units;

6. The use of the hand cymbals, the ching, to mark off the metrical structural points of the melodic units;

7. The ensembles of instruments, the sound texture of which is the result of the particular function of individual instruments within the ensemble, the total sound texture differing from that of ensembles of the other gong-chime cultures in Southeast Asia.

Chapter V

Forms and Compositional Techniques

Composition in Thai music for the most part has been more a matter of arranging existing material than creating new, original compositions. As one result, to honor and remember composers as such has not been a longstanding tradition. Most of the oldest compositions in the repertory are anonymous. With changing custom somewhat in the late nineteenth and twentieth centuries, however, for more recent compositions the composer or "arranger" is often known.

A. RŪANG

The oldest compositions in the Thai repertory of traditional instrumental music are those grouped together in what might be called "suites"—in Thai, "rūang." The age of these rūang is not known exactly; since Thai musicians say they are "old," most if not all were probably put together in the nineteenth century. Some of the compositions themselves in the rūang may well be survivals from the eighteenth century or even earlier.

In the manuscript collection (discussed in Chapter I) twenty-nine rūang have been notated; others are said to have existed but to have been lost. In former times when ceremonies or functions took place in the royal households in which Buddhist monks usually participated, the ensemble belonging to the household was expected to furnish music during the time before the monks arrived and the ceremony started. Gradually certain compositions began to be played together as a group and thus became associated as a unit, being unified by a common tempo or formal structure, a mutual general style and mood, similar titles, or titles referring to similar objects.[1] Though the unifying factor in many suites is clear, in some it is not.

The compositions in a rūang are grouped into divisions according to tempo, with the number of compositions in each tempo varying from one rūang to another; most rūang are closed with a standard "farewell" song, called in Thai "Lā," which also varies slightly. The rūang generally have three main divisions—in slow (prop kai), medium (sǒng mai), and fast tempo (phlēng reo)—the ching patterns for which were illustrated in Chapter II (pp. 41-42). Some rūang, however, have compositions in only one or two tempos; whether this is the true form of the particular rūang or it was not notated completely is not known.

Since the decline of the royal households (1932) occasions for playing the rūang are rare, and few musicians today know any of them or anything about them. During the two years I was in Bangkok, I heard only two rūang—the shorter, simpler type—played, at one of the ceremonies still observed.

A tabulation of the structural make-up of the rūang is given in chart 29.

The chart can be summarized as follows:

Content:	Number of rūang:
prop kai only	3
sǒng mai only	3
phlēng reo only	2
prop kai and sǒng mai only	1
sǒng mai and phlēng reo only	1
all three tempos	19

| No. of compositions in each tempo | | | | No. of rūang of that type |
prop kai	sǫng mai	phlēng reo	"La"	
0	0	11	0	1
0	0	12	0	1
0	3	0	0	1*
0	4	0	0	1
0	6	0	0	1
0	8	1	1	1
1	1	1	1	4
1	2	1	1	1
1	3	1	1	1
1	3	3	1	1
2	0	0	0	1
2	2	2	1	1
2	3	1	1	1
3	1	1	1	5
4	0	0	0	1
4	1	1	1	1
4	2	1	1	1
5	1	1	1	1
5	2	1	1	1
6	5	2	0 (rua)	1
7	0	0	0	1
8	1	4	1	1

total   29

(* This rūang is incomplete in the manuscript copy; the ching part is missing, so it is not clear what the formal structure is. However, in comparing some of the compositions in this rūang with the Thao versions that were created from them, it is probable that the originals were in the sǫng mai tempo, though the possibility that they were in prop kai must not be excluded. Whatever the interpretation, it is the only rūang with only three compositions, all in the same tempo.)

Chart 29. Classification of rūang.

As can be seen from the tabulation in chart 29, the rūang vary greatly despite a so-called standard or "ideal" form: aside from the two types for each of which several rūang exist, every rūang is a single one of its type.

Compositions in the prop kai and sǫng mai tempos are much like the compositions discussed in the previous chapter, except that they perhaps vary somewhat more and many of them are longer. The phlēng reo sections in the rūang are much longer than the chan dio (fast) sections of the Thao compositions (to be discussed shortly), though the tempo and ching structure are the same. The reason is that the chan dio are a reduction from a specific number of measures originally existing, while the phlēng reo are a composition or series of compositions forming a climax section to a suite of compositions. The phlēng reo compositions generally reach a level and intensity of true virtuoso style; they make a fitting climax to the series of tempo changes from slow to fast broken suddenly at the end for the final "La," sixteen measures long, played in the initial slow prop kai tempo.

The longest rūang composition is "Tao Kin Phak Bung," the first and only composition in prop kai in the rūang of the same name—it has six hundred and eighty-four measures exclusive of repeats. The shortest composition actually having a specific name is only eight measures long, but it is not really an independent composition; the title indicates that it is to be played as the conclusion or coda to the preceding composition. The average length for most compositions in the rūang is forty to sixty measures. Long compositions are generally broken up into sections, in come cases indicated in the manuscript; other compositions are not so marked but are divided by repeat signs. Since these compositions are on the whole longer than those considered in the last chapter, a good deal more repetition is found in them—often long passages within a section, or even whole sections, may be repeated at another pitch level. A good deal more use of metabole is also characteristic of the rūang compositions. But aside from these structural differences, the style of music is identical to that dealt with in the previous chapter. Compositions using a simple 123 56 pitch pattern, pitch supply, or mode are present, as well as compositions in mǫn style.

Other than the occasional repeats of phrase-units of one section in another section and the repeat of a complete section at another pitch level, the general style of the rūang compositions is through-composed, with liberal use of similar motives or melodic species. Other than cadences that are sometimes identical at the end of each section (though just as often different), the Thai forms do not exhibit the rounded quality of Western forms, so many of which return to material stated at the beginning of the composition (or part of a composition, such as a movement of a symphony) after a section of contrasting material.

Generally the rŭang is known by the name of its first composition—or, occasionally, its most important composition if other than the first.[2]

"Lā" (Farewell Song)

To show the amount of variability allowable in Thai traditional compositions without destroying the identity of a composition, the nineteen versions of the main melody of the final composition, "Lā," will be discussed as it appears in the manuscript copies of the various rŭang with which it is used. The pitch outline is in chart 30.

	o	+	o	⊕	
HK:	3	6	6	(2)	2
	1	3	6	(3)	3
	2	2	2	6	
	1	6	3	(1)	1

Chart 30. Pitch outline—"Lā" (Farewell Song), prop kai structure.

In the first, second, and last phrase-units a variation in the pitch used among the different versions is found on the second unaccented ching stroke, but on all other ching strokes the pitches are identical in all versions even though the melodies for that motive or phrase vary.

Two main types of variation are to be found, and further, variations of these two types exist; in example 90 the main variation types have been labeled "A" and "B," and the various versions of each measure are numbered with Arabic numerals. Each measure differing in any detail is notated separately. One version, labeled "C," has a final cadence different from the two main versions.

Of the versions of each measure, one is used more than any other. Taking these measures, an "ideal" "Lā" could be created as shown in example 91.

No one version in any rŭang is exactly like this "ideal." In Appendix B the actual version of each "Lā" is given by indicating the letter and number of each version of each measure from example 90 which is used in each "Lā."

B. THAO

The Thao or variation form already mentioned in preceding chapters is a unique handling of the variation form, incorporating specific and characteristic uses of the principles of augmentation and diminution.

The technique of Thao composition arose in the late nineteenth century and reached its height probably in the twentieth century during the reigns of Rama VI and Rama VII (from about 1910 to 1930). Because royal patrons often took their own musicians along when visiting other royal households, a spirit of friendly rivalry grew up among resident and visiting musicians. Soon definite contests were arranged. Besides rivalry as to which ensemble could play the best and which solo players could demonstrate the most skill as virtuosos, musician-composers began to devise special works for these contests. In about the middle of the nineteenth century[3] they began in earnest to conduct their adaptation and rearrangement of existing compositions according to specific rules so that the original compositions would be difficult to ascertain; hundreds of these "new" compositions were created. If an opposing group of musicians failed to identify the original composition, it lost face as well as the contest. Great lengths were resorted to by groups to try to discover in advance what rival groups were going to play for a contest—spies tried to get into rival households or were sent to loiter nearby in the hope of overhearing a rehearsal. If one team's composition could be discovered beforehand the other team could compose another version of the same composition, and after the opposing team had played its version they could counter with theirs. From all reports this subterfuge fortunately was never other than friendly and only the end result of entertainment and fun was desired.[4]

The Thao technique (and form) is based on two main principles: (1) the technique of augmentation and diminution of a given composition, and (2) the constant doubling of tempo—that is, doubling the

Example 90. "Lä" (Farewell Song).

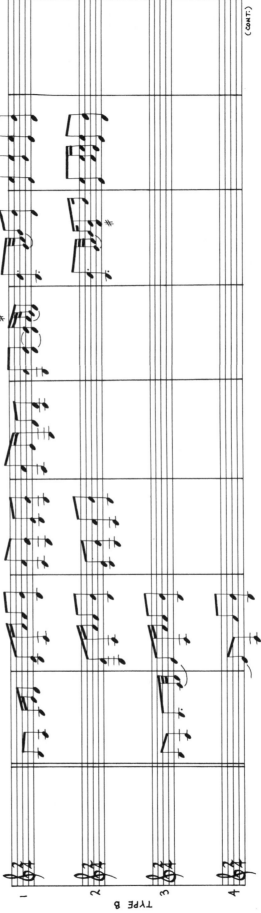

Example 90 (continued).

Example 91. "Lā" ("ideal" form).

number of ching strokes per measure, which gives a feeling of doubling the tempo. These two principles in themselves are neither new nor revolutionary, but the way the Thai have used them to create a specific form is unique. Because of the custom in Thai music not to create new and original compositions, this technique of composing was and is admirably suited to the Thai music system and customs.

Let us look at the process in general outline. An already existing composition—usually an old traditional one, or perhaps one that might be considered a folksong, or sometimes a simple melody borrowed from a neighboring country—is selected, and an "augmented" and a "diminished" version of it are composed. Because of the limit of available material some old compositions were used by more than one composer, but generally one version was considered superior and remained in the repertory while the others were sooner or later abandoned. Occasionally a Thao has divisions composed by different composers, or one composer's version will be used for the first playing and another composer's

version for the repeat. Sometimes if a composer composed only the augmented, or extended, version—which was all that was played when the style first became popular for contests—a later composer may have added the short, diminished version so that the whole Thao with three complete divisions might be played.

When the style first arose only the augmented or extended version was played for the contest, for naturally if this were followed by the original composition the rival group would recognize it. But after the extended version had once been played, if it was popular the composer might then make a short version and the complete Thao could be played on subsequent occasions.

The composition selected as a basis for a Thao generally has one to three sections. Each section contains a number of measures that is usually a multiple of four; it is usually sixteen measures long, although some are eight to twelve and others twenty-four to thirty-two. Whatever the original length, the extended version must cover twice the number of measures. This is why a section of sixteen measures seems an ideal length, the resulting extended version of thirty-two measures seeming long enough for artistic and aesthetic purposes——a greater length is unwieldy, and if the complete Thao is played it is regarded as being too long for truly pleasurable listening. A few Thao compositions exist, however, well-known and still popular, the sections of whose extended versions are longer than thirty-two measures. For example, one of the famous Thao compositions of Rama VII, "Rātrī Pradap Dāo," has two sections whose extended versions are each forty-eight measures long. It should be pointed out here that each instrumental section is generally repeated and is also preceded by a vocal section (accompanied only by the rhythmic percussion instruments) of the same length; thus the complete composition is much longer than a simple adding together of the single instrumental sections would indicate. A complete short Thao in performance lasts from ten to fifteen minutes and a long one twenty to thirty.

After the composition has been selected on which the Thao set is to be composed, the composer changes the ching pattern to sǭng mai if it is not already that. Then he examines the pitches falling on the accented ching strokes (at the beginning of each measure in Western notation). In the extended version these pitches will occur twice as far apart, at the beginning of even-numbered measures starting with measure two, as illustrated in the following diagram:

What occurs between these points is up to the composer, and here his creative ingenuity is brought into play: he must create music in the style and mood of the original composition with these original pitches occurring both smoothly and naturally in the melody and coinciding with the proper ching strokes.

Often the composer retains certain outstanding motivic phrases of the original at important structural points, as illustrated in example 92, which gives the music for the ching strokes and key pitches shown in the diagram above.

In this example the composer has chosen to retain the initial thao on pitch 6. (This incidentally ties in with the final cadence 3216 and helps to unify the composition as well as give it, to the Western ear, a "minor," "melancholy" quality. If a mode 6 exists in Thai music this composition is in that mode, although many passages in the body of the composition for contrast modulate—in the fundamental meaning of the word—to mode 1 (on high phīang ǭ). After the thao the composer has inserted entirely new music to fill the required number of measures up to the "half-cadential" motive $\overline{5}|\overline{1}\cdot\overline{3}\overline{2}\overline{1}\overline{2}|3$, which he has transferred intact from the original composition to the extended version. The new music consists of ascending and descending passages using all five pitches of the pentatonic mode 1 (123 56 1) and/or mode 6 (6 123 56) on high phīang ǭ, centered first around pitch 6 and then around pitch 1. These passages are in the general style and mood of the original composition.

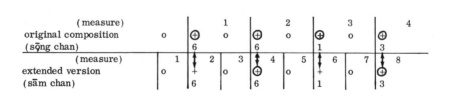

Example 92. "Khamēn La Ō Ong" (Thao)·(*Silpakǫn Magazine,*
1 (March 1958), 50; ms. coll. no. 375).

(Beginning of Section 1) (measure numbers above staff)

(N.B. These two versions are, of course, played not simultaneously but successively; they are shown here one under the other for comparison.)

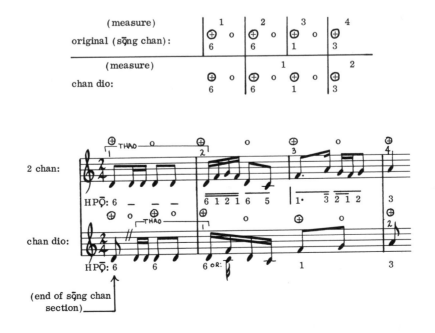

In the short, contracted version the same process is followed in reverse—diminution rather than augmentation: the pitches on the ⊕ strokes in the original, middle version which cover a space of four measures now are compacted into two measures, falling at the beginning and middle of each. In diagram and notation this is as follows:

The composition used for illustration here presents a rather ideal example of the Thao technique in that the four pitches occurring at structural points in the original (6-6-1-3) are transferred intact to both the extended and short versions. As might be expected in a highly developed music, there are exceptions to such rigid structural formulas. Indeed, when a composer feels a phrase is appropriate for the music with which he is dealing, he is in a sense under aesthetic compulsion to use that phrase whether it embodies the correct pitch at the specific structural point or not. These deviations are more the exception than the rule, however, and though they may occur on the unaccented ching strokes in the extended and short versions, they rarely occur on the first accented ching stroke. Almost never does a deviation occur on the second accented ching stroke (accompanied by the gong in the extended version), which is a crucial cadential point. A deviation here would destroy the unity of the Thao. Some of these deviations will be pointed out as they occur in later examples.

In brief, the construction of a Thao may be described as follows: the pitches used at the ends of the first two phrase-units of the original composition (second and fourth measures) become the pitches at the ends of the first two phrase-units of the extended version (four measures each); and the pitches at the ends of the second and fourth phrase-units in the original version (fourth and eighth measures) become the middle and end pitches of measures two and four of the short version. They may be shown more clearly in diagram form. Chart 31 shows the first section of "Nok Khao Khamāē,"[5] composed by Luang Pradit Phai Rǫ (Sǭn Silapabanleng), in skeletal form with only the pitches on the structural ching strokes indicated for the original and short versions but all ching-stroke pitches indicated for the extended version.

Some of the shorter compositions from the rȳang which have been used as bases for Thao compositions will now be examined.

The prop kai division of the rȳang known as *Khāēk Sai* (ms. coll.: Rȳang 12), according to the list in the Department of Fine Arts, consists of three compositions. The names for the first two are missing, and the point at which the second one begins is not indicated in the manuscript; the third composition is designated as "Khāēk Sai." It is notated in low phīang ǭ (IV), and this pitch level is retained for the entire Thao. The rȳang composition has two sections of one phrase-block each in the prop kai structure. In order for the composition to be used as a middle version in sǭng chan form, the metrical structure is changed to the sǭng mai pattern. Nothing else is changed, however; the music remains the same (except for occasional minor changes such as thao fill-ins and so forth). The original pitch outline of the rȳang composition is shown in chart 32.

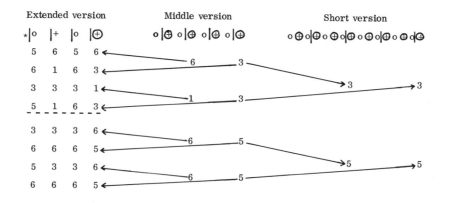

*Vertical lines indicate measure.

Chart 31. Pitch outline—"Nok Khao Khamāē" (Thao),
(ms. coll. no. 381).

```
                    o    +    o    ⊕
                   ┌─thao─┐
Section 1:   LPO̱: ‖:6/5 6/5  6    1
                     2    6    6    2
                     2    2    3    1
                     2    6    3    5:‖

                   ┌─thao─┐
Section 2:         ‖:5/1 5/1  6    5
                     6    3    2    5
                     5    5    6    5
                     6    3    3    1:‖
```

(N.B. In Section 1 the thao on pitch 6 is changed to pitch 5 and in Section 2 pitch 5 is changed to pitch 1 for the repeat, the thao in the repeat being a continuation of the final pitch of the section.)

Chart 32. Pitch outline—"Khaēk Sai" (Rüang 12, 3rd composition of 3 in prop kai division).

When the pattern is changed to sǭng mai, the ching-gong strokes are doubled—in the pitch outline the pitches on all the ching strokes, accented and unaccented, in the prop kai pattern become the pitches on ching-gong strokes in the sǭng mai pattern; that is, the first phrase-unit in prop kai in chart 32:

```
        |o  |+  |o  |⊕
         6   6   6   1
```

becomes, in sǭng mai:

```
    o |⊕  o |⊕  o |⊕  o |⊕
       6      6      6      1
```

Both patterns cover only four measures, as has been explained. The sǭng mai version now becomes as shown in the pitch outline given for the entire Thao in chart 33.

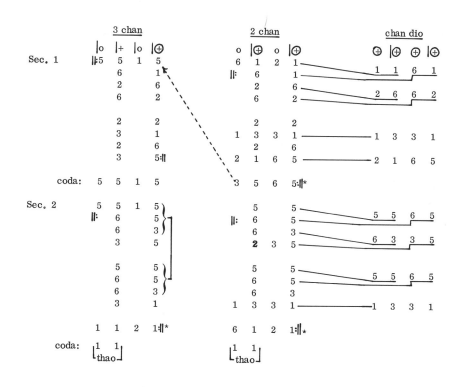

*Substituted for phrase-unit one for the repeat.

Chart 33. Pitch outline—"Khaēk Sai" (Thao), (ms. coll. no. 329.)

In this chart of structural pitches the arrangement of sām chan and sǭng chan give the impression that the two are identical. It must be remembered, however, that one line of numbers in this chart in sām chan covers four measures of music, while one line in sǭng chan (and chan dio) covers only two measures. It is set up this way to show clearly the correspondence of pitches among the three divisions.

Frequently the first phrase-unit will be varied for the repeat of a section. In the first section of sǭng chan in this composition the phrase-unit used for the repeat (3 5 6 5) is used for the extended version (5 5 1 5) both times (that is, the structural pitches 5 – 5 are used); but in chan dio the first version of the first phrase-unit of sǭng chan (6 1 2 1) is used.

A few deviations occur in this Thao: in the last phrase-unit of the first section the original version has pitch 1 on the penultimate ⊕ stroke, while in the extended version this is changed to pitch 3 (on the penultimate accented ching stroke). However, this is not a primary structural point, and variation here is not unusual. In the second phrase-block of the first section of the short version, rather than retain the primary structural pitches (2-2-3-1, the + strokes of sǭng chan) for the first two phrase-units, the composer-arranger used pitches of the entire second phrase-unit, 1-3-3-1. The same also holds true for the last two phrase-units of the section, as well as for the last two phrase-units of Section Two. At the end of the first phrase-block of Section Two (phrase-unit four), instead of the theoretically correct pitches 2 and 5, the last two pitches of the phrase unit (3 and 5) are used. This is a rather common occurrence: the cadence at this point in sǭng chan is moved intact to chan dio, and instead of subjecting the phrase-unit in sǭng chan to the process of diminution, the first half of the phrase-unit is discarded and the entire second half of the phrase-unit, with the cadence, used as is.

The notation for this Thao is shown in example 93, using a four-part open score so that cross-divisional comparisons may be seen more easily.

The composition "Ānū" is the only one in the sǭng mai division of Rɥ̄ang Čhin Sǣ Mai (Rɥ̄ang 16). The compositions in this rɥ̄ang are Chinese in style, indicated by the word "Čhin"—the Thai word for "China"—in the title. This rɥ̄ang contains three compositions in the prop kai division, this single sǭng mai composition, the phlēng reo division, and the final "Lā." As is often the case, the phlēng reo division is not separated into separate compositions with names; the whole division is designated "phlēng reo."

In the rɥ̄ang, "Ānū" is played and notated at the high kruat level (I). The pitch outline appears in chart 34.

		o	⊕	o	⊕
Section 1:	HK:	‖:1	6	1	6
		6	3	3	(3)𝄇
		‖:6	5	6	5
		5	2	2	(2)𝄇
		‖:5	2	1	6
		5	1	1	(1)𝄇
Section 2:	‖:3	3	1	1
		5	5	1	1 𝄇
		3	3	3	3
		3	3	3	3
		‖:5	2	1	6
		5	1	1	(1):‖

N.B. The last two phrase-units of the two sections are the same; this often occurs in Thai compositions as a unifying technique.

Chart 34. Pitch outline—"Ānū" (sǭng mai from Rɥ̄ang 16), ms. coll. no. 111.

Instead of the high kruat level (I) of the rɥ̄ang version of "Ānū," for the Thao version it is transposed down to the low kruat level (IV). Since the original composition is already in the sǭng mai pattern, the metrical pattern need not be altered for its use in the sǭng chan position in the Thao. The essential structural pitches for the first four phrase-units are:

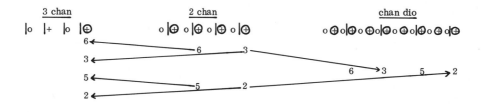

Example 93. "Khāek Sai" (Thao).

Section 1.
(Numbers above staff are measure numbers)

Example 93 (continued).

Example 93 (continued).

(Because there is no vocal section in the Rụ̈ang separating the two sections, the thao at the end of Section 1 acts as a bridge to Section 2.)

(cont.)

Example 93 (continued).

Here, as in the pitch outline for "Nok Khao Khamāē" given earlier (chart 31), only the essential structural pitches are indicated. The accompanying pitch outline for the full Thao version of "Ānū," shown in chart 35, is more complete: the pitches on all ⊕ strokes in the middle and short versions are given. This more complete outline is presented in order to show that in some compositions many pitches in addition to the essential structural ones are retained from version to version, a procedure that naturally makes for a more tightly knit and unified composition.

at the top covers a space of four measures in the extended version as notated in Western notation, but only two measures in the middle and short versions, the same amount of time is required to play four measures in each version. The music in each succeeding version is collapsed into half the number of measures of the preceding—for example, 32 – 16 – 8—and the ching strokes in each succeeding version are increased to twice the number per measure. Therefore, although the same amount of playing time is required to cover the four measures in each version, each succeeding version lasts half as long

		3 chan				2 chan				chan dio	
		Extended version				Middle version				Short version	
		|o	|+	|o	|⊕	o	|⊕	o	|⊕	⊕	|⊕
Section 1:	LK:	‖: 1	1	2	6	‖: 1	6	1	6	‖: 1	6
		6	3	1	3:‖	6	3	3	(3):‖	3	(3) :‖
		‖: 6	5	6	5	‖: 6	5	6	5	‖: 6	5
		6	5	3	2:‖	5	2	2	(2):‖	2	(2) :‖
		‖: 3	2	1	6	‖: 5	2	1	6	‖: 1	6
		1	1	1	1:‖	5	1	1	(1):‖	1	(1) :‖
Section 2:		‖: 3	3	1	1	‖: 3	3	1	1	‖: 3	1
		5	1	1	1:‖	5	5	1	1 :‖	5	1 :‖
		3	3	3	3	3	3	3	3	3	3
		3	1	1	3	2	5	3	(3)	3	(3)
		‖:(3)	2	2	6	‖: 5	2	1	6	‖: 1	6
		1	1	1	1:‖	5	1	1	(1):‖	1	(1) :‖

*Vertical lines are bar lines indicating measures.

Chart 35. Pitch outline—"Ānū" (Thao), ms. coll. no. 348.

Attention is again drawn to the following factor: although in the above diagram the ching-gong pattern

as the preceding because it is half the number of measures long. For example:

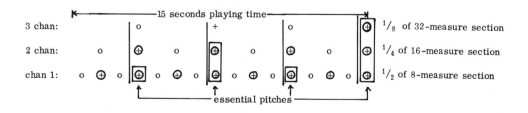

The structural pitches occur twice as far apart in sām chan as in the original, a phrase-unit in sǫng chan being two measures long and in sām chan four measures. In chan dio the phrase-unit is one measure, half as long as in sǫng chan. The ratio then is 4:2:1—2 doubled and 2 halved.

The ⊕ pattern does not follow this same ratio, and one must not confuse the two patterns. The *ratio* of ching strokes, however, is the same—doubled between adjoining patterns—two per measure in sǫng mai, one per measure in prop kai, and four per measure in phlēng reo (and chan dio). But in sǫng mai, instead of the gong occurring on every other accented ching-stroke—o|+ o|⊕ (which would be the theoretically correct pattern if the prop kai pattern were played twice as fast)—it occurs with every accented ching-stroke, o|⊕ o|⊕. The phlēng reo (chan dio) pattern follows the theoretically correct pattern: the sǫng mai pattern is doubled, o⊕o|⊕.

In the brief historical survey of the development of the Thao form given earlier in this chapter, it was mentioned that the same original composition was sometimes used by more than one composer as the basis of a Thao composition. Two versions of the same composition will now be examined.

The rūang called *Khamēn Yai* (Rūang 8) consists partly of three prop kai compositions: "Khamēn Yai," "Khamēn Nǫi," and "Khamēn Klāng" (ms. coll. nos. 61, 62, and 63)—the words *yai, nǫi,* and *klāng* mean basically "large," "small," and "medium," respectively. (This method of labeling sets of three compositions also occurs in a few other rūang, but the three words as used here refer not to the length or importance of the compositions but to tribal or ethnic groups.) The first two compositions (Yai and Nǫi) are of average length, sixty-four measures, and are different from each other; the third (Klāng) is half that length, thirty-two measures, and is made up of material from the first two. The rest of the rūang consists of one sǫng mai composition and a phlēng reo and "Lā" finale. This phlēng reo composition or division is one of the few with a specific name; it is called, picturesquely, "The Fruit-bat (or Flying Fox) Eats Bananas."

This rūang, and *Rūang Khāek Sai* described earlier, are both of the type shown in chart 29 for which there are five examples, structured as 3-1-1-1. In the manuscript collection of Thai compositions

there is a sām chan version of "Khamēn Yai" (ms. coll. no. 378), based on the composition from the rūang. Another composition—called "Khamāe Thom" (ms. coll. no. 382)—whose pitch outline resembles that of "Khamēn Yai" was found on further investigation to be indeed based on the same rūang composition. The word *"khamēn,"* as was explained, is the Thai version of the word written in Roman letters as "Khmer" (pronounced "k'mare" in English). As discussed in Chapter I, the Khmer people were the inhabitants of Angkor in what is now northwestern Cambodia; their culture reached a high state of development between 800 and 1450, at about which time they were finally conquered by the Thai. The Thai pronunciation of "Khmer," because of the requirements of the language, must be "khamēn"—a final "r" sound does not exist in spoken Thai, being replaced by the "n" sound. The word *khamāe(r)* is another Thai word for "Khmer." The word *thom* is listed in the Thai dictionary as an adjective derived from the Cambodian language meaning "big" or "large." The two titles are therefore synonymous. This technique for duplicating with other words an existing title is frequently found among Thai compositions.

These two sām chan compositions, based on this same rūang composition, are examples of compositions played only in the extended version; they are not followed by the original composition, nor is there any short version.

The original composition in the rūang has four sections. The first half of Section One is in high kruat (I), and the second half shifts to low kruat (IV) by means of a pivot pitch—pitch 5 in high kruat becoming pitch 2 in low kruat. Section Two remains in low kruat except for a four-measure thao in the middle of the section which is possibly a metabole back to high kruat. Section Three returns to high kruat. Section Four is Section Three transposed to low kruat.

The original composition exhibits a peculiarity in the colotomic structure also found in at least one other rūang: the first ⊕ stroke in the prop kai pattern falls on the second full measure of the score. Since the prop kai division ends on a ⊕ stroke at the conclusion of a regular four-measure phrase-unit, the first phrase-unit is altered or defective and the melody starts in the middle of the phrase-unit in relation to the colotomy. The two missing beginning

```
                                    "Khamēn Yai"                    "Khamāē Thom"
                                              3 chan
                                              HPŌ
                o  +  o  ⊕                     only            o  +  o  ⊕
Section 1:                    HPŌ: ‖:1  1  2  1 (thao)   1    HPŌ:‖:3  5  1  1
          HK:   (1) ‖:6  1         3 3/6 5  1 LK         5         6  3  3  5
                              LK:  1  3  3  1            5         1  2  5 (5)
                1  1  2  5         3  1  6  5            2         6_ 3 (3) 2_

                                   3  5  5  1            5        (2) 6  6  5
                5  1  1 5/2 LK      3  1  1 5/2 HPŌ       2         2  5  5  6*
                              HPŌ: 3  1  3  2            2        (6) 3  3  2
          LK:   1  2  6  1         1  3  3  1:‖          1         5  2  6  1:‖

                1 1/4:‖ HK    coda: 1  1  2  1 (thao)                (*deviation)

Section 2:                    HPŌ: ‖:1  1  2  1          1    HPŌ:‖:1  6  5  1
          LK:   (1) ‖:1  3         5  1  1  3            3         5  1  1  3
                                   3  6  6  3            3         3  6  5  3
                6  3  3  1         1  3  3 1/4 LK        1         5_ 3 (2) 1_

                5  5  5  2    LK:  1  1  1  1 (thao)     5         6 (1) 3  5
(or HK:         1  1  1  5)        3  1  6 5/2 HPŌ       2         3 (5) 5  2
                1  2  6  1    HPŌ: 3  1  3  2            2        (2) 5  5  2
                                   1  3  3  1:‖          1         3  1 (2) 1:‖
                1  1:‖
                1/4 HK – to    coda: 1  1  2  1
                Section 3:

Section 3:                    LK: ‖:1  1  2  1           5    HPŌ: 1 (1) 3  1
          HK:   (1) ‖:2  6         5  2  2  6            3       ‖:6  6  6  3
                                   3  2  1  6            3        (3) 6  3  3
                2  6  6  2         3  6  6  2            6         3  3 (2) 6

                6  2  2  6         3  5  4  2            6         3  2  1  6
                                   5  2  2  6            3         6  6  6  3
                1  5  5  1         6  6  6  5            2        (3) 3 (2) 6
                                   1  3  3  1:‖          5        (6) 6  6  5
                1  1:‖
                1/5 LK – to    coda: 1  1  2  1          5         5  5  6  5:‖
                Section 4:

Section 4:                    HPŌ: ‖:1  1  2  1
          LK:   (1) ‖:2  6         5  2  2  6
                                   3  2  1  6
                2  6  6  2         3  6  6  2
                                                         (If analyzed in LK, the numbers
                6  2  2  6         3  5  4  2             will be the same as in Section 3
                                   5  2  2  6            of "Khamēn Yai.")
                1  5  5  1         6  6  6  5             No thao introduction.
                                   1  3  3  1:‖
                1  1:‖                                    If analyzed in LPŌ, the numbers
                              coda: 1  1  2  1            are the same as in Section 3 above.
                                                         If analyzed in HPŌ, the numbers
                              final coda: 6  3  3  6      will be the same as in Section 4
(No coda, as the Rɨ̄ang                   6  6  5  6     of "Khamēn Yai."
proceeds directly to the                  6  3  3  6
second composition. )                     -  6  5  6     No final coda is given.

                                          6  3  3  6
                                          6  2  2  6
                                          6  3  3  6
```

Chart 36. Pitch outline—"Khamēn Yai" and "Khamāē Thom" (Rɨ̄ang and 3 chan).

measures are supplied at the end by repeating the last two measures of the section or with a thao; in this way the colotomic structure is filled out and completed.

The rŷang composition is in the prop kai pattern, so this must first be replaced with the sǫng mai pattern to make the composition into sǫng chan. In composing the extended version the two measures at the end of the section of the rŷang composition were considered to exist at the beginning, as they do when the section is repeated; that is, the final + stroke of the rŷang composition becomes the first ⊕ stroke of the extended version, as can be seen from the pitch outline in chart 36. The extended versions are laid out evenly with two phrase-blocks in each section. The pitch level is also changed for the extended versions, both of which are basically on the high phīang ǫ level (VII). Also, as is usual in extended versions, more use is made in them of metabole than in the original composition; in fact, in the first section of the sām chan version that retains the original name a clever technique is used in the metabole: the same pitches, soundwise, of the original are retained in the extended version, but the *functional* position of the pitch in relation to the mode on the new pitch level is different — the structural pitches in the first two phrase-units of the original composition are HK 1-1-1-5 (the pitches occurring on the accented ching strokes of the prop kai pattern). In the extended version the first pitch 1 is retained at the end of an introductory thao one phrase-unit long. The next three ⊕ strokes in the extended version have the pitches 5-5-2 when they are analyzed all on high phīang ǫ without a metabole. What actually happens here is that a metabole is made to the pitch level a fifth above, high phīang ǫ (VII) to low kruat (IV), and the pitches 5-5-2 in high phīang ǫ are identical in sound to the pitches 1-1-5 on low kruat. At the end of the section the melody returns to the original pitch level (high phīang ǫ), and the last two structural pitches — 2 and 1 — are on the original starting pitch level.

In "Khamǣ Thom," on the other hand, no metabole is used in Section One—it remains on high phīang ǫ throughout the section. This composition was probably written after the other extended version, the reasoning being that the composer-arranger has used for his structural pitches in Section One not those of the original composition—1-1-1-5

1-5-2-1—but those of "Khamēn Yai" (3 chan), analyzed on only high phīang ǫ throughout— 1-5-5-2 5-2-2-1 (with one deviation in the second phrase-unit of phrase-block two where pitch 2 is replaced by its fifth, pitch 6), shown in the pitch outline in chart 36 in the single column headed "HPǬ only" to the right of "Khamēn Yai" (3 chan). The same thing happens in Sections Two and Three. This might be called a Thai method of parodying another composition or composer's work, not in a derogatory way, but to show subtlety and add interest to the composition.

In the original composition Section Three is on the original starting pitch level, high kruat, and Section Four is Section Three transposed down a fifth to low kruat. In "Khamēn Yai" (3 chan) Section Three is shifted to the auxiliary level, low kruat, and Section Four is Section Three now on the home level of high phīang ǫ. In "Khamǣ Thom" Section Three is on the home level, high phīang ǫ, while Section Four is Section Three transposed down a fifth to low phīang ǫ.

In the pitch outlines in chart 36 the few deviations in the essential structural pitches can be seen. One instance should be especially pointed out: in Section Four of "Khamǣ Thom" the introductory thao phrase-unit is missing in the manuscript. The section, therefore, starts on phrase-unit two and the first phrase-block is deficient, having only three phrase-units. The thao phrase-unit appears at the end of the section and so occurs in the repeat. Perhaps the most interesting feature here is that, contrary to the technique mentioned above of using the same sounds, but on an auxiliary pitch level, at this point the structural pitch numbers are those of the basic pitch level of the extended version (high phīang ǫ), but the melody of the section is on the auxiliary pitch level a fifth below—low phīang ǫ. In low phīang ǫ these pitches, 1-6-6-2 2-6-5-1 in high phīang ǫ, have the numbers 5-3-3-6 6-3-1-5. Only three pitches are involved here: 3, 5, and 6 in low phīang ǫ, which are 6, 1, and 2, respectively, in high phīang ǫ. This technique of what might be called musical *double entendre* shows another example of the ingenuity of some of the Thai composers.

The treatment of the final cadence in each extended version is noteworthy. In "Khamēn Yai" (3 chan) the final cadence is the usual 5321 in open position followed by the coda for the section, 1-1-2-1, which leads into the coda of the entire

Example 94. "Khamēn Yai"—"Khamāe Thom."

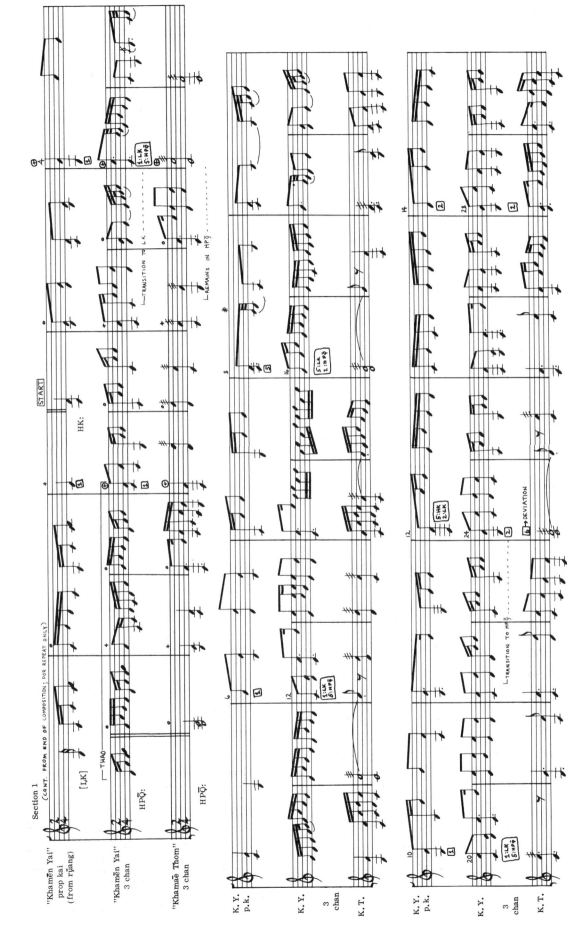

Example 94 (continued).

Example 94 (continued).

(cont.)

Example 94 (continued).

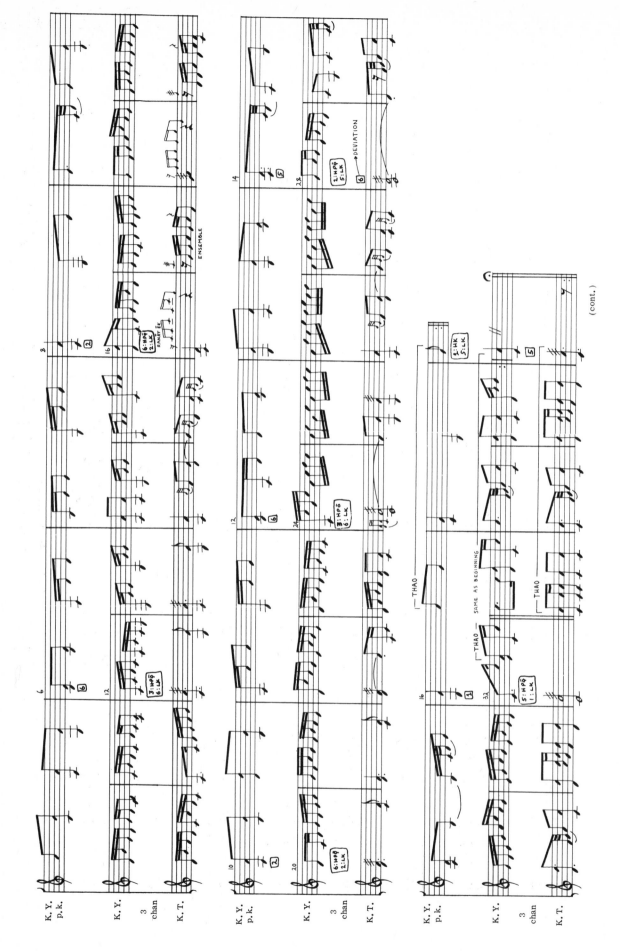

Example 94 (continued).

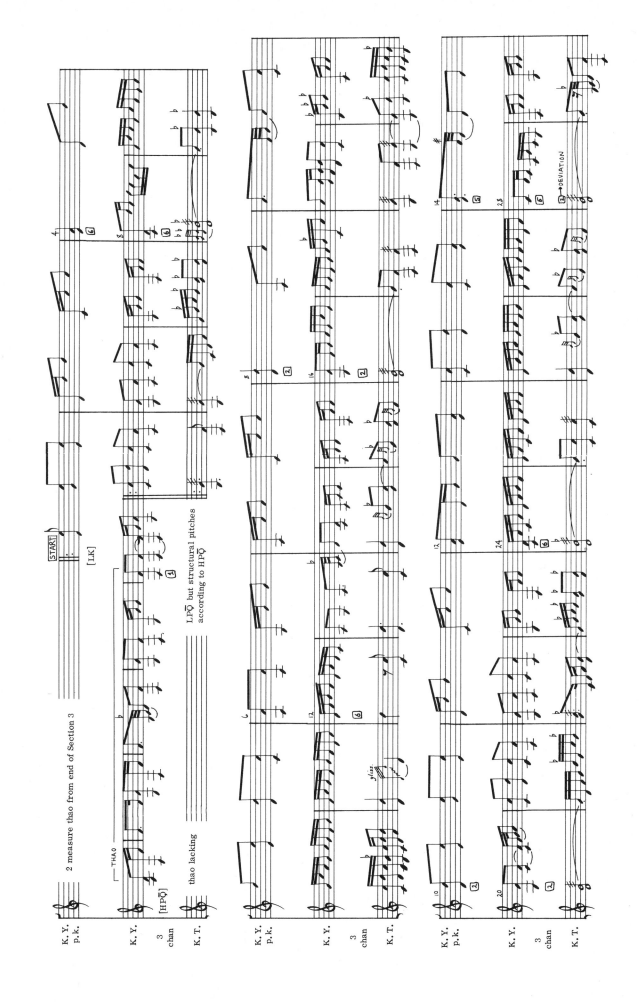

Example 94 (continued).

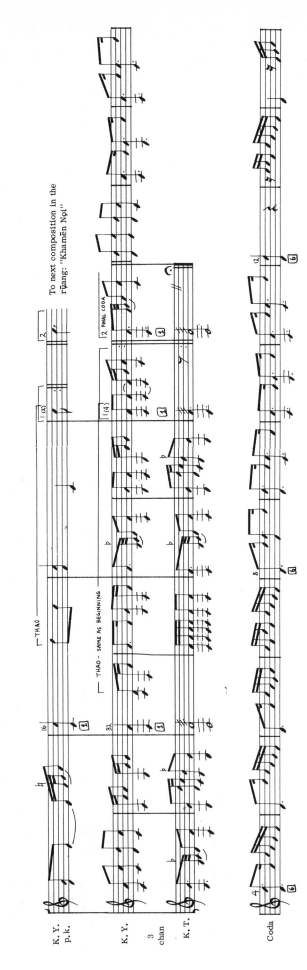

To next composition in the
rŭang: "Khamēn Nọi"

composition. This coda contains seven phrase-units and is one of the few final codas of a composition in high phīang ǭ which stays on that pitch level for the entire coda, ending on pitch 6, rather than progressing through a metabole and ending on pitch 2 in low phīang ǭ. In "Khamāē Thom" the final cadence of the composition, as well as of the appended thao phrase-unit, is 2-1-6-5 in closed position in low phīang ǭ. The essential structural pitches, however, are those of high phīang ǭ, and therefore the composition actually ends on pitch 1 of that pitch level. As was pointed out when this composition was used for illustration in the previous chapter (pp. 141 ff.), this is a unifying device.

In the notation for the three compositions in example 94 the numbers above the staff indicate the measures. The numbers in squares between the staves of the two extended versions at measures 4, 8, 12, 16, and so forth indicate the essential structural pitches at these points—two numbers sometimes appear in these boxes because, though the pitch is the same, two pitch levels are involved, as reference to the pitch outline will show. The numbers for the pitches for the prop kai version appear beneath the staff for that version.

The three compositions often do not coincide in pitch level; care must be taken not to confuse the pitches as indicated by notes on the Western staff. A convenient procedure is to treat HK (high kruat) as the key of G, HPǬ (high phīang ǭ) as the key of F, LK (low kruat) as the key of C, and LPǬ (low phīang ǭ) as the key of B♭ and transpose as one would in reading a Western orchestral open score in which the parts for the instruments are not all written at concert pitch.

Sections Three and Four of "Khamēn Yai" (3 chan) may be compared by consulting example 94.

Besides the ingenious handling of the structural pitches, attention should be drawn to a few other features found in these compositions which are characteristic of Thai music.

The melody of "Khamēn Yai" (3 chan) is in the simple Thai style; it progresses at a fairly even pace with the eighth note being the basic pulse and with a few running passages in sixteenth notes for contrast. The melody of "Khamāē Thom," on the other hand, is much slower in feeling, accomplished by the use of longer note values played in the krǭ style (that is,

with rolls, indicated by three lines on the note stems in the notation in ex. 94).

In "Khamēn Yai" (3 chan) the final cadence is in open position for each section; in "Khamāē Thom" the closed position is used. The last two phrase-units of Sections One and Two are the same; this is also true of Sections Three and Four since the complete sections are identical.

Occasionally motives are transferred from one version to another, particularly a thao and cadential sections.

Some examples of standard sām chan phrase-units of four measures expanded from sǭng chan phrase-units of two measures are found in these compositions. In Section Two in measures four to six in prop kai, the phrase in both prop kai and sǭng mai patterns would be as shown in example 95.

Example 95.

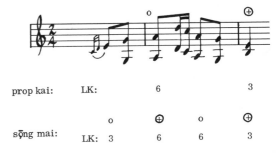

It was pointed out earlier that phrase-units for the extended version consisting of a pair of two ciphers representing the interval of a fifth, mirrored, as in the form shown above, 3-6-6-3, are very common in Thai music. Likewise, the expanded form of this phrase as used in "Khamēn Yai" (3 chan) at this point—Section Two, measures eight to twelve—is one of the standard melodic species of Thai music (ex. 96).

In "Khamāē Thom" several of the typical ornaments are notated.

The examples examined so far in this chapter have been of compositions basically in the simple Thai pentatonic style. An example of a full Thao composition in mǭn style will now be discussed.

The original composition entitled "Khāēk Tǭi Mǭ" is the second of two compositions in the sǭng mai division of *Rฺยang Mǭn Plāeng* (Rฺยang 3). All the

Example 96.

HPǭ: 3   6   6   2
[or LK: 6   2   2   6]

compositions in the Ryāang (except the final "Lā") are in mǭn style: four in the prop kai division, the two in sǫng mai, and the nondifferentiated phlēeng reo division. The final "Lā" is one of the standard versions.

An examination of many of the phlēeng reo sections shows that they ordinarily have no thematic connection with the rest of the compositions in the ryāang. *Ryāang Mǭn Plāeng,* however, is an exception: the first part of the phlēeng reo division is a short version of "Khāek Tǫi Mǭ," thus both the middle and short versions of the composition already existed. All that was needed for a full Thao was the extended version (and the vocal sections).

The extended version for "Khāek Tǫi Mǭ" was composed in 1929 by Montri Tramote, head musician of the music section of the Department of Fine Arts,

already mentioned in previous chapters. The complete Thao of this composition has been printed in the *Silpakǭn Magazine,* published by the Department of Fine Arts, in the issue for November 1960 (vol. 4, no. 4). With the notation was included a brief commentary (in Thai), portions of which are quoted here in my translation:

> The middle and short versions of this Thao are old Thai compositions, being part of the old suite, *Ryāang Mǭn Plāeng* (sǫng mai and phlēeng reo divisions). Both versions have a basic melody suitable for that particular use. Later, the middle version was sometimes used in the khǭn and lakhǭn dramas, generally in the parts where the actor began to change his posture or action-movement, such as entering, leaving, or assuming a disguise.
>
> In 1929 I made an extended version of the composition, retaining the khāek (mǭn) style in the melody, so that the whole might be played as a Thao. But

	3 chan				2 chan				original sǫng mai				chan dio		original phlēeng reo	
[all LK]	o	+	o	⊕	o	⊕	o	⊕	o	⊕	o	⊕	⊕	⊕	⊕	⊕
Sec. 1	3	5	2	3	–	5	2	3	5	5	5	3	–	3	2	3
	(3)	5	5	6	3	5	5	6	1	5	6	6	5	6	5	6
	1	4	2	6	–	4	4	6	6	4	5	6	–	4	4	6
	5	4	2	2	6	5	3	2	6	4	3	2	–	2	4	2
Sec. 2	3	1	3	–	–	–	1	3	3	1	1	3	–	3	1	3
	5	3	1	1	3	2	1	1	6	3	5	1	–	1	3	1
	4	5	–	6	5	–	4	–	5	1	1	3	–	4	3	5
	4	2	(2)	(2)	6	5	3	2	3	5	4	2	2	2	4	2
									go directly to phlēeng reo				add coda		go directly to next part of phlēeng reo	

(N.B. The dashes (–) indicate rests in the published version. In the manuscript collection copy, the notes are tied over from the previous note.)

Chart 37. Pitch outline – "Khāek Tǫi Mǭ (Thao), (*Silpakǭn Magazine,* 4 (Nov. 1960), 49, and ms. coll. no. 389).

Example 97. "Khāek Tǫi Mǭ"

(cont.)

Example 97 (continued).

(cont.)

Example 97 (continued).

Example 97 (continued).

when I surveyed the words and melody, I saw that the original basic melodies, when played with the newly created extended version in the khāēk (mǭn) style, were not well matched. So I altered the middle and short versions to give them a mǭn flavor also, making all three parts matched in style. The Thao became very popular.

This is one of the most interesting mǭn compositions because, using six pitches prominently, it can be analyzed in either of two pitch levels—high phīang ǭ with a finalis on pitch 6 and liberal use of pitch 7 as a passing tone, or low kruat with a finalis on pitch 2 and liberal use of pitch 4 as a passing tone. Since pitch 4 is perhaps more common in mǭn style than pitch 7, the composition is analyzed here in low kruat with a cadence on pitch 2.

The pitch outlines for the various versions laid side by side are shown in chart 37. The various versions are notated in example 97 in open score for

purposes of comparison. As in previous examples, numbers above the staves indicate measures and numbers in boxes under the staves or between staves are the pitch numbers for the structural points. Since all the compositions are in low kruat, there is no need for transposing.

In some of the versions, instead of spacing the notes evenly on the staff, motives are put directly under identical ones in other versions.

As an examination of the part will show, in Section Two of the sǭng chan division of the Thao, for purposes of artistic interest pulses and phrases have occasionally been shifted or "dislocated" by a measure or part of a measure. A comparison of this line with that of the sǭng mai version beneath it will reveal the changes made by Mr. Tramote of which he spoke in the quotation.

Example 98. "Khāēk Mǭn Bang Khun Phrom"

One possibility in enlarging a phrase from sǫng mai to prop kai (from sǭng chan to sām chan) is that of utilizing a full-scale metabole in the extended version which may be inherent in the middle version, but only suggested. This is illustrated in example 98, an excerpt from the famous Thao known as "Khāek Mǭn Bāng Khun Phrom" *(Silpakǫn Magazine,* 2 (July 1958), 59), composed by one of the Thai princes. The first eight measures of the middle version are given in example 98 to show the diversity of pitch level that can be developed in the extended version out of a simple short phrase of the middle version. The matching four measures of the short version are included to show how, in reverse, in the short version, the middle version is subjected to greater unity and uniformity of pitch level.

C. DEVELOPMENTAL SĀM CHAN

Before leaving the subject of Thao compositional techniques, one more important one should be discussed. It has been explained how, often, only the extended version of a Thao composition remains in the repertory, the original middle version and the short version (if there was one) having been abandoned. The form of these compositions is called simply "sām chan."

In composing this type of composition (occasionally for the first section of the extended version of a full Thao as well), for purposes of variety, interest, and virtuosity a section of development is sometimes interpolated in the central part of Section One. Since Thai music is linearly oriented, this development is of course not of a harmonic nature such as is found in Western forms but proceeds in a purely melodic or linear way. To accomplish this type of development Thai composers follow a method of exploiting one important pitch of the main part of the section by a process of constantly diminishing the length of a motivic phrase. The technique of "question and answer" is usually used, and each phrase ends with this emphasized pitch (or alternate phrases end with the pitch a fifth above the principal pitch if a fifth polarity is used for contrast). The initial phrase generally is four measures long, divided into a two-measure phrase played by the ranāt ēk—which starts the developmental section—followed by the ensemble answering with

the same phrase. (If the repetition is exact, it is called "lūk lǭ"—"like a wheel." Another example of this may be seen in ex. 53.) Or the initial phrase can be four measures long for the ranāt ēk and can be answered by a different, contrasting four-measure phrase by the ensemble. (If the "answer" is different, it is called "lūk khat"—"to oppose.") These are followed by two-measure phrases (or four-measure phrases if that is the format), played first by the ranāt ēk and echoed by the ensemble; then the phrases begin to be diminished, becoming proportionately shorter by half as the development progresses, until the short closing motivic fragments overlap in a stretto; finally two pitches are reiterated in what might be called an elongated trill, ending on the principal exploited pitch itself.

To illustrate this technique, an excerpt from the famous composition "Khāek Lopburī" *(Silpakǫn Magazine,* 4 (Sept. 1960), 57; ms. coll. no. 301) is shown in example 99. This composition has one long section that has been composed in two different versions, one for the first playing and another for the repeat. The two vocal sections are forty and forty-four measures long, respectively. The first instrumental section, from which the following excerpt is taken, is one hundred and forty-eight measures long, the first four measures of which overlap with the end of the vocal section. The excerpt is of the developmental part between measures sixty-four and one hundred and four, in which this technique of diminishing in ratio is used. The exploited pitch is pitch 2 in low kruat. The composition is in a khāek or mǭn style.

D. TAP

Another type of suite found in the Thai repertoire is called "Tap." A Tap consists of compositions in the original or sǭng chan form which have been extracted from a music drama and are played, with or without the vocal sections, as one group. In the manuscript collection of the Department of Fine Arts eight of these Tap have been notated; others exist. The number of compositions in a Tap will vary—two of the Tap in the manuscript collection have only four compositions, one has thirty-four; five or six seems an average number. No regulations seem to exist as to the performance of a Tap; all the compositions may be played, or only a few.

Example 99. "Khāek Lopburī" (3 chan); excerpt from Section 1.

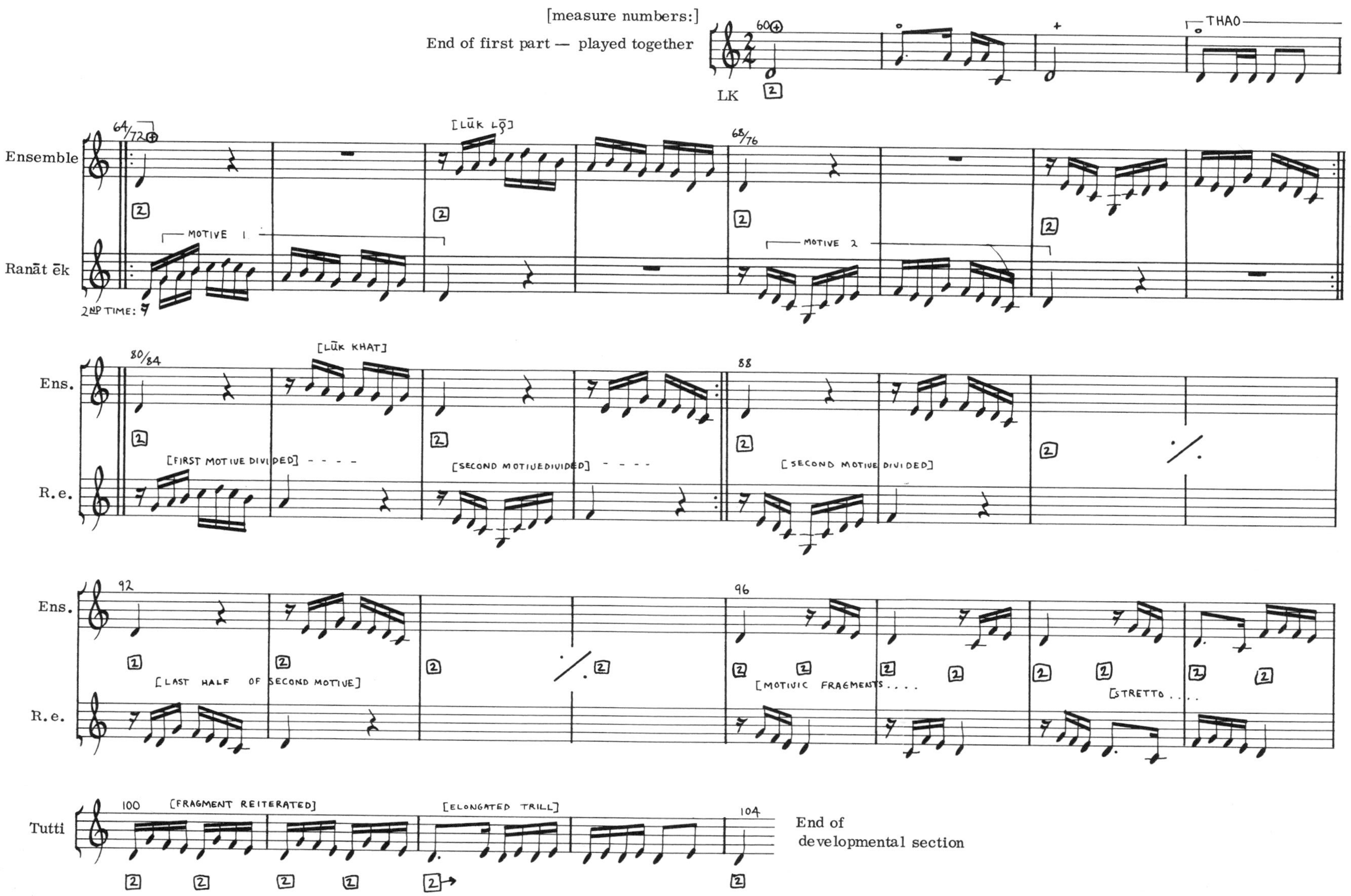

The compositions, being in the sǭng chan form, are relatively short. One of the shortest, if not the shortest composition in the Thai repertoire, "Lāo Khruan"—only eight measures long—is the last composition of seven in a Tap in simple Thai style (Tap Pralǭ; Tap, no. 30; ms. coll. nos. 209-216). The compositions in this Tap have been taken from a drama set in northern Thailand or Laos. "Lāo Khruan" was given in its complete form in Chapter IV, example 54, page 139.

Some of the compositions in the Tap are also found in the rǖang. In the Tap the metrical structure is sǭng mai, but in the rǖang some of the compositions appear with the prop kai pattern.

All compositions in a Tap often have the same prefix in their titles. For example, Tap Khamēn (Tap, no. 35; ms. coll. nos. 245-248) contains four compositions the titles of which all start with the word khamēn. The Tap extracted from the drama Ābūhāsan (Tap, no. 33; ms. coll. nos. 234-239) has six compositions whose titles all begin with the prefix khāek. The fourth composition in this Tap is "Khāek Tǭi Mǭ," the Thao version of which was given earlier in this chapter (ex. 97). The form of this composition in the Tap is practically the same as the sǭng mai form in the rǖang; but the Tap and rǖang versions, given in example 100, show how alternate motives—one perhaps an elongated form, one a condensed form—may be used interchangeably at given points in a composition without changing its essential structure.

E. OTHER FORMS

1. Sǭng chan

Three more forms and compositional techniques should be commented on briefly. The first, already mentioned many times, is the sǭng chan form per se. Occasionally composers have written compositions in this form which, contrary to the general custom, are new creations not based on pre-existing material. Of course, all so-called original compositions were newly created by some composer in the past whether or not his name is still known. These more recent sǭng chan compositions are not numerous, however. Of the one hundred and fifty-four sēphā compositions notated in the manuscript collection, only eight are indicated as being in sǭng chan. There are a few other well-known

compositions in sǭng chan form which are not in the manuscript collection——three famous ones are "Lāo Kham Hǭm," "Lāo Duang Dǖan," and "Lāo Damnǒēn Sāi." "Lāo Kham Hǭm" was recorded on a cylinder by Stumpf (1901: 123), later transcribed, and subsequently analyzed by Hornbostel (1919/1920). This version varies slightly from the version I learned, which is practically the same as the version published in the Silpakǭn Magazine (6[July 1962], 52).[5] These three compositions are in the simple Thai style; the melodies supposedly came from the country of Laos or were original melodies of the composer written in the style of Laotian compositions, which is synonymous with the simple Thai pentatonic style. The three compositions have vocal sections just as do the Thao compositions, and the instrumental sections may be played separately as an instrumental suite.

The structure and length of these three compositions are as follows:

"Lāo Kham Hǭm"
    Section 1: 32 measures
    Section 2: 24 measures
    Section 3: 32 measures
"Lāo Duang Dǖan"
    Section 1: 16 measures
    Section 2: 24 measures
    Section 3: 28 measures
"Lāo Damnǒēn Sāi"
    Section 1: 24 measures
    Section 2: 46 measures

Each composition is about the length of the usual extended version of a Thao and is therefore rather too long to lend itself comfortably to enlargement. At least two of the three compositions, however, have been used for Thao treatment. Luang Pradit Phai Rǭ (Sǭn Silapabanleng) made a Thao of "Lāo Kham Hǭm"; "Lāo Duang Dǖan," composed by one of the younger sons of King Rama V, was used as the basis for a Thao treatment by Montri Tramote, who called his Thao version "Sōm Sǭng Saēng." The original title, "Duang Dǖan," means "the moon"; the title "Sōm Sǭng Saēng" means "the moon shines."

The matter of titles was mentioned briefly in connection with the compositions "Khamēn Yai" and "Khamāe Thom," but a word more may be said about them here. If a synonymous title cannot be found, the title for a new composition based on another will often be a rewording of the idea of the

Example 100. "Khāēk Tǭi Mǭ," sǭng mai versions.

title of the original, or the same idea using a different type of language. That is, the original title might be in informal words, and the complementary title in formal words. The words "duang dᵮan" are ordinary Thai words, whereas the word "sǭm" is a formal word for "moon," of Pali origin. Thai borrows words from both Sanskrit and Pali for its formal language, just as English does from Latin and Greek.

Although "Laō Duang Dɥan" has three sections, whereas "Laō Damnoēn Sāi" has only two, the sections of "Laō Duang Dɥan" are shorter than those in the other two compositions in this group, so of the three, it is the one that most lends itself to Thao development. "Sōm Sɔ̄ng Saēng" was published in the *Silpakɔ̄n Magazine* (2 (Nov. 1958), 49).

2. Sī chan

Another compositional technique, rarely used, is to expand the extended version, using the same techniques of augmentation as used between sɔ̄ng chan and sām chan, into another version twice as long as sām chan, called sī chan ("fourth level or degree"). Only a gifted composer could do this without resorting to undue repetition and monotony. Composing such a section is a true *tour de force*. Only one such composition has come to my attention—a sī chan version by Luang Pradit Phai Rɔ̄ (Sɔ̄n Silapabanleng) of the composition "Khamēn Sai Yōk" (3 chan), composed by Prince Narit (half-brother of King Rama V) and mentioned in preceding chapters. The notation of the sī chan version is in the possession of the Silapabanleng family. For his large version Luang Pradit used the prop kai metrical pattern for the sī chan. Then he changed the prop kai pattern originally used with the Prince's sām chan version to the sɔ̄ng mai pattern so that this version then became the sɔ̄ng chan or middle version. Finally Luang Pradit wrote an original short version to make the complete Thao. In this special Thao, then, there are twice as many measures as in the usual Thao: 64 – 32 – 16.

F. CEREMONIAL AND THEATER MUSIC

Two final categories of Thai instrumental music should be mentioned: ceremonial music and theater music. These compositions are in the same general styles and have the same characteristics as the music that has been presented in this study. There is instrumental music used specifically for ritual purposes in ceremonies of a religious and semi-religious nature; it is not considered part of the repertory of entertainment music, of course, the music with which this study has been concerned. But the music is based on the same principles and is played by the same instruments.

All the compositions from the Tap suites presented in this study—"Laō Khruan" and "Khaēk Tɔ̄i Mɔ̄," for instance—are examples of theater music. There are other compositions that, though they may be considered as part of the repertory of entertainment music in a general sense, are used today mainly as theater music. Each composition has become identified with a certain action, event, stage movement, character, and so forth, and is used as background music to the drama in a manner comparable to Wagner's system of *leitmotifs* in his music dramas.

G. VOCAL MUSIC

As was mentioned in the Preface, this study has been concerned only with the fundamentals of the Thai traditional music system and the instrumental music. Vocal sections are an inherent part of the Thao form, however, and at least a brief explanation should be made of vocal practice and of the relationship of the vocal sections of the Thao to the instrumental part. An initial study of the vocal practice has been made,[6] but a thorough depth analysis remains to be done.

The Thai language is a tonal language, like many of the Chinese dialects, to which it is related. Each word has its own inherent inflection which must always be observed in speaking the word, or it cannot be understood. Such a tonal language has its own built-in melody, so to speak, and to be understood when sung, must be sung to a melody that has the same inflection as the words: if a word has a rising tone, for example, the melody must also rise, and vice versa:

khao   khao
(rising)   (falling)

It is not known when the practice of separating the vocal from the instrumental music occurred with the Thai, but it is highly likely that it was when they were still inhabiting southern China (prior to about 1250).[7] The requirements of a tone language limit the melodic possibilities, and the freedom of the instruments would be greatly restricted if they accompanied the vocal line. For this reason, I was told by several Thai musicians, the separation was made. Another factor not to be discounted is the use of vocal pitches or tones[8] not in the fixed tuning system (that is, the tuning system found on the instruments of fixed pitch: xylophones, metallophones, and sets of gong-kettles); the use of the heavy-sounding instruments with the subtle vocal line would blur and confuse it. Traditionally in Thai music the vocal part is accompanied by only the ching and drum; occasionally a single stringed instrument is added in the background for special effect.

If the tone (inflection) of a word is crucial,[9] it will be sung with that inflection. If the tone is not crucial, that is, if there is no possibility of confusing the word with another of the same basic sound but a different inflection, a certain amount of flexibility of melody to which it is sung is allowable. To give further freedom for melodic possibilities, after the tone of the word is sung the voice may continue with a free melody. Also, meaningless or vocalizing syllables (like "oh" and "ah" in Western languages) are interspersed among the words of the Thai text. These syllables ("ōe"—pronounced something like "er" in the British fashion with a dropped "r"—and "ōe-i," for example) may be sung to any melody.

A composer-arranger of a Thao creates the vocal as well as the instrumental sections. The vocal section is based on the same skeleton of structural pitches as the corresponding instrumental section. Because of the numerous ornamentations used with the vocal melody, the structural pitch may not always occur in the vocal section precisely on the ching stroke, and to have a good melodic line, secondary structural pitches may not always be strictly observed.

To show how the vocal and instrumental parts correspond, these parts for Section One for all three divisions of the Thao "Khamēn Pāk Thǭ" are given in example 101 one part under another, as has been done in previous Thao examples:

3 chan	vocal—28 measures (1st phrase-unit missing) (vocal sections are not repeated) instrumental—32 measures, which is repeated
2 chan	vocal—16 measures instrumental—16 measures, which is repeated
chan dio	vocal—8 measures instrumental—8 measures, which is repeated

An attempt has been made in this Western notation (published in the *Silpakǭn Magazine,* 10 [May 1966], 86) to show the ornaments for the voice. Where the structural pitches do not coincide with the ching stroke, a small arrow points to them. The "correct" structural pitches occur at structural points in the middle version. If structural pitches in the other parts do not match these, no mark is made—the deviations can be clearly seen, both there and in the pitch outline.

As can be seen in the notation, the vocal part of the extended version does not start at the beginning of the thirty-two-measure pattern, but at the second ⊕ stroke. The vocal parts of the middle and short versions start with an instrumental introduction one phrase-unit long called in Thai *"song rǭng"*—literally, "to send off the singing."

This composition also has a finalis on pitch 3 and a descending cadence 1653. As can be seen from the pitch outline in Chart 38 the 6-3 polarity is the primary one, supported by pitches 2 (6-2 polarity) and 1 (3-1 polarity). Pitch 5, though used on ching strokes, is slighted.

The sǭng chan version of this composition is one of the old Thai traditional melodies, written in khamēn (Cambodian) style. It was composed in honor of the Khmer people of the district of Pāk Thǭ in the province of Ratburi (about 100 miles southwest of Bangkok). The idiom of the melody shows that it was composed during the Bangkok period, that is, sometime after 1782; however, the composer is unknown. Up to the time of King Rama VI (1910—1924) this composition had been made into a Thao by many composers, but Luang Pradit's, composed about 1921, became the most popular. The text usually used for this composition is from the drama *Phraruang* or *Khǭm Dam Din,* written by King Rama VI, because it was the sǭng chan melody of "Khamēn Pāk Thǭ" to which the words were sung in the performance of the drama. The words did not fit too well with the Thao composition, however, and around 1930 King Rama VII (brother of King Rama VI) altered them to make them fit better. This revision has been used since.[10]

A transliteration of the Thai text has been given here to show the sounds of the Thai words and their pronunciation. The tone marks are as follows: no mark = level; ⁄ = high tone; ＼ = low tone; ˅ = rising tone; ˄ = falling tone. Refer also to the explanation of the transliteration system in Appendix A.

Example 101. "Khamēn Pāk Thǫ" (Thao).

Example 101 (continued).

Example 101 (continued).

Example 101. (continued).

	Extended Version (32 measures)								Middle Version (16 measures)						Short Version (8 measures)				
	Vocal				Instrumental				Vocal		Instrumental		Vocal		Instrumental			
	|o	|+	|o	|⊕	|o	|+	|o	|⊕	o |⊕	o |⊕	o |⊕	o |⊕	o ⊕	o |⊕	o ⊕	o |⊕		
HPŌ:					3	3	6	3	(3	3)	3	3	(	3)		3		
				3	3	1	1	3	1	3	6	3		3		3		
	-	3	6	2	3	3	3	2	(3)	2	-	2		2		2		
	1	2	1	6	5	2	1	6	2	6	2	6		6		6		
	(6)	6	(1)	⁶5*	(6)	6	5	5	(6)	5	-	5		(6)		5		
	5	5	(1)	6	6	3	6	(6)	5	6	5	6		5		6		
	6	3	3	6	3	2	1	6	3	6	3	6		(6)		(6)		
	1	6	(6)	⁵3	(6)	6	6	3	(6)	⁵3	6	3		⁵3		3		

*The small number is the pitch sounding on the ching stroke, the initial pitch of an ornamentation ending on the principal pitch.

Chart 38. Pitch outline – "Khamēn Pāk Thŏ" (*Silpakŏn Magazine*, 10 (May 1966), 86 and ms. coll. no. 3349).

Chapter VI

Conclusion

The traditional instrumental music of Thailand as it is known today is a product of the Bangkok period of the nineteenth and twentieth centuries. Thai history prior to the establishment of Bangkok as the capital is usually divided politically into the Sukhothai period (1250–1350) and the Ayuthaya period (1350–1767). Since we know little of the actual music of those times, it is impossible to classify the history of Thai music by "periods" on the basis of the music itself. Change in the high-art music of Asian nations seems to have been slow, probably as a result of the oral tradition and lack of rapid communication systems. There is no evidence that traditional Thai music in its evolution has shown such major changes as have occurred in the evolution of Western music.

Simplicity of principles characterizes Thai music. Chinese, Javanese, and Indian music—the musics of the three great musical cultures surrounding Thailand—present a formidable array of musical elements that might conceivably have been taken by Thai musicians and composers and integrated into their system; yet strangely enough Thai music seems to have evolved centripetally, ever simplifying its materials, rather than centrifugally by expanding its boundaries and adding more and more elements to its available musical resources. It has been created out of a relatively small and restricted group of musical elements: the tuning system of only seven fixed pitches, one basic pentatonic mode, the prevalence of a finalis on pitch 1 of this mode, an elementary or even vague modal practice, and only a few musical forms.

Despite the two references quoted in Chapter I (pp. 3, 13) to great musical activity in former times, traditional Thai music was a hot-house art from the beginning, having grown up as an aristocrat's music performed at the courts by court musicians for court functions. With the abolition of the monarchy in 1932 the traditional social foundation for the music disappeared and its practice and performance came to a more or less abrupt halt. And no other element of the social structure has taken over the function of the courts as patron of the traditional arts. In the West the Catholic Church had a leading role for centuries in the development, performance, and preservation of Western sacred music; so far as a non-Buddhist foreigner can determine, the Buddhist religion—which in some of its forms, at least, stresses wordly renunciation and meditative contemplation—did not perform a comparable role in the history of Thai music. The general populace by reason of religious philosophy is not equipped to do so. The Thai Department of Fine Arts and a few other groups are trying to provide a kind of patronage but receive little governmental or popular support. Aside from the few musicians' posts at the department, the television station, and the schools that give shows for tourists, little or no employment is available for a practitioner of the traditional music. In recent years the music has not played a significant part in the lives of a majority of the people, which perhaps in part explains the apathy of the general public toward it today. Western music and Western-style Thai popular music, fostered by commercial interests, are rapidly replacing the traditional music, and nothing at present suggests that this trend will be reversed.

One solution to the problem would seem to be for the traditional music to be carried forward to new stages of development beyond that reached in the golden age of the courts. Such an achievement would be difficult at best without some strong new revitalizing stimulus. Within the system as it stands today little more seems likely to be accomplished than the continual restatement of well-tried musical material, and it appears doubtful that the fresh material and social circumstances and the fresh creative outlook that could stimulate musical practice to evolve will be forthcoming in the near future——they certainly have been lacking during the past forty years.

Thus the path of traditional Thai music lies in deep shadows, at a creative crossroads that could lead to new popularity or to the museum. Hopefully there will appear within the Thai culture itself those who will become active practitioners of their traditional music and assure its further development lest it become extinct.

Notes

CHAPTER I

1. The material in this general introduction pertaining to the historical references to Thai music has been liberally drawn from the introductory part of the book *Thai Musical Instruments* by Dhanit Yupho, which I translated from the Thai when I was in Bangkok. The translation was published in Bangkok in 1960 by the Department of Fine Arts of the Thai government. Mr. Yupho did exhaustive research on the history of Thai music, and what is known about early Thai music is in his book. Rather than footnote in this introduction each separate item taken from this source, acknowledgment is herewith made to it as the primary reference on the history of Thai music.

A companion source is the article by Montri Tramote, "The Evolution of Thai Music," which appeared in the Thai language in the *Thai Culture Journal* (2 [Dec. 1, 1954] 6–11). Acknowledgment of this article is also made here. Mr. Tramote is head musician of the music section of the Department of Fine Arts.

2. For two pertinent views on tradition in artistic expression see Sachs (1943: 52–53) and Hood (1954: 1).

3. Schafer's *Golden Peaches of Samarkand* contains much of the remnants of factual material known about Nanchao.

4. For some pictorial reconstructions of scenes of Khmer life based on the carvings at Angkor, some of which include musicians and musical instruments, see W. R. Moore (1960: 516–569).

5. For a short, concise account of "Cambodia's Debt to India" see Bernard Groslier (1957: 19 ff.).

6. For a brief description of this instrument see Aalst (1884: 57–58) and Sachs (1940: 208–209).

7. The Thai retained a large portion of the Khmer territory in present-day Cambodia (including Angkor) as part of their kingdom until they were forced to cede it to the French in 1907.

8. See, for example, le May (1954). This book is a cross-cultural study of Burma, Thailand, Cambodia, Malay, and Indonesia; it contains a large section of photographs and a good bibliography on these areas.

9. Mr. Silapabanleng holds a degree in Western music from a Japanese university and is the son of one of the most illustrious Thai musician-composers of the twentieth century, Luang Pradit Phai Rọ (Sọn Silapabanleng).

10. After many border disputes Thai independence and national boundaries were arranged in 1896 by the Anglo-French Convention.

11. For a discussion of oral tradition see Hood (1959: 201–209).

12. Verbal communication from Prasidh Silapabanleng. Being the son of a famous court musician of the time, who with his family lived in the palace compound, Mr. Silapabanleng was in a position to witness much of it in his early life (c. 1915–30).

13. The musicians and dancers of the Institute have given several performances outside of Thailand, not only in Asia but also on two tours to the West in 1961-2 and 1970. A short biography of Luang Pradit appears in *Selected Reports* II, 2 (Morton, 1975).

14. Verbal communication from Prasidh Silapabanleng. A picture of an ensemble that substitutes a Western instrument for a Thai instrument may be seen in the Duriyanga pamphlet (1956).

15. See further in Hood (1963: 240, 290 ff.).

16. When I met Pringsheim in 1960 in Bangkok, he told me he had been in Bangkok at that earlier time for only a short period and did not consider his article to be in any way a depth study. Nonetheless, I consider it one of the best essays of a general nature on Thai music.

17. V. Vichitr-Vadakarn, "The Evolution of Siamese Music," *Siam Today* (July 1937: 71-80). An off-print of this article was published by the Department of Fine Arts, Bangkok in 1942. The copy of the article in my possession was a reprint in a short-lived publication called *Thai Digest* in the issues of February 8 and 15, 1957, where, because of the official change in the name of the country, the title was changed to "The Evolution of Thai Music."

18. This booklet was selected by the Royal Institute on command of the King to be printed for distribution at the cremation of a lady-in-waiting to the Queen, the distribution of commemorative booklets at cremations of the upper classes and royalty being a Thai custom. After its first publication in Thai the booklet was published in a French translation (Extrême-Asie, Sept. 1928) and a Dutch translation (*Nederlandsch-Indië Oud & Nieuw,* July 1929). The text as printed in the first edition was somewhat incomplete, and the illustrations were not so good as might have been desired. For the commemorative issue—which was the second edition, appearing in 1931—the text was revised and enlarged, the illustrations improved, and an English translation provided. Unfortunately the booklet has long been out of print.

19. As no Thai system of notation existed, one had to be devised; the solution was the adoption of the Western staff of lines and spaces—the coincidence of seven pitches in the Thai tuning system and seven pitches in conventional Western scales made this possible. In order to show that a pentatonic scale (or mode) of the 123 56 1 variety was intended in certain instances where the music shifts to another pitch level, the

Thai notators added accidentals above certain notes — principally sharps above *f* and *c*, flats above *b* and *e*. The musical examples presented in this study are given as they appear in the manuscript collection, with, however, the melodic line transcribed in most instances in cipher notation below the staff.

The reader must constantly bear in mind that although Western notation is used, neither the pitches represented by the notes on the staff nor the intervals between the pitches are an accurate representation of the actual sound of Thai music.

Further comments on the notation will be made as the need arises.

20. Full scores of two of the suites have been published by the Department of Fine Arts. No date is given, but the publication was after the end of World War II. A recent publication of a collection of Thai compositions, mostly in the Thao and sām chan forms, is given in the bibliography under *Thai Classical Music, Book I.* These are reprints of compositions and explanatory articles by Montri Tramote which first appeared in the *Silpakǭn Magazine.*

CHAPTER II

1. Kunst coined the term "nuclear theme" for the main melody in Javanese music (see Kunst 1949: 157); Hood (1954) continued its use, though more recently he has begun to use the term "fixed melody." These terms are not used in this study because in Thai music the theme is not a nucleus of pitches often of relatively long duration with little rhythmic variety as it generally is in Java (see Hood: 1954 for examples), but more a melody in the Western sense with some rhythmic variety. For this reason it is called here the "main melody."

2. For a discussion of this term in relation to Javanese music see Hood (1963, "Polyphonic Stratification . . .").

3. After considerable thought it is my speculation that equidistant tuning evolved in Southeast Asia when the Chinese tuning system, said to be based on acoustical intervals

(Pitches 4 and 7 are *pien* tones. See further in Aalst, for example.)

collided and blended with nonequidistant tunings (or one tuning) used by the Khmer (and possibly the Mồn also), which may have been derived from Indian tunings and early raga developments brought by the colonists. A number of tunings approximately but not exactly alike would undoubtedly have led to confusion, and the solution—perhaps accelerated by the blend of several musical systems and practices—may have been the combining of all the tunings into one equidistant one.

4. Tables of these figures are given in Appendix B.

5. Ellis (quoted by Verney, pages 23-24, with slightly different c.p.s.) lists the names of the pitches as follows (1885: 1105):

i.	Thang = sound	285	middle C Sharp
ii.	Rong thang = second, or under sound	315	D Sharp
iii.	Oat = voice	347	Between E and E Sharp
iv.	Klang = centre or middle, from its position	383	F Sharp
v.	Phong Oar, merely a name, without any other special significance	423	G Sharp
vi.	Kruert = sharp sound	467	Between A and A Sharp
vii.	Nork = outside	516	Between B and B Sharp

6. Since there are no "half-steps" in Thai tuning, there cannot be both E and E♭, for example. The choice of which "key" to use for notation depends on the intent of the shift ("modulation"), and the fifth relationships. For example, if a composition started in III/B♭ and shifted down a fifth, it would be appropriate to notate the new level as E♭, a fifth from B♭, to show the fifth relationship. If the music shifted down another fifth, it would be appropriate to notate the new level as A♭, the fifth below E♭, not as A. However, if the composition started in G, shifted to D (an ascending fifth), and then shifted again to the fifth above D, it would be appropriate to notate the new level as A, the fifth above D, not as A♭.

7. When a sound-producing object is struck, besides the pitch that the ear hears and registers as the fundamental pitch of the sound, other more or less inaudible sounds related to the fundamental—sometimes referred to as sympathetic vibrations—are also generated; the presence or absence of these and the relative strength or weakness of the ones that are present give the resulting quality.

A harmonic series of overtones or partials is one in which the numbers are relatively small, producing what are called small-number ratios. If the fundamental is given the number 1, 2 represents a wave motion twice as fast—that is, two complete cycles of the wave motion in the time it takes for the fundamental to complete one cycle. The number 3 represents a wave motion or cycle three times as fast, and so forth. The resulting ratios of these simple whole numbers and the familiar intervals that they represent in Western music are:

2:1 = octave		5:3 = major sixth
3:2 = fifth		8:5 = minor sixth
4:3 = fourth		9:5 = minor seventh
5:4 = major third		15:8 = major seventh
6:5 = minor third		

It is on these ratios that the harmonic system of the West is based.

A series of partials or overtones that cannot be represented by a series of simple whole numbers is termed, in contradistinction, a nonharmonic or inharmonic series. It has been shown, for instance, that the relative frequencies of the first five upper partials of a sound produced by a metal rod attached at one end bear the relations given by the numbers 1, 6.25, 17.5, 34.4, 56.5, 84 (Culver 1956: 238). A rod supported at the acoustical nodes and free at both ends gives a series corresponding approximately to the numbers 1, 2.76, 5.4, and so forth (Culver 1956: 239).

The fewer the number of partials or overtones present with a fundamental pitch, the "purer" the sound is said to be; the more partials present and the stronger they are, the more "complex" the sound is. A flute usually produces a relatively pure sound; an oboe and other double-reed type instruments generally produce a complex sound. (See further in Culver 1956: 102 ff.)

8. Further description and an illustration of the instrument can be found in Culver (1956: 98-101).

9. Ellis describes his cent system in two articles (1884: 368 ff.; March 25, 1885: 485 ff.); the system is also described by Kunst (1959: 2 ff.).

10. For further discussion of this matter see Hood (1963: 269).

11. According to a verbal communication from Hood.

12. See Kunst (1949) for a thorough discussion of surupan. According to a verbal communication from Hood, Balinese paired instruments average six to seven cycles per second difference between high and low instruments.

13. The phonetic form of this word (mōn), usually transliterated as "Mon" or "Môn," will be used in this study when referring to the style of music. For reference to the ethnic group the usual "Môn" will be retained.

14. This sound can be written in different ways in Thai. The inflection or tone is dependent on which letter for "th" is used. There are several symbols in the Thai alphabet for the soft "t" consonant. (See Appendix A for the discussion of the Thai language and transliteration system used here.)

The word "thao" referring to these fill-in phrases or motives is pronounced with a falling tone and is written:
เทา , while the word "thao" referring to the variation form is pronounced with a rising tone and is written: เถา , and means "a set of something in gradated sizes." These words will both be used a good deal in this study. To differentiate them on the printed page without the use of tone marks, the word for the fill-in motive will be printed entirely in lower case letters, thao; the word for the form will be printed with an initial capital letter, Thao. The Thao form is treated in detail in Chapter V.

15. Mode in Thai music will be the subject of a subsequent chapter. In this chapter the term "mode" should be understood to be used in its simplest, most basic meaning of "a set of pitches" or "a pattern of intervals"—that is, a theoretical concept existing apart from specific compositions. The term "scale" is often used in this context, but as I consider this confusing usage it will be avoided here. "Scale" will be used here to refer to "those pitches used in one specific composition, placed in arbitrary ascending and/or descending order." Since we are not speaking here of specific compositions, the term "scale" is not in order.

16. Transposition in Thai music is comparable to transposition in Western music, where for example a popular song may be performed in G major, F major, C major, B♭ major, and so forth—except that where twelve keys or tonalities are available in Western music, in Thai music only seven are available and not all seven are used with equal frequency.

Both Prince Narit with his short-lived theatrical venture called "Dykdamban" and V. Vichitr-Vadakarn (see Note 17, Chapter I) in his songs experimented with nontraditonal methods. It may have been one of these compositions that Sachs transcribed and included a portion of in his book (1943: 132). I have seen no notations of any of the compositions of these two men.

17. For a short discussion of an old genre of Thai songs (with instrumental interludes) in 7/4 meter see: S. Moore (1969). Since these are reputedly old songs dating back to the Ayuthaya period or before they may be a borrowing from the Khmer, in turn representing a remnant of an additive meter from India.

18. In Thai there is a term, "čhangwa," which is confusing at best because it can refer to several different functions—"beat," "pulse," "meter," and "rhythm," for example; for that reason I have decided to avoid it in the body of this work.

Tramote in his booklet of terms gives several definitions (1964: 8-10), which may be summarized as follows:

1. Ordinary (čhangwa sāman) = meter, or pulse. Even though there may not be an instrument keeping time (rare in Thai traditional music), a sense of pulse must be maintained by the performers in their consciousness. Metrical divisions occur in halves and duples of a given pattern. Thus, čhangwa can mean a metrical-rhythmical pattern (for the drum) of a specific length. For example, if a composition having 128 beats has 8 čhangwa, each čhangwa has 16 beats; if each čhangwa has 8 beats, there are 16 čhangwa in the composition.

2. Ching pattern (čhangwa ching). The pattern of unaccented and accented ching strokes.

3. Length of a composition (čhangwa nā thap). Calculating the length of a composition by the number of čhangwa cycles it contains, that is, that occur during the playing of a composition (or section): the length of one cycle of the nā thap (rhythmic-metrical pattern of the drum) = one čhangwa.

The prop kai nā thap pattern is twice as long as the sŏng mai nā thap pattern. These are correlated with the ching strokes, but Tramote does not show these. S. Moore (1969) understands this to mean that the prop kai pattern has 8 ching strokes, regardless of the particular form. (Moore says "tempo," rather than "form"; this has just been discussed in the main part of this study.) The sŏng mai pattern has 4 ching strokes.

According to this, then, in the prop kai nā thap in sām chan (extended version of the Thao) the cycle has 8 ching strokes and, in Western notation, 8 measures

|o |+ |o |⊕ |o |+ |o |⊕

or on two lines

|o |+ |o |⊕
|o |+ |o |⊕

and prop kai in sŏng chan (middle version of Thao) would have 8 ching strokes also, covering 4 measures

o |⊕   o |⊕   o |⊕   o |⊕

and in chan dio (short version of Thao), 2 measures

o ⊕   o |⊕   o ⊕   o |⊕

The drum patterns for these cycles are given in the discussion of the taphōn, pages 69-71.

In sŏng mai nā thap in sām chan there would be only 4 ching strokes and 4 measures

|o |+ |o |⊕

and in sŏng chan, 4 strokes and 2 measures

o |⊕   o |⊕

and in chan dio, 4 strokes and 1 measure

o ⊕   o |⊕

As I understand it, the Thao are in prop kai.

19. For a discussion of the Javanese system of rhythmic emphasis see Hood (1954: 12 ff.).

20. A verbal communication from Prasidh Silapabanleng also supports this view. When I was in Bangkok and discussed with him this aspect of Javanese meter and the possibility that the same might also obtain in the Thai music system, Silapabanleng agreed, saying that Thai music notated in Western style did not "look" or "feel" right to him. When he began to study Western music, Silapabanleng said further, he felt that the system of metrical emphasis in Western music differed from that of the Thai music with which he had grown up.

CHAPTER III

1. Much of the information in this chapter is taken from Yupho's book on Thai instruments.

2. Besides the number of the principal figure illustrating the instrument, following the semicolon are listed the figure numbers of the illustrations of the ensembles in which the instrument is included. The page adjoining these ensemble illustrations identifies the location of the instrument in the ensemble.

3. The nine kettles may be a mistake, or they may represent an octave and one pitch or of course some other tuning.

4. An illustration may be found in Kunst (1949: II, ill. 108).

5. See Hood (1970).

6. Occasionally an instrument has only seventeen kettles, in which case there is only one dummy kettle.

7. For illustrations see Kunst (1949: II, ill. 14 and 47).

8. See for example Condominas (1952: 359 ff.) and Schaeffner (1951: 1 ff.).

9. This is discussed by Tramote in two short explanatory notes to songs published in the *Silpakŏn Magazine* (3 [Sept. 1959], 43-44; 3 [Jan. 1960], 43-44). See also Note 20, Chapter I. Also included in his booklet of terminology (1964: 1 and 2).

10. The kings of Thailand all had proper names, but for this study, for convenience, all will be referred to by the name "Rama" and a Roman numeral, as is sometimes done. See for example Wilson (1959: 4, footnote 2).

The kings of the last half of the nineteenth and the twentieth centuries are:

Mongkut (1851–1868) (King Rama IV)
Chulalongkŏn (1868–1910) (King Rama V)
Wachirawut (1910–1925) (King Rama VI)
Prachatipok (1925–1935) (King Rama VII)
Anan Mahidon (1935–1946) (King Rama VIII)
Phumiphon Adunyadet (1946–   ) (King Rama IX)

11. For some notations of the nuclear themes of Javanese compositions see Hood (1954: 266-308).

12. The word "lek" (เหล็ก) used with the name of this instrument has a low tone in the Thai language and means "iron." The word "lek" (เล็ก) used in the name "khŏng wong lek" has a high tone and means "small."

13. Some are mentioned briefly by Tramote in his discussion of "changwa" (1964: 9) He gives these:

chīn or *yuan:*   o   o |⊕   o   o |⊕   etc.

"chīn" means "Chinese"; the dictionary translates "yuan" as "Annamese," but it would also seem to relate to the name "Yuan" of the Mongol or Yuan Dynasty of China (1280–1368), the advent of which drove the Thai southward into present-day Thailand (see Chapter I).

The ching pattern for the 7/4 songs according to Tramote is:

+   o   +   o
1 2 3 4 5 6 7

S. Moore (1969) gives it as:

o   x   o   x
1 2 3 4 1 2 3
       (5 6 7)

(S. Moore, for some reason, uses the ching marks in the opposite way from this study—o for damped, accented and x for open, unaccented.)

14. See note 7, Chapter II.

15. See also the discussion of changwa and ching patterns, note 18, Chapter II.

16. For example *darabuka* (alternate spellings: *darbuka, darabouka, daraboukkeh, tarabuka*) and *tindi* in Arabic-Moslem regions, *tombac (dombek)* in Persia.

17. *Python reticulatus* and *Acrochordus javanicus,* respectively.

18. The instrument is known by various names, all similar — for example *zurna, zurnai* (Near East), *sanai, senai, surna, shahnai, sahnai* (North India), *sona* (China). It is called *nagaswaram* in South India. In Cambodia the contemporary name is *sra lai.*

19. Cf. the Dutch transliteration of the Javanese pronunciation "Djåwå."

20. See Sachs (1940: 231) for drawings of the Indian, Thai, and Javanese double-reed instruments.

21. For a full account see Yupho (1960: 87 ff.).

22. For illustrations of the Javanese kachapi see Kunst (1949: II, ill. 144).

23. For a short account and picture see Kunst ("Notes" for the record *Indonesia*).

24. The name of this instrument is sometimes written *takhe* or some version thereof, but it is not considered to be the correct traditional spelling; the first syllable should be "cha," not "ta."

25. Many of the readily available books on Indian music include illustrations of the instruments. The taus is illustrated in two of the books on India already mentioned in this study, Popley (1950: 102, 106) and Fyzee-Rahamin (1925: 54). A drawing of the taus can be found also in Edgerly (1942: 175). A photograph of a small Burmese "crocodile zither" with the front actually carved in the shape of a crocodile's head appears in Sachs (1917: pl. 12).

26. Nielloware refers to a type of engraving on a processed-tarnished silver; a great deal of jewelry is made today in Thailand by this process.

27. Islam reached India in the thirteenth century and Indonesia in the fourteenth and fifteenth centuries. Despite the fact that Islam frowns on music and its practice, the Islamic invasions of Asian areas are considered by many to be the vehicle by which musical instruments and musical ideas were carried from the Near East to Asia.

28. According to a verbal communication from Hardja Susilo, a Javanese musician who did graduate work in ethnomusicology at UCLA and later began teaching at the University of Hawaii.

29. See Daniélou (1957: 19-20); in this book are also to be found illustrations of the Cambodian versions of many Thai instruments.

30. "Phrayāsōk" (พระยาโศรก), Record Number CTR-125, issued by Crown Brand, Bangkok, Thailand.

31. The material on all the ensembles is drawn liberally from Damrong (1931) and Tramote (1954, and "Notes" from the pamphlet accompanying the records of Thai music).

32. More information has come to light recently on the origins of sēphā. The following, by Ayumongol Sonakul, is taken from the section "Cultural and Social Notes from Member Countries" of the *ASPAC Quarterly of Cultural and Social Affairs*, II (Winter, 1970), 86.

No one is quite sure how—or when—*sebha* [transliterated "sēphā" in this study] began; or even what the word *"Sebha"* means. H.R.H. Prince Damrong, great historian and student of antiquities, who is much believed in matters of this nature, thought it began with professional storytellers who plied their trade at religious ceremonies and in temple pavilions as a form of entertainment, from the earliest times of Siamese civilization.

Prince Damrong surmised that the earliest storytellers told their tales in prose, while their successors gradually began to work in a few verse passages to break the monotony and to achieve a more pleasant sound. Gradually, the sebha verse form was born.

Sebha verse is not recited in normal speech tone, but chanted to the accompaniment of clicking sticks, and "received" at certain intervals by a full piphat ensemble....

The use of piphat with sebha recitation began only in the Bangkok era, quite lately; in the Ayudhya [Ayuthaya] era it was voice only.

Sebha is basically "folk" as opposed to "formal" verse, thus sharing a common quality with such folk verse arts as pleng choi and pleng rua [phlēng]. However, pleng choi and pleng rua are spontaneous verses sung by men and women to wittily woo and insult each other; sebha, on the other hand, is narrative.

Being a folk art, sebha tends to be a little on the bawdy side: but only permissibly so, not bawdy enough to incur police attention upon its reciters, unlike pleng choi performed in its full glory by professionals.

Originally, all sebha told the story of "Khun Chang-Khun Phaen," an epic tale of heroism, intrigue, love, sex, and sadism. In recent decades, however, poets have adapted the form to tell other tales.

"Khun Chang-Khun Phaen" is based on a true story that probably occurred during the Ayudhya era. Though the written sebha version names the king at the time only as "Phra Phanvasa" ("Lord of a Thousand Years") a mere honorific title as opposed to a name, Prince Damrong has tentatively dated the occurrence to the reign of King Ramathibodi II (1491−1529); he believed that the tale was told in prose until the reign of King Narai in the 17th Century, when it was versified and gave birth to sebha.

The present written sebha version, however, is a comparatively recent work. It was begun at the court of King Rama II (1809−1824) right here in Bangkok; the final portions were probably not finished until the reign of King Mongkut (1851−1868).

It was written by a group of poets at court, including King Rama II himself, who was one of the leading poets of his time. It is not known which other poets collaborated, but they definitely included Sunthorn Phu, one of the greatest poets in Thai literature.

33. See also Sachs (1940: 224); for another illustration see Sachs (1917: pl. 2) and Scott (1924: photograph facing page 232).

CHAPTER IV

1. Several books make reference to a certain grouping of compositions. This was probably stated for the first time by Vichitr-Vadakarn in the first printing of his article on the evolution of Thai music (1937)—this was quoted by both Pringsheim (1944) and Thompson (1941), for example. Vichitr-Vadakarn says that there are more than 1200 melodies composed since the Ayuthayan period and that these ready-made melodies are divided into 36 groups. Each group is to be used for one particular purpose. For example, 13 are for the expression of anger, 21 for sorrow and affliction, 4 for joy, 7 for reflection and contemplation, 4 for excitement, and so

forth. This list, which was said to be in the Department of Fine Arts, could not be located when I was in Bangkok in 1958–1960. That is unfortunate, for it might have served as a starting point in the search for modal criteria in Thai music: if a number of compositions are considered appropriate for a given mood, for example, they all perhaps contain elements similar among themselves that unite them and set them apart as a group from compositions in the other groups. If these are old compositions they may also possibly contain elements of the raga system, borrowed or not from the Khmer, which classifies each raga as pertaining to a particular mood or emotion. It may also be that Vichitr-Vadakarn is referring to compositions used in the dramas as leitmotif compositions; see the last paragraph in the main text of this chapter.

2. A recording of this composition is contained in the two-record album "Thai Traditional Music" (with an accompanying booklet of commentary and analysis by me) issued in 1968 by the Institute of Ethnomusicology, UCLA, Los Angeles, California 90024.

CHAPTER V

1. Stated by Tramote in explanatory articles accompanying the compositions published in the *Silpakǭn Magazine,* for example Vol. 5 (July 1961), 60.

2. A recording of a simple rǔang is included in the album of Thai music listed in Note 2, Chapter IV and in the Discography. Besides recordings of Thai music, available from the Department of Fine Arts in Bangkok, are complete scores of two rǔang. These are listed in Bibliography I under "Bangkok, Thailand. Department of Fine Arts."

3. Stated by Tramote in several of the explanatory articles accompanying compositions published in the *Silpakǭn Magazine.*

4. Verbal communication from Prasidh Silapabanleng.

5. See Note 2, Chapter IV.

6. Sidney Moore (see Notes 18 and 19, Chapter III and the Bibliography) has made a preliminary study of vocal practice, but the entire results have not yet been published. Stanley Mendenhall (1975) has investigated the relationship of words and music when the Thai tonal language is sung.

7. Two recent sources on Chinese opera describe local genres of Cantonese opera in which vocal and instrumental sections are separated, the vocal sections being unaccompanied; these sources by Hsing K'o Lee and Pei Lun Wong are listed in the second part of the Bibliography.

8. When I was in Bangkok in 1969, I recorded specially, without accompaniment, the vocal sections of a composition in lament style for use on the Melograph machine at UCLA in the Institute of Ethnomusicology—a machine that tracks a single pitch line, dynamics, and the spectrum of tone quality. Vocal tones are clearly apparent to the ear in this vocal style; the melograms show one lying between pitch 2 and 3 of the mode on 2 (23 56 12) about 86 to 90 cents above the tonic (pitch 2) and a descending portamento from pitch 1 to pitch 7 decorating pitch 6 and an ascending portamento from pitch 7 to pitch 1. This lament style seems allied to, if not the same as, mǭn style. A full report on this can be found in the 1974 issue of the Institute of Ethnomusicology's *Selected Reports.* Ornaments in the simple Thai style seem to be basically the pitches of the fixed tuning system.

9. For example, the following different versions of the sound "my":

ไม้ = mái: wood

ไม่ = mâi: no, not

ไหม้ = mâi: to burn

ไหม = mǎi: silk; final word at the end of a question sentence

ใหม่ = mài: new

มาย = māi: calculation, measurement

ม่าย = mâi: to turn away (verb)
        widow, widowhood (noun)

หมาย = mǎi: to intend, imagine, expect (verb)
        a notice, decree (noun)

10. Information extracted from Tramote's explanatory article, *Silpakǭn Magazine,* Vol. 10 (May 1966), 84.

Appendix A

Phonetic Transliteration of Thai

The system of transliteration of Thai into Roman letters in this study was originally published by the Library of Congress in 1948 but was never adopted by the Library because of certain inadequacies. The system was adapted by Professor Robert B. Jones, Professor of Linguistics in the Department of Asian Studies, Southeast Asia Program, Cornell University, for use by the Cornell Library. This system was devised to make use only of symbols found on a typewriter (with the exception of "čh") and to be easily alphabetized on library cards.

In many instances the true Thai sounds cannot be shown in Roman letters or in English syllables; when such is the case, the sound is described as closely as possible.

CONSONANTS

Thai consonants are reasonably close to the Roman letters used to represent them except for the following:

čh — pronounced like the "j" in judge (ch, without the mark — pronounced like the "ch" in church)

ng — as an initial consonant, pronounced like "ng" in song

ph — pronounced like "p" in pen

th — pronounced like "t" in top

kh — pronounced like "k" in king

p, t, and k are unexploded, voiced consonants, in contradistinction to the exploded forms listed immediately above. The unexploded forms do not really exist in English; the nearest equivalent pronunciations in English words might be the following:

p — pronounced like "p" in top

t — pronounced like "t" in hat

k — pronounced like "g" in hug

One part of the Cornell system has not been followed here. In Thai a word in the written language may not begin with a vowel, so a silent consonant is used. The Cornell system employs the letter "q" to show this silent consonant; for this study it was considered unnecessary––"Ānū," for example, is the actual sound, and "qānū" seems rather confusing.

VOWELS

Vowels with a macron (a line over) are long; those without are short. The following vowels are reasonably close to English:

i — pronounced like "i" in hit

ī — pronounced like "ee" in meet

e — pronounced like "e" in met

ē — pronounced like "a" in gate (but not the diphthong sound of the English vowel)

ae, āe — pronounced like "a" in hat

a, ā — pronounced like "a" in father

o, ō — pronounced like "o" in go (but not the diphthong sound of the English vowel)

u, ū — pronounced like "oo" in moon

ǫ, ǭ — pronounced like "aw" in law

The short forms of these last five vowels are the same sounds as the long form, but of very short duration. Linguists say also that they are stopped with a glottal stop.

The following vowels are not found in English:

y, ȳ — pronounced something like the French "u" and German "ü"

oe, ōe — pronounced something like the British pronunciation of the syllable "er" as in the word "term," that is, with a dropped "r" also something like the German "ö"

The following diphthongs are reasonably close to English equivalents:

īa — pronounced like "ia" in Australia

ai, āī — pronounced like "y" in sky

ao, āo — pronounced like "ow" in now

ōi — pronounced like "oy" in boy

The following diphthongs can only be represented by combinations of English vowel sounds:

āeo — a-o ("a" in hat)

eo, ēo — ay-o ("ay" in day)

ǭi — aw-ee

iu — ee-oo

ōei — "er"-ee (see "oe" above)

ua — oo-ah

uai — oo-ay ("ay" in day)

ui — oo-ee

ȳa — u-ah (see "u" above)

ȳai — u-ay ("ay" in day)

Appendix B

Measurements of Tunings

In Bangkok in 1960 I purchased from diverse places instruments for a pī phāt ensemble. Before they were sent to the United States, the melodic percussion instruments (xylophones and gong-kettle sets) were tuned to the Phakavali tuning by their instrument tuner. The tunings of these instruments were subsequently checked with the Stroboconn after they had arrived at the University of California, Los Angeles. When the Phakavali musicians and dancers were in Los Angeles in November, 1962, during their tour of the United States, the tunings of the two instruments of fixed pitch which they carried with them were checked with the Stroboconn.

Since the monochord readings are less accurate than those of the Stroboconn, we may dispense with them except for two representative sets given here in a "master tuning chart," Table A in this Appendix, for comparative purposes. The monochord readings do not in any way refute the principle of tuning shown by the Stroboconn readings.

The tunings of the instruments sent to UCLA were checked on the Stroboconn at different times and by different persons. The figures are almost identical, indicating that the instruments, when not moved and used—when the tuning waxes remain undisturbed—hold their tuning extremely well. The instruments appeared to have suffered no alteration during their trip across the Pacific Ocean except for three tuning waxes that fell off the wooden bars of the ranāt thum (low-pitched xylophone). The readings for the ranāt thum in 1961 and 1962 (except for the pitches of the three damaged keys) are given in Table B to show the relative permanence of tuning when the instrument is undisturbed.

For the ranāt ēk (high-pitched xylophone with wooden bars), khǭng wong yai (large circle of gong-kettles), and khǭng wong lek (small circle of gong-kettles), two separate checks of the tuning were made—by me and by Max Harrell, a graduate student in Ethnomusicology at UCLA; both of these readings are given to show the closeness of the tunings made by different persons. They are for the most part identical or within one or two cycles per second of one another. A few deviate by four cycles per second; none deviates more than four. An average of these is taken for each of the instruments. The figures are shown in Table C.

The averages for the four instruments are now placed together in one table with corresponding pitches side by side.

A comparison of the corresponding pitches of these four instruments shows that the instruments of the ensemble are closely in tune with one another. The averaged pitches, given with the intervallic structure in Table D, represent a typical tuning of a Thai ensemble.

Some observations and generalizations may be drawn from the figures in Table D. First, in the two-octave range between 275 cycles per second and 1203 cycles per second (of the averages)—involving pitches represented on three or four instruments—the intervallic structure is fairly stable. The intervals are within about 10 cents above or below the theoretically correct interval of 171.4 cents. Two intervals may be said to be exact: 171 and 172 cents. Of the other thirteen intervals, more are too small than too large—eight and five intervals respectively. No clear pattern of large and small intervals obtains. Second, intervallic structure above and below this central section—represented by only one, or the average of two, instruments—shows more variety. It may be that the extreme highs and lows of the range are harder for the tuner to tune.

The tunings of the two instruments of the Phakavali Institute, treated in like manner, are given in Table E. The tunings of these instruments were made jointly by Max Harrell and me. This set of tunings shows greater deviations from a theoretical standard than the UCLA ensemble, probably a result of the greater travel to which these instruments had been subjected. The instruments were not tuned before the readings were taken—they were tested in the condition in which they had been used for the concert the night before.

TABLE A
MASTER TUNING CHART
(continued on next page)

Ranāt Thum

Strobocomm		Monochord	
1961	1962	P (9)	Show
665	665	678	680
605	605	619	610
–	–	555	560
494	494	493.3	508
448	449	447.5	453
407	407	409	410
368.5	369	369	372
336	335	339.5	343
–	–	307	310
273	273.5	278	280
247.7	248	247.5	254
–	–	223	226
199.5	200	204	204.5
189	189	184.5	185
168	167.3	167.7	170
153	153	150.5	153.5
136.5	137	–	138.5

Ranāt Ēk

Strobocomm			Monochord	
MH 1962	DM 1962	PS 1962	P (14)	Show
1204	1208	1220	1226.5	1236
1102	1100	1098	1112	1124
990	990	998	990.5	1016
894	896	896	898.5	906
812	812	818	818.5	826
735	736	740	740.5	746
664	665	672	674.5	680
602	604	604	612.5	616
545	545	550	556	560
494	492.5	498	494	506
448.5	451	450	446.5	447
406.5	409.5	411	407.7	411
372	372	371	368.8	370
335	335.5	334	336	336
302	302.5	305	305	308
274	273	277	277.5	280
244.5	245	246	246.7	253
223	223.2	225	223	223.5
201.5	204	204	203.5	205.5
182	182.5	185	184	185
169	168.7	170	–	167

Khong Wong Yai

Strobocomm		Monochord	
MH 1962	DM 1962	P (6)	Show
1199	1200	1228	1240
1092	1092	1112	1116
984	986	996	1012
896	897	896	914
811	812	819.5	824
735	736	738	744
662	662	674.5	682
603	603	614.5	622
543	543	556	562
491	491	492	508
447	448	446.3	453
408	409	409.3	413
372	373	369	370
334.5	335.5	336	338
302	305	306	312
278	278	278	282

Khong Wong Lek

Strobocomm			Monochord	
MH 1962	DM 1962	PS 1962	P (4)	Show
2444	2448	2396	2456	2472
2232	2236	2224	2224	2248
2000	2004	2020	1976	2024
1826	1828	1812	1810	1816
1648	1650	1636	1638	1652
1478	1480	1482	1486	1488
1336	1340	1364	1364	1360
1202	1202	1224	1228	1236
1094	1094	1106	1112	1120
984	986	994	986	1008
896	897	894	898	908
812	813	812	820	820
733	734	738	741.5	744
660	660	664	681	680
600	601	602	618	618
Dummy kettles, not used			555	556
			502	504

Averages

Strobocomm Average	Intervals in Cents	Intervals in Cents	Monochord Average
2446	162	168	2464
2230.7	180	193	2236
2008	170	171	2000
1822	176	168	1813
1644.7	165	177	1645
1480	187	153	1487
1347	165	174	1362
1207.5	180	171	1232.4
1097.2	172	187	1116
989	171	178	1001.4
895.7	170	166	903.4
812.7	178	175	821.3
736	167	156	742.3
664	175	166	678.7
603	171	171	616.2
545.2	165	190	558
493.5	178	186	500.2
448.8	167	157	448.9
408.7	176	178	410
371	172	157	369.8
335	168	161	338
303.3	194	171	308
275.2	167	190	279.3
246.2	177	190	250.3
223.7	145	158	224
201.8	166	178	204.4
185.5	167	160	184.6
168.5	195	175	168.2
153		161	152
136.7			138.5

MH refers to the readings made by Max Harrell.
DM refers to the readings made by David Morton.
Dates refer to the years in which the readings of the tunings were made.
P refers to the instruments of the Phakavali Institute of Dance and Music in Bangkok. The number in brackets indicates the number of instruments whose tunings were averaged. "Show" refers to the instruments used in pub-lic for accompanying the performances given by the Phakavali Institute in Bangkok. PS refers to the instruments used in the Phakavali touring show brought to the United States.
All figures are cycles per second except the two columns of cents figures for intervals.

TABLE B

Ranāt Thum

No. of bar	1961	1962	Average	
17	665	665	665	Cycles per second
16	605	605	605	
15	-	-	-	
14	494	494	494	
13	448	449	448.5	
12	407	407	407	
11	368.5	369	369	
10	336	335	335.5	
9	-	-	-	
8	273	273.5	273	
7	247.7	248	248	
6	-	-	-	
5	199.5	200	200	
4	189	189	189	
3	168	167.3	168	
2	153	153	153	
1	136.5	137	137	

TABLE C

	Ranāt Ēk				Khǫng Wong Yai				Khǫng Wong Lek		
No. of bar	Max Harrell	David Morton	Average	No. of kettle	Max Harrell	David Morton	Average	No. of kettle	Max Harrell	David Morton	Average
21	1204	1208	1206	16	1199	1200	1200	15	2444	2448	2446
20	1102	1100	1101	15	1092	1092	1092	14	2232	2236	2234
19	990	990	990	14	984	986	985	13	2000	2004	2002
18	894	896	895	13	896	897	896.5	12	1826	1828	1827
17	812	812	812	12	811	812	811.5	11	1648	1650	1649
16	735	736	735.5	11	735	736	735.5	10	1478	1480	1479
15	664	665	664.5	10	662	662	662	9	1336	1340	1338
14	602	604	603	9	603	603	603	8	1202	1202	1202
13	545	545	545	8	543	543	543	7	1094	1094	1094
12	494	492.5	493	7	491	491	491	6	984	986	985
11	448.5	451	450	6	447	448	447.5	5	896	897	896.5
10	406.5	409.5	408	5	408	409	408.5	4	812	812	812
9	372	372	372	4	372	373	372.5	3	733	734	733.5
8	335	335.5	335	3	334.5	335.5	335	2	660	660	660
7	302	302.5	302	2	302	305	303.5	1	600	601	600.5
6	274	273	273.5	1	278	278	278				
5	244.5	245	245								
4	223	223.2	223								
3	201.5	204	203								
2	182	182.5	182								
1	169	168.7	169								

Cycles per second

APPENDIX B

236

TABLE D

Chart of Averages of the Tunings
and Intervallic Structure

Cycles per second

Ranāt Thum	Ranāt Ēk	Khong Wong Yai	Khong Wong Lek	Average	Interval in cents
			2446	2446	158
			2234	2234	190
			2002	2002	156
			1827	1827	180
			1649	1649	186
			1479	1479	174
			1338	1338	184
	1206	1200	1202	1203	161
	1101	1092	1094	1096	181
	990	985	985	987	168
	895	896.5	896.5	896	171
	812	811.5	812.5	812	172
	735.5	735.5	733.5	735	178
665	664.5	662	660	663	165
605	603	603	600.5	603	178
–	545	543		544	170
494	493	491		493	162
448.5	450	447.5		449	166
407	408	408.5		408	161
369	372	372.5		371	176
335.5	335	335		335	174
–	302	303.5		303	168
273	273.5	278		275	186
248	245			247	177
–	223			223	175
200	203			201.5	148
189	182			185	162
168	169			168.5	167
153				153	191
137				137	

TABLE E

Chart of the Tunings of the Instruments of the
Phakavali Institute of Dance and Music

Cycles per second

Ranāt Ēk	Khong Wong Lek	Average	Interval in cents
	2396		
			129
	2224		
			167
	2020		
			188
	1812		
			177
	1636		
			173
	1482		
			144
	1364		
			190
1220	1224	1222	
			178
1098	1106	1102	
			176
998	994	996	
			187
896	894	895	
			160
818	812	815	
			167
740	738	739	
			175
672	664	668	
			177
604	602	603	
			159
550			
			172
498			
			175
450			
			157
411			
			177
371			
			182
334			
			157
305			
			166
277			
			205
246			
			155
225			
			170
204			
			169
185			
			146
170			

Appendix C

Structure of the Versions of "Lā" (Farewell Song)

(The structure of each of the 19 interpretations of the "Lā" according to the versions of the measures in figure 147)

Rŭang No.	[Measure number]	1	2	3	4	5	6	7	8	9	10	11	12	13	14	15	16
1	A3	A1	B1	B1	A2	A1	B1	B2	A1	A1	A1	A1	A3	B1	A1	A1	A1
2	A2	B1	B1	B1	A2	A1	A1	A1	A1	A1	A1	A1	A1	A1	A1	A1	A1
3	A1	A1	B2	B1	A1	B1	B1	B1	A1	A1	A1	A1	A5	A1	B2	B1	B1
4	A1	A1	A2	A2	A1	A1	B1	B1	A1	A1	A1	A1	A5	B1	A1	A2	A1
5	A1	A1	A1	A2	A1	A1	B1	B1	A2	A1	A1	A1	A2	A1	B3	A3	A1
8	A2	A1	A1	A2	A1	A1	B1	B2	A1	A1	A1	A1	A2	A1	B2	B1	B1
9	A1	B3	B3	B1	A2	A1	B1	B2	A1	A1	A1	A1	A1	A1	A2	A1	A1
10	A1	B3	B3	B1	A2	A1	B1	B2	A1	A1	A1	A1	A1	A1	A2	A1	A1
11	A1	B3	B3	B1	A2	A1	B1	B2	A1	A1	A1	A1	A1	A1	A2	A1	A1
12	A1	A1	A1	A2	A1	A1	B1	B1	A1	A1	A1	A1	A2	B1	A1	A1	A1
13	A2	A1	A3	B2	A1	A2	A1	A1	A1	A1	A1	A1	A1	B1	A1	A1	A1
14	A1	A1	B3	A2	A1	A1	B2	B2	A1	A1	A2	A2	B1	A1	B2	B1	B1
15	A1	B3	B4	B1	A1	A1	B1	B1	A1	A1	A1	A1	A6	A1	C1	C1	C1
16	A3	A1	A1	A1	B1	A1	A2	A1	A1	A1	A1	A2	A4	A1	B2	B1	B1
17	A1	A1	A1	A2	A1	A1	B1	B2	A1	A1	A1	A1	A5	B1	A1	A2	A1
18	A1	A1	A1	A2	A1	A1	B1	B2	A1	A1	A1	A1	A2	A1	B2	B1	B1
19	A1	A1	A1	A2	A1	A1	B1	B1	A1	A1	A1	A1	A2	B1	A1	A2	A1
23	A1	B3	B3	B1	A2	A1	B1	B2	A1	A1	A1	A1	A1	A1	A2	A2	A1
27	A1	A1	A1	A2	A1	A1	B1	B2	A1	A1	A1	A1	A1	B2	B1	B2	B2
Ideal	A1	A1	A1	A2	A1	A1	B1	B2	A1	A1	A1	A1	A1	A1	A2 / B2	A2 / B1	A1 / B1

(The numbers of the rŭang are those in the manuscript collection. The first column of letters is the anacrusis.)

Glossary of Thai Words

The glossary contains the directions for correct pronunciation of all Thai words and titles of compositions used in this book with the exception of proper names of people and places—pronunciation of these will be indicated following the name in the entry in the index. The pronunciation chart for the letters is in Appendix A.

Thai is a tonal language. There are five main inflections, indicated by the following marks above the vowels in the transliterations:

no mark (other than the macron indicating the long vowel) = level tone

ʹ = high tone ⎫ (high and low short vowels are
ˋ = low tone ⎭ stopped glottally)

ˇ = rising tone (not to be confused with ch, which indicates the English "j" sound)

ˆ = falling tone

The Thai written language has no capital and small letters—there is only one form of the letter. Here, however, titles of compositions and literary works are capitalized, names of compositions further being enclosed in quotation marks and names of literary works being italicized. Common words are spelled without capitals with three exceptions: thao/Thao, rŷang/Rŷang, and Tap, to differentiate two uses of the first two words, and to differentiate the third word from the English word of the same spelling.

A

"Ābūhāsan" (Tàp) อาบูฮาซัน

"Ānŭ" อาหนู

B

"Bāi Klāng" ใบ้คลั่ง

bandỏ บัณเฑาะว์ (a small, hand drum)

bua lọi บัวลอย (an old ensemble)

C

chán ชั้น (degree, level, storey)

chán dio ชั้นเดียว ("first level"; third and final section in a Thao, which may be followed by a coda)

"Chāng Prasǎn NGā" ช้างประสานงา

chàp ฉับ (onomatopoeic—sound of the damped ching)

chàp lék ฉับเล็ก (medium-sized cymbals)

chàp yài ฉับใหญ่ (large-sized cymbals)

cháwā ชวา (Java)

"Chīn Sǎe Mài" (Rŷang) จีนแส่ใหม่ (เรื่อง)

chìng ฉิ่ง (small hand cymbals)

"Chom Sǔan Sàwǎn" ชมสวนสวรรค์

239

ČH (= English j)

čhá ฉุ่ย   (a drum stroke)

čhàkhê่ จะเข้   (a zither-type stringed instrument)

čhangwà จังหวะ   (rhythm/meter)

čhangwà sǎman จังหวะสามัญ   (a kind of rhythm/meter)

čhangwà nâ tháp จังหวะหน้าทับ   (a kind of rhythm/meter)

čhǫrákhê่ จรเข้   (crocodile)

D

"Dǫ̀k Mái Sai" ดอกไม้ไทร

dùkdamban ดึกดำบรรพ์   (a recent theatrical form, now obsolete)

H

"Hòk Bòt" หกบท

"Hǒmrōng Yen" โหมโรงเย็น   ("Evening Prelude")

"Hǒng Thǭng" หงษ์ทอง

K

kèp เก็บ   (a technique of playing on melodic percussion instruments)

kin nǭn (sometimes pronounced "kin nara") กินนร   (a mythical figure, half woman, half bird)

klāng กลาง   (middle, medium)

klāng hǎep กลางแหบ   (a pitch——D in Western notation)

klǭng กลอง   (generic word for "drum")

klǭng chātrī กลองชาตรี   (a drum of southern Thailand)

klǭng cháwā กลองชวา   ("Javanese drum"——that is, a Javanese-derived drum)

klǭng khǎek กลองแขก   ("foreign drum")

klǭng mālāyū กลองมลายู   (Malayan drum)

klǭng mārígan กลองมริกัน   (American bass drum)

klǭng thát กลองทัด   (large barrel-shaped peg-headed drum)

klǭng yāo กลองยาว   (long drum)

kràjàppī กระจับปี่   (a plucked lute-type stringed instrument)

krāo ram กราวรำ   (a composition to accompany fight scenes or marching)

kràp กรับ   (a wooden percussion instrument; a pair is held in each hand)

kràp phuang กรับพวง   (a percussion instrument of loose pieces tied together; held in the right hand and slapped against the palm of the left)

kràp sěphā กรับเสภา   (a wooden percussion instrument; see kràp)

krǫ̀ เกราะ   (an old bamboo percussion instrument)

krǭ กรอ   (the "roll" technique of playing on the ranāt ēk)

krǫ̀ng โกร่ง   (an old bamboo percussion instrument)

krùat กรวด   (a tuning level for instruments)

KH

khǎek แขก   (foreign, exotic; Indian, Javanese, etc.)

"Khǎek Lopburī" แขกลพบุรี

"Khǎek Mǭn Bāng Chǎng" แขกมอญบางช้าง

"Khǎek Mǭn Bāng Khǔn Phrom" แขกมอญบางขุนพรหม

"Khǎek Sai" แขกไทร

"Khǎek Tǫ̀i Mǭ̂" แขกต่อยหม้อ

"Khǎek Thǭn Sǎi Bua" แขกถอนสายบัว

khāen แคน   (a wind instrument; free-beating metal reeds in bamboo tubes with a common mouthpiece)

"Khàmāe(r) Thom" ขะแม(ร)ทม

"Khàmě̄n Klāng" เขมรกลาง

"Khàmě̄n Lá Ǭ Ong" เขมรละออองค์

"Khàmě̄n Nǭi" เขมรน้อย

"Khàmě̄n Pǎk Thǫ̂" เขมรปากท่อ (or จ๋อ)

"Khàmě̄n Sai Yǫ̂k" เขมรไทรโยก

"Khàmě̄n Yài" เขมรใหญ่

khàp mái ขับไม้   (an old ensemble)

khǐm ขิม   (a zither-type stringed instrument = the Chinese yang ch'in)

khlùi ขลุ่ย   (the bamboo flute)

khlùi líp ขลุ่ยหลีบ   (the small-size bamboo flute)

khlùi phīang ǭ ขลุ่ยเพียงออ   (the medium-size bamboo flute)

khlùi ū̂ ขลุ่ยอู้   (the large-size bamboo flute)

khǒn โขน   (the theatrical form using masks)

Khǫ̌m Dam Din ขอมดำดิน   (a drama)

"Khǫ̌m Sǫng Khrǘ̄ang" ขอมทรงเครื่อง

khǭng ฆ้อง   (a gong or gong-kettle)

khǭng hùi ฆ้องหุ่ย   (a gong on a tripod stand)

khǭng khū̂ ฆ้องคู่   (a pair of gong-kettles)

khǭng mě̄ng ฆ้องเหม่ง   (a small, suspended, hand-held gong)

khǭng mǭn ฆ้องมอญ   (gong-circle on a crescent-shaped rack)

khǭng rábēng ฆ้องระเบง   (an old style gong)

khǭng rāng ฆ้องราง   (row of gong-kettles on a rack)

khǭng rāo ฆ้องราว   (set of gongs on a stand)

khǭng wong lék ฆ้องวงเล็ก   (small gong-circle)

khǭng wong yài ฆ้องวงใหญ่   (large gong-circle)

khrų̄ang เครื่อง   (a generic word for instruments or tools, equipment)

khrų̄ang hā̂ เครื่องห้า   (a small ensemble—"of five instruments")

khrų̄ang sāi̇ เครื่องสาย   (the ensemble composed of stringed instruments, flute, and rhythmic percussion)

khū̇ คู่   (a pair)

Intervals in Thai music are called by this word plus the number of the pitch in the series of the scale/mode; the number, of course, refers to the interval between the two pitches in the Thai tuning system:

khū̇ pàet	คู่แปด	octave
khū̇ čhèt	คู่เจ็ด	7th
khū̇ hòk	คู่หก	6th
khū̇ hā̂	คู่ห้า	5th
khū̇ sī̇	คู่สี่	4th
khū̇ sāṁ	คู่สาม	3rd
khū̇ sǫ̌ng	คู่สอง	2nd

L

"Lā̄" ลา

lákhǭn ละคอน   (theatrical form without masks)

lákhǭn nai ละคอนใน   (indoor lakhǭn)

lákhǭn nǭ̂k ละคอนนอก   (outdoor lakhǭn)

lákhǭn nōrā ละคอนโนห์รา (theatrical form of southern Thailand)

"Lāo Chǐang Tàt Sǫ̂i" ลาวเฉียงตัดสร้อย

"Lāo Damnōen Sāi" ลาวดำเนินทราย

"Lāo Duang Dų̄an" ลาวดวงเดือน

"Lāo Kham Hǫ̌m" ลาวคำหอม

"Lāo Khruan" ลาวครวญ

"Lāo Sīang Thīan" ลาวเสียงเทียน

líkē (sometimes yǐkē) ลิเก (ยี่เก)   (a popular burlesque theatrical form)

"Līlā Kràthúm" (sometimes "Kàthúm") ลีลากระทุ่ม

lū̂k khàt ลูกขัด   (a compositional and instrumental playing technique involving "question and answer")

lū̂k lǫ̀ ลูกล้อ   (a compositional and instrumental playing technique involving "question and answer")

lū̂k òt ลูกโอด   (a pitch—A/A♭ in Western notation)

M

máhǭrī̇ มโหรี   (an ensemble composed of melodic and rhythmic percussion instruments and flute)

mái ไม้   (wood; see note 7, Chapter V, page 230)

mōng โหม่ง   (a large gong)

Mǭn; mǭn มอญ   (the Mȏn or Peguan people; not capitalized: a style of music)

"Mǭn Chom Čhan" มอญชมจันทร์

"Mǭn Phlāeng" (Rų̄ang) มอญแปลง (เรื่อง)

"Múlōng" มุล่ง

N

nai ใน   (inside; indoors)

nai lót ในลด   (a pitch name—F in Western notation)

"Nâk Phan" นาคพันธ์

nǎng หนัง   (leather; also the shadow play. A drum stroke)

nǎng yài หนังใหญ่   (large leather shadow puppets)

"Nāng Khruan" นางครวญ

"Nārāi Phlāeng Rū̂p" นารายณ์แปลงรูป

"Nók Khǎo Khàmāe(r)" นกเขาขะแม(ร)

nōrā โนห์รา   (southern Thai theater)

nǫ́i น้อย   (little, less; few)

nǭk นอก   (outside; outdoors)

nǭ̂k tàm นอกต่ำ   (a pitch name—B♭ in Western notation; another name for phiang o bon)

P

pá ป๊ะ   (a drum stroke)

"Páe" แป๊ะ

pōeng māng เป๊งมาง   (a small, thong-wrapped barrel-shaped drum)

pōeng māng khǭ̂k เป๊งมางคอก   (a set of drums and their stand)

pī̇ ปี่ (double-reed instrument)

pī̇ chànǎi ปี่ไฉน   (early double-reed instrument)

pī̇ cháwā ปี่ชวา   ("Javanese pī̇")

pī̇ klāng ปี่กลาง   (medium-sized pī̇)

pī̇ mǭn ปี่มอญ   (mǭn-style pī̇)

pī̇ nai ปี่ใน   (indoor pī̇)

pī̇ nǭ̂k ปี่นอก   (outdoor pī̇)

pī̇ phāt ปี่พาทย์   (an ensemble composed of melodic and rhythmic percussion instruments and the pī̇)

pī̇ phāt mái nuam ปี่พาทย์ไม้นวม   (the pī̇ phāt ensemble using padded sticks)

pī̇ phāt nǎng hǒng ปี่พาทย์นางหงส์   (the pī̇ phāt funeral ensemble)

pròp kài ปรบไก่   (a metrical pattern)

PH

"Phắt Chā̃" พัดชา

"Pháyā (Phráyā) Khruan" พญา(พระญา)ครวญ

"Pháyā Ram Phụng" พญา (พยา)รำพึง

phía เพียะ   (a stick zither-type stringed instrument)

phīang ǭ   เพียงออ   (a tuning; a type of khlui)

phīang ǭ bon   เพียงออบน   (a pitch——B♭ in Western notation; same as nōk tam)

phīang ǭ lâng   เพียงออล่าง   (a pitch——F in Western notation)

phīn   พีณ   (a stick zither-type stringed instrument)

phīn nám tão พีณนำเต้า   (a type of phīn)

phīn phía พีณเพียะ   (a type of phīn)

phlēng chā̃ เพลงชา   ("slow song",–i.e., slow tempo)

"Phlēng Chìng Práchǎn" (Rûang)เพลงนิ่งพระจันทร์

phlēng reo เพลงเร็ว   ("fast song"–i.e., fast tempo)

"Phrálǭ" (Tap) พระ ลอ (ตับ)

"Phrárām Dōen Dong" (Rûang) พระรามเดินดง

Phrárûang พระร่วง   (a drama)

"Phráyā Sǒk" พระญา (พยา)โศก

phring พริ่ง   (a drum stroke)

phrôeng เพริ่ง   (a drum stroke)

phrôet เพริด   (a drum stroke)

phrÿt พรี่ด   (a drum stroke)

"Phuang Rǒi" พวงร้อย

R

rá รย   (a syllable only)

rammánā รำมะนา   (a small frame drum)

ránât ẽk ระนาดเอก   (high-pitched xylophone)

ránât ẽk lèk ระนาดเอกเหล็ก   (high-pitched metallophone)

ránât kãeo ระนาดแก้ว   (early form of the gong-circle?)

ránât thǭng ระนาดทอง (a metallophone; original name of the ránât ẽk lèk)

ránât thúm ระนาดทุ่ม   (low-pitched xylophone)

ránât thúm lèk   ระนาดทุ่มเหล็ก (low-pitched metallophone)

"Rásàm Rásǎi" ระส่ำระสาย

rāt ราด   (a syllable)

"Rātrī Pràdàp Dāo" ราตรีประดับดาว

rua รัว   (a rubato section of a composition)

rûang } เรื่อง   (literally, "subject matter, the thing in
Rûang }   question." With a small initial "r" it refers to the suites in general; with an initial capital letters it refers to a specific suite.)

S

sàbàt สะบัด   (a playing technique on melodic percussion instruments)

sǎm สาม   (three)

sǎm chán สามชั้น   (third degree, level, storey; extended version of a Thao)

"Sǎm Mái Nai" สามไม้ใน

sǎng สังข์   (a wind instrument——a curved metal horn)

"Sǎo Sǒt Wǎen" สาวสอดแหวน

Sàp Sǎngkhít ศัพท์สังคีต   ("knowledge about music")

sēphā เสภา   (an old style of chanting; entertainment repertoire)

sǐang เสียง   (sound)

sǐang เสียง   (to prophesy)

Silpakorn, Silpakǭn (pronounced sǐnlápākǭn or sǐnpākǭn) ศิลปา   ("fine arts")

"Sǒm Sǒng Sǎeng" โสมส่องแสง

sòng rǭng ส่งร้อง   (to begin, or join with, the singing)

sǭ ซอ   (a generic term for bowed stringed instruments)

sǭ dûang ซอด้วง   (a stringed instrument——two-stringed bowed lute with cylindrical resinator)

sǭ sǎm sǎi ซอสามสาม   (a stringed instrument——three-stringed bowed lute with triangular sound box)

sǭ thai ซอไทย   (old name for sǭ sǎm sǎi)

sǭ û ซออู้   (a stringed instrument——two-stringed bowed lute with half coconut shell sound box)

"Sǒi Máyúrā" สร้อยมยุรา

sǒng สอง   (two)

sǒng chán สองชั้น   (second degree, level, storey; middle or original version of a Thao)

sǒng mái สองไม้   ("two beats"; middle section of a rûang)

sǒng nâ สองหน้า   (a medium-sized, hand-played drum)

sÿng ซึง   (a plucked lute-type stringed instrument)

T

"Tào Kin Phàkbûng" เต่ากินผักบุ้ง

Tàp ตับ   (a suite or medley of compositions from a musical drama)

tàphōn ตะโพน   (a barrel-shaped drum on a stand)

tàphōn mǭn ตะโพนมอญ(the mǭn model of the taphōn)

ting ติง   (a drum stroke)

tùt ตุ๊ด   (a drum stroke)

"Tǒi Rûp" ต่อยรูป   (a drum stroke)

"Tôn Nāng Nâk" ต้นนางนาค   (a drum stroke)

"Tôn Phlēng Ching" ต้นเพลงนิ่ง

"Tuang Phrá Thât" ดวงพระธาตุ

túp ตุ๊บ   (a drum stroke)

TH

thà เถะ (a drum stroke)

"Tham Khwăn" (Rŷang) ทำขวัญ (เรื่อง)

thāng ทาง ("a way, method"; generic term for pitch or tuning level)

thâo เท่า (a fill-in, extending phrase)

Thǎo เถา (the telescopic variation compositional form)

tháp ทับ (pertaining to meter/rhythm)

thêng เท่ง (a drum stroke)

thòe เถอะ (a drum stroke)

thôeng เถิ่ง (a drum stroke)

thôet เถิด (a drum stroke)

thōn โทน (a goblet - or inverted vase-shaped drum with a single head)

thōn chātrī โทนชาตรี (a drum of south Thailand; small-size klǫng that)

thōn mahōrī โทนมโหรี (the thōn drum used in the mahōrī ensemble)

W

wâi khrū ไหว้ครู (the ceremony of paying respect and homage to teachers of music, theater, and dance)

"Wíwêk Wēhǎ" วิเวกเวหา

Y

yài ใหญ่ (large)

"Yǒng (Yûng) NGìt" ย่อง (ยุ่ง) หงิด

Bibliography

The bibliography is divided into two parts. Part I includes the references cited in this study and those other references (not specifically cited) that I consider to be the important references on Thai music existing, with a few exceptions, prior to 1958.

Part II includes other references mentioning Thai music, but which I consider of secondary importance. Some of these references contain material on Thai music other than the court repertory. In the light, however, of my statement in the Preface that "Western writing on Thai music previous to this study is a hodge-podge of opinions and statements that are conflicting, generally subjective, and sometimes even patronizing" (p. vii), it was felt necessary to include these sources so that any interested reader could check them for himself.

Annotations and special information are included where it is deemed useful.

I

Aalst, J. A. van. Chinese Music, Chinese Maritime Customs II, Special Series no. 6. Shanghai: Statistical Dept., Inspectorate General; London: P. S. King and Sons, 1884. Stereotyped reprint issued by the French Book Store, Peiping, 1933 and 1939. 84 pp.

Apel, Willi, ed. Harvard Dictionary of Music. 2nd ed., revised and enlarged. Cambridge: Harvard University Press, 1969.

Ayer, Margaret. Made in Thailand. New York: Knopf, 1964. 245 pp. I examined the chapter on music before this book was printed, and except for a minor error or two in printing, it is accurate.

Bake, Arnold. "The Music of India," in Egon Wellesz, ed., The New Oxford History of Music; Vol. I: Ancient and Oriental Music. London: Oxford University Press, 1957. Pp. 195-227.

Bangkok, Thailand. Chulalongkorn University Library. Bibliography of Material about Thailand in Western Languages. 1960 (B.E. 2503).

——. Department of Fine Arts. "Hōmrōng Yen" (เพลงชุดโหมโรงเย็น) [n.d.] The "Evening Prelude" — full score and part books.

——. Department of Fine Arts. Thai Classical Music (โน้ตเพลงไทย) Book I. 1961. Contains 15 compositions, main melodic line only; commentary and texts for the vocal sections are in Thai only.

——. Department of Fine Arts. "Tham Khwan (เพลงชุดทำขวัญ) Musical suite to be performed during a ceremony for invoking spiritual bliss." 1954.

Bangkok World, May 4, 1959. "This Wonderful World." This column this day was about Luang Pradit Phai Rǭ.

Blanchard, Wendell, ed., and others. Thailand; its People, its Society, its Culture. New Haven: Human Relations Area Files, 1958. 525 pp.

Bowers, Faubion. Theatre in the East. New York: Nelson, [1956] . 374 pp.

Bowring, John. The Kingdom and People of Siam. London: Parker and Son, 1857. 2 vols.

Brailoiu, Constantin. "Un problème de tonalité," in Mélanges d'histoire et d'esthétique musicales ... Vol. 1. Paris: Bibliotheque d'études musicales, 1955. Pp. 63-75.

Brandon, James R. Theatre in Southeast Asia. Cambridge: Harvard University Press, 1967. 370 pp.

Brown, Robert. "Introduction to the Music of South India," in Festival of Oriental Music and the Related Arts, Program. Los Angeles: UCLA, 1960. Pp. 47-53. This collection of essays on non-Western musics and arts is available from the Institute of Ethnomusicology, UCLA, Los Angeles, California 90024.

Colston, E. J. A Monograph on Tanning and Working Leather in the Province of Burma. Rangoon, 1903. One illustration of a Burmese ensemble (Fig. 116 in this book) has been reprinted in the New Oxford History of Music (see the listing under Bake, Arnold) facing page 214. Both illustrations from this book showing the instruments are reproduced here (figs. 115, 116).

Condominas, G. "Le lithophone préhistorique de Ndut Lieng Krak," L'Ecole Française d'Extrême Orient, Bulletin, XLV (1952), 359-392.

Culver, Charles A. Musical Acoustics. 4th ed.; New York: McGraw-Hill, 1956. 305 pp.

Damrong (Rajanubhab), Prince. Siamese Musical Instruments. 2nd ed.; Bangkok: The Royal Institute, 1931. 12 pp., 16 pls. The text is in both Thai and English. This important little pamphlet has unfortunately been long out of print.

Daniélou, Alain. La musique du Cambodge et du Laos. Publications de L'Institut Française d'Indologie, 1957. 32 pp.

Dhaninivat Sonakul, Prince (Prince Dhaninivat Kromamun Bidyalabh Bridyākọn). "An Outline of Siamese Cultural History," Thai Digest, I (Feb. 8, 1957), 2-10. Prince Dhani has written many articles on aspects of Thai arts and culture. Some of the others are listed in Part II of this bibliography.

Duriyanga (Phra) Chen. "A Talk on the Technique of Siamese Music in Relation to Western Music," African Music Society, Newsletter, I, No. 4 (June 1951), 2-8. This talk was originally presented to the Siam Society in 1947. It formed the basis for the following pamphlet. An undated, unpublished typescript of this is in the Library of Congress.

—. Thai Music. Thailand Culture Series, no. 8.

4th ed.; Bangkok: National Culture Institute, 1956. 56 pp. The first edition of this pamphlet was: "Siamese music in Theory and Practice as compared with that of the West and a description of the piphat band" (Bangkok: Department of Fine Arts, 1948 [B. E. 2491], 32 pp.). In 1962 (B.E. 2505) most of this series was reprinted by the Department of Fine Arts under the heading "Thai Culture, New Series." This pamphlet is number 15 in this new series.

—. Thai Music in Western Notation. Thai Culture, New Series, no. 16. Bangkok: Fine Arts Department, 1962 (B.E. 2505). 16 pp. Phra Chen was the son of a Thai mother and a German father who came to Thailand as a band master. Phra Chen's writings on Thai music are rather simple, as he was educated in Western music methods and did not investigate Thai music in any analytical way. His writings are not much help in knowing essential factors about Thai music, but are important historically as some of the first that even attempted to treat the music in any detail at all. These initial pamphlets are written from the viewpoint of trying to explain Thai music in terms of Western music, which, as any ethnomusicologist knows, can lead to great difficulties and misunderstandings.

Ellis, Alexander J. "Appendix to Mr. Alexander J. Ellis's Paper on 'The Musical Scales of Various Nations' read 25th March, 1885," Society of Arts, Journal, XXXIII (Oct. 30, 1885), 1102-1111.

—. "On the Musical Scales of Various Nations," Society of Arts, Journal, XXXIII (March 25, 1885), 485-527.

—. "Tonometrical Observations on Some Existing Non-harmonic Scales," Society of Arts, Proceedings (1884), 368-385.

Finney, Theodore M. A History of Music. Rev. ed.; New York: Harcourt, 1947. 720 pp.

Foran, William Robert. Malayan Symphony. London: Hutchinson, 1935. 302 pp.

Fyzee-Rahamin, Atiya (Begum). The Music of

India. London: Luzac, 1925. 95 pp.

Gervaise, Nicolas. The Natural and Political History of the Kingdom of Siam A.D. 1688. Translated into English from the original French by Herbert Stanley O'Neill. Bangkok: [Printed at the Siam Observer Press], 1928. 150 pp.

Graham, Walter Armstrong. Siam. 3rd ed.; London: Moring, 1924. 2 vols. As stated in Chapter I, this book contains a lengthy bibliography of books on Thailand during the early period.

Groslier, Bernard, and Jacques Arthaud. Angkor; Art and Civilization. Translated from the French by Eric Ernshaw Smith. London: Thames and Hudson, 1957. 230 pp. This book contains what are probably the most beautiful photographs of Angkor in print.

Groslier, George. Recherches sur les Cambodgiens. Paris: A. Challamel, 1921. 432 pp. This work contains drawings of the instruments in the Angkor carvings.

Helmholtz, Hermann L. F. On the Sensations of Tone. Translated by A. J. Ellis. 3rd ed.; New York: Longmans, 1895. 576 pp. In the appendix are found some of the early readings made of the tunings of Thai instruments.

Hood, Mantle. "The Effect of Medieval Technology on Musical Styles in the Orient," in Selected Reports (Institute of Ethnomusicology, UCLA), Vol. I, No. 3 (1970), 147-170.

—. The Ethnomusicologist. New York: McGraw-Hill, 1971. 386 pp.

—. "Music, the Unknown," in Musicology. Englewood Cliffs, N.J.: Prentice-Hall, 1963. Pp. 215 - 326.

—. The Nuclear Theme as a Determinant of Patet in Javanese Music. Gröningen: J. B. Wolters, 1954. 323 pp.

—. "Polyphonic Stratification in Javanese Music," IFMC, Program. Israel: August 1963. Unpublished.

—. "The Reliability of Oral Tradition," American Musicological Society, Journal, XII (1959), 201-209.

Hornbostel, Erich M. von. "Foranalysen an siamesischen Orchesterstücken," Archiv für Musikwissenschaft, II (1919/1920), 306-333.

Kunst, Jaap. Ethnomusicology. 3rd ed.; The Hague: Nijhoff, 1959, 303 pp.

—. Music in Java. 2nd ed.; The Hague: Nijhoff, 1949. 2 vols.

—. "Notes" for the record: Columbia World Library of Folk and Primitive Music, vol. VII, Indonesia.

—. "Een overwalsche bloedverwant van den Javaanschen gamelan; geschiedenis van het Siameesche orkest," Nederlansch Indië Oud und Nieuw, XIV (1929/1930), 79-96, 354.

LeMay, Reginald Stuart. The Culture of South-East Asia; the Heritage of India. London: Allen and Unwin, 1954. 218 pp.

Low, (Capt.) James. "On Siamese Literature," Society for Asiatic Researches, Transactions, XX, Part II (1839), 333-392. (The publication is sometimes referred to as: Asiatic Society of Bengal, Asiatic Researches

Luang Pradit Phairo. "Introduction" to Selected Reports (Department of Music, UCLA), Vol. II, No. 2 (1975).

Mendenhall, Stanley T. "Interaction of Linguistic and Musical Tone in Thai Song," in Selected Reports (Department of Music, UCLA), Vol. II, No. 2 (1975).

Moore, Sidney. "Thai Songs in 7/4 Meter," Ethnomusicology, 13 (May 1969), 309-312.

Moore, W. Robert. "Angkor, Jewel of the Jungle," National Geographic Magazine, 117 (April 1960), 516-569.

Morganthaler, Hans O. Matahari. New York: Doran, 1923. 240 pp.

Morton, David. "An American Discovers Thai Music." Arts of Asia. I (Sept.-Oct. 1971), 11-15.

—. "Polyphonic Stratification in Traditional Thai Music; A Study in Multiple Tone Color." Asian Pacific Quarterly of Cultural and Social Affairs. III (Summer, 1971), 70-80.

—. "Thai Traditional Music: Hothouse Plant or Sturdy Stock," Siam Society, Journal, LVIII, Part 2 (July 1970), 1-44.

—. Thailand. Harvard Dictionary of Music. 2nd

ed.; Cambridge: Harvard University Press, 1969. Pp. 842-843.

Morton, David. "The Traditional Instrumental Music of Thailand." (Paper read at an International Music Symposium, Manila, April 1966), in: The Musics of Asia, published by the National Music Council of the Philippines and UNESCO National Commission of the Philippines, 1971.

—. The Traditional Music of Thailand. Los Angeles: Institute of Ethnomusicology, UCLA, 1968. 47 pp. This is a booklet of commentary and analysis which accompanies the two-record album of traditional music of Thailand issued by the Institute (see the Discography).

—. "Vocal Tones in Traditional Thai Music," in Selected Reports (Institute of Ethnomusicology, UCLA), Vol. II, No. 1 (1974), 89-99.

—. "Instruments and Instrumental Functions in the Ensembles of Southeast Asia: A Cross-Cultural Comparison," in Selected Reports (Department of Music, UCLA), Vol. II, No. 2 (1975).

Moule, A. C. "A List of the Musical and Other Sound-producing Instruments of the Chinese," North China Branch of the Royal Asiatic Society, Journal, XXXIX (1908), 1-160. 13 pls.

Parry, Charles Hubert Hastings. The Evolution of the Art of Music. New York: Appleton, 1917. 342 pp.

Picken, Laurence. "The Music of Far Eastern Asia: 1. China," in Egon Wellesz, ed., The New Oxford History of Music; vol. I: Ancient and Oriental Music. London: Oxford University Press, 1957. Pp. 83-134. (I do not consider Picken's article on "Siam" in this book to be a prime source of information on Thai music. See the annotation of the entry in Part II.)

Pischner, Hans. Musik in China. Berlin: Henschelverlag, 1955. 152 pp. Illus.

Popley, Herbert A. The Music of India. 3rd ed.; Madras: Modern Book Printers, 1966. 184 pp. This little book is one of the best of the small general books on Indian music. The au-

thor was a director of the Y.M.C.A. in India, and the book was originally published by the Y.M.C.A. Publishing House. This new edition (which is a reprinting of the earlier editions) is now available from the Crescendo Publishing Co., 48-50 Melrose Street, Boston, Mass. 02116.

Pringsheim, Klaus. "Music of Thailand," Contemporary Japan, XIII (July/Sept., 1944), 747-767. Essentially the same material in German was contained in Pringsheim's "Musik in Siam," in Stimmen I (Dec., 1947), 46-51.

Sachs, Curt. The History of Musical Instruments. New York: Norton, 1940. 505 pp.

—. Die Musikinstrumente Birmas und Assams im K. Ethnographischen Museum zu München. Sitzungsberichte der K. Bayerischen Akad. der Wissenschaften, Phil.-phil. und hist. Kl., Jahrgang 1917, 2. Abhandlung. Munich: K. Bayerischen Akademie der Wissenschaften, 1917. 47 pp. 19 pls.

—. The Rise of Music in the Ancient World East and West. New York: Norton, 1943. 324 pp.

Satow, Ernest Mason. "Essay Towards a Bibliography of Siam," Royal Asiatic Society, Straits Branch, Journal, XVII (1886), 1-85, 163-189.

Schaeffner, André. "Une importante découverte archéologique: le lithophone de Ndut Lieng Krak (Vietnam)," La Revue de Musicologie, XXXIII (1951), 1-19.

Schafer, Edward H. The Golden Peaches of Samarkand; A Study of T'ang Exotics. Berkeley: University of California Press, 1963. 399 pp.

Scott, James George. Burma; from the Earliest Times to the Present Day. New York, Knopf, 1924. 372 pp.

Seelig, Paul. Siamesische Musik. Bandoeng: Editions Matatani, 1932. 155 pp. This collection of melodies of Thai compositions is more important historically than otherwise. It was issued before the project of notation done in the Department of Fine Arts. There are some melodies in this book which do not appear in the Department's notations; these are perhaps more folk melodies than high-art. The notations in the Department's collection are notated more completely and in more detail. This collection is useful, however, for comparing different versions of melodies, for, from one standpoint, there is no one absolutely "authentic" version of a Thai melody.

Silapabanleng, Prasidh. "Music in Thailand," First Regional Music Conference of Southeast Asia, 1955, Document 11.4 (mimeographed), 5 pp.

—. "Thai Music at the Court of Cambodia — A Personal Souvenir of Luang Pradit Phairoh's Visit in 1930," Siam Society, Journal, LVIII, Part I (January 1970), 121-124.

Stumpf, Carl. "Tonsystem und Musik der Siamesen," Beiträge zur Akustik und Musikwissenschaft, 3 (1901), 69-138. Reprinted in Sammelbände für Vergleichende Musikwissenschaft, I (1922), 122-177. Also issued separately by J. A. Barth, Leipzig, 1901.

Tramote, Montri. "A Description of Thai Musical Ensembles," in Notes on Thai Songs, pamphlet accompanying Series Two of phonograph records released by the Department of Fine Arts, Bangkok, 1959.

—. "The Evolution of Thai Music" (in Thai), Thai Culture Journal, 2 (Dec. 1, 1954), 6-11.

—. Sap Sangkhit (ศัพท์สังคีต). Bangkok: Department of Fine Arts, 1964. 62 pp.

Trần Văn Khê. La musique vietnamienne traditionelle. Paris: Presse Universitaires de France, 1962. 384 pp.

—. "Vietnam," Harvard Dictionary of Music. 2nd ed.; Cambridge: Harvard University Press, 1969.

Verney, Frederick. Notes on Siamese Musical Instruments. London: Wm. Clowes and Sons, 1885. 26 pp.

Vichitr-Vadakarn, (Luang) V. "The Evolution of Thai Music," Thai Digest, I (Feb. 8, 1957), 42-54; I (Feb. 15, 1957), 12-17.

First appeared in Siam Today (July 1937), 71-80; issued separately by the Department of Fine Arts in 1942.

Yupho, Dhanit. Classical Siamese Theatre. Bangkok: Hatha Dhip, 1952. 168 pp.

—. The Custom and Rite of Paying Homage to Teachers of Khon, Lakon and Piphat. Thai Culture, new series, no. 11. Bangkok: Department of Fine Arts, 1962. 16 pp.

—. The Khon and Lakon. Bangkok: Department of Fine Arts, 1963. 260 pp.

—. The Preliminary Course of Training in Siamese Theatrical Art. Thailand Culture Series, no. 15. Bangkok: National Culture Institute, 1956. 68 pp. Reprinted: Thai Culture, new series, no. 13. Bangkok: Department of Fine Arts, 1962. (In the title, "Siamese" is changed to "Thai" in the 1962 edition.)

—. Thai Musical Instruments. Translated from the Thai by David Morton. Bangkok: Department of Fine Arts, 1960. 104 pp. A 2nd edition in Thai only appeared in 1967. A few minor changes were made in the text of the second edition.

Zarina, Xenia. "The Thai Royal Ballet," Asia, XLI (June 1941), 285-287. Illus.

II

Aab, (Nai). "Siamese Music," Harvard Musical Review, I (1913), 14, 22.

Balfour, Henry Lucas. "Report on a Collection of Musical Instruments from the Siamese Malay States and Perak," Fasciculi Malayenses . . . Anthropology, Pt. II (a) (1904), 1-18.

Bangkok, Thailand. Department of Fine Arts. Ramwong Songs (รำวง). 1957 (B.E. 2500). A collection of folksongs and folk-like songs used as accompaniment for the national ballroom dance.

Beaumont, A. G. "Siam's Musical Heritage," Inter-Ocean, VIII (Oct. 1927), 561-564.

Bidyalankarana, Prince. "The Pastime of Rhyme-making and Singing in Rural Siam,"

Siam Society, Journal, XX (1926), 110-113.

Bock, Carl. Temples and Elephants: The Narrative of a Journey of Exploration Through Upper Siam and Lao. London: Sampson Low and others, 1884. 438 pp.

Boulle, Pierre. Le Siam. Lausanne: Librairie Payot, [1955]. 81 pp. Illus. The color illustrations are from the Walt Disney production, some of which include instruments. An English version appeared in 1958 (Switzerland: Nouvelles Editions S.A.), translated by Gordon Graham.

Bowers, Faubion. "Twins of Siamese Theatre," Saturday Review, XXXVIII (June 11, 1955), 31-32. A short article on the popular theatrical form likē.

Bokofzer, Manfred F. "The Evolution of Javanese Tone-Systems," in Papers Read at the International Congress of Musicology, held at New York, Sept. 11-16, 1939. New York: Music Educators' Natl. Conference, for the American Musicological Society, [1944]. Pp. 241-250. Bukofzer discusses the Javanese tuning systems and their possible relation to Thai music. He says sléndro tuning is equidistant and spread to Thailand.

Busch, Noel Fairchild. Thailand; an Introduction to Modern Siam. 2nd ed.; Princeton: Van Nostrand, [1964]. 166 pp.

Campbell, John Gordon Drummond. Siam in the Twentieth Century . . . London: Arnold, 1902. 332 pp.

Chandruang, Kamut. "If Music be the Food of Love," Thai Pictorial, I (Sept. 1941), 47-54. Illus.

—. My Boyhood in Siam. New York: John Day, [1940]. 226 pp. Previously published as a serial in Asia (1938). Mr. Chandruang is the brother-in-law of Prasidh Silapabanleng and a son-in-law of Luang Pradit Phai Rǫ, having married one of Luang Pradit's younger daughters. The book is a narrative of everyday life in Bangkok (although, as the author told me, somewhat exaggerated for commercial reasons). A number of the events and ceremonies and daily happenings concern the household of Luang Pradit.

Closson, Ernest. "Un Principe exotique inconnu d'organologie musicale," La Revue musicale, XIII (sept./oct., 1932), 200-204. Closson seems to be mistaken about the name of the instrument he describes. The klui [sic] has no reed; it is played like a recorder. The instrument that Closson describes is a folk instrument of the north with one free-beating metal reed. His discussion is about the possibility of adding it to some Western ensembles.

Cowell, Henry. "Music; Oriental," Encyclopaedia of the Social Sciences, XI (1933), 152-155.

Davis, Hal. "Benny and the King of Siam," Saturday Review, XL (Jan. 12, 1957), 64-65. A short article describing experiences of Benny Goodman and his jazz ensemble in Thailand. The king of Thailand (King Rama IX) is a devotee of Western jazz and popular music.

de Rosny, Leon. Le Peuple siamois ou thaï. Paris: Librairies de la Société d'Ethnographie, 1885. 120 pp.

Dhaninivat Sonakul, Prince (Prince Dhaninivat Kromamụm Bidyalabh Bridyākǫn). The Khon. Thai Culture, new series, no. 6. Bangkok: Department of Fine Arts, 1962.

—. The Nang. Thai Culture, new series, no. 3. Bangkok: Department of Fine Arts, 1962.

—. "Pageantry of the Siamese Stage," National Geographic Magazine, XCI (Feb. 1947), 209-212. Illus.

Dhuraratsadorn, Boriphandi. "The White Meo," Siam Society, Journal, XVII (1923), 153-199. Concerns the tribal group in northern Thailand.

Döhring, Karl. Siam. Munich: Müller, 1923.

Draws-Tychsen, Helmut. Siamsänge. Leiden: Brill, 1955. 86 pp. Concerns poetry and poetic forms.

Dyck, Gerald P. "The Vanishing Phia: An Ethnomusicological Photo-Story," in Selected Reports (Department of Music, UCLA), Vol. II, No. 2 (1975).

Dyck, Gerald P. "Lung Noi Na Kampam Makes a Drumhead for a Northern Thai Long Drum," in Selected Reports (Department of Music, UCLA), Vol. II, No. 2 (1975).

—. "They Also Serve," in Selected Reports, Vol. II, No. 2 (1975).

Edgerly, Beatrice. From the Hunter's Bow. 2nd ed.; New York: Putnam, 1942. 491 pp.

Gordon, Wilhelm Friedrich. Thailand: das neue Siam. Leipzig: Goldmann, [1939]. 155 pp.

Haas, Mary Rosamund. "Siam (Thailand)," Collier's Encyclopedia, XVII (1954), 567-573. Haas is noted for her work in Thai linguistics. Brief mention is made here of the "art, music and literature," page 572.

Hipkins, Alfred James. Musical Instruments: Historic, Rare and Unique. London: Black, 1921. xxiii, 123 pp. Illus.

Hood, Mantle. "Improvisation in the Stratified Ensembles of Southeast Asia," in Selected Reports (Department of Music, UCLA), Vol. II, No. 2 (1975).

Kosiyabongs, Kim, and Jaivid Rangthong, comp. A New Guide to Bangkok. 3rd ed., revised and enlarged; Bangkok: Hatha Dhip, [1954]. 281 pp. New editions of this are issued from time to time, though not necessarily incorporating all the material from previous editions. This third edition contains a list and brief description of Thai instruments with illustrations (pp. 51 ff.).

Kurosawa, Takatomo. Investigation of Musical Instruments in Thailand. Bangkok: Nippon-Tai Bunka Kenkyujo, 1941. This small book of badly printed illustrations of Thai instruments in the National Museum, without text, was issued shortly after the Japanese took over Thailand during World War II. Kurosawa was a sincere research worker and was attempting, while in Bangkok under war conditions, to make Thai culture more widely known. The edition of the book was small, and it has long been out of print.

LaBarre, H. "Fortress of Freedom in Southeast Asia," Cosmopolitan, CXXXIX (Nov. 1955), 55-57.

Lee, Hsing K'o. Tsen yang hsin shang chung-kuo hsi ("How to Appreciate Chinese Opera"). (In Chinese.) Singapore: World Book Co., 1957.

LeMay, Reginald Stuart. An Asian Arcady. Cambridge (England): Heffer, 1926. 274 pp. This book is particularly good for its intelligent, comprehensive treatment of the instruments of the northern area of Thailand, pages 114-116.

Loti, Pierre (pseud.). (Louis Marie Julian Viaud). Siam. (Translated from the French by W. P. Baines.) London: Laurie, [1913]. 182 pp. Also published in New York: Stokes, 1930.

Marshall, Harry Ignatius. "The Use of the Bronze Drum in Siam," Burma Research Society, Journal, XXII (1932), 21-22.

Meyer, Max F. The Musician's Arithmetic, Drill Problems for an Introduction into the Scientific Study of Musical Composition. University of Missouri Studies. Boston: Ditson, 1929. 149 pp. Contains a discussion of the Thai tuning; uses it as an example of an equidistant scale.

Moore, W. Robert. "'Land of the Free' in Asia," National Geographic Magazine, LXV (May 1934), 531-576. Illus.

—. "Scintillating Siam," National Geographic Magazine, XCI (Feb. 1947), 173-208. Illus.

Picken, Laurence. "Siam (Thailand)," in Egon Wellesz, ed., The New Oxford History of Music; vol. I: Ancient and Oriental Music. London: Oxford University Press, 1957. Pp. 162-163. The several short sections on musics of Asia contained in this book, written about 1956-57, are to my mind good examples of the type of article that should never be attempted before a music has been adequately researched. While knowledge is fragmentary and incomplete, full description cannot be undertaken — the result, such as this (slightly more than one page with one music example taken from Seelig's book of melodies, and no pictures), may well do more damage than printing nothing at all.

Pringsheim, Klaus. "Siamesische Oper," Stimmen, Heft 18 (1950), 520-521.

Roberts, Edmund. Embassy to the Eastern Courts of Cochin-China, Siam, and Muscat . . . during the Years 1832-3-4. New York: Harper, 1837. 432 pp.

Sachs, Curt. Our Musical Heritage. New York: Prentice-Hall, [1948]. 400 pp.

Sahni, Jogendra Nath. Across the Twentieth Parallel. New Delhi: Press News Features, 1954. 164 pp.

"Siam," Riemann's Musik Lexikon. 11th ed.; II (1929), 1699.

Smyth, Herbert Warrington. Five Years in Siam. London: John Murray, 1898. 2 vols. The five years in question were from 1891 to 1896. The music discussion offers good material on the folk music of the northern areas, including a good discussion of the "ken" (khāen) (Vol. II; pp. 289-295, 301-307).

Sommerville, Maxwell. Siam. Philadelphia: Lippincott, 1897. 237 pp.

Sterling, Adeline. "Drama and Music in Siam," Inter-Ocean, XIII (1932), 139-144. Illus. Music.

—. "The Shadow Play in Siam," Inter-Ocean, XIII (1932), 57-60.

Strickland, Lily. "Music and Dancing in Siam," Etude, LVI (July 1938), 440, 488. Illus.

Tanaka, Shohei. "An Investigation of the Tuning of the Siamese Seven Tone Equal Tempered Scale," Society for Research in Asiatic Music, Journal, 9 (March 1951), 1-2. A short article describing how to achieve a seven-pitch equidistant tuning without the aid of a mechanical measurer, using only the ear.

"Thailand," Encyclopedia Americana, XXVI (1957), 486-486h. I have included this reference as a typical example of the amount of space and discussion given to music in general articles about countries in encyclopedias. Thai "Theatre and Music" are mentioned briefly on page 486e.

Thompson, Peter Anthony. Siam: An Account of the Country and People. Boston and Tokyo: Millet, [1910]. 330 pp. Also published by Lippincott (Philadelphia) under the title Lotus Land.

Thompson, Virginia. Thailand: The New Siam. New York: Macmillan, 1941. 865 pp.

Uhle, M. "Sur quelques tam-tams siamois," Société des études japonaises, Mémoires, IV (1885), 153-156.

Wong, Pei Lun. Hsih ch'u tz'e tien (Dictionary of Chinese Operas). (In Chinese.) Taipei: Chung Hua Publishing Co., 1969.

Yasser, Joseph. A Theory of Evolving Tonality. New York: American Library of Musicology, 1932. 381 pp. A scholarly and scientific treatment of tonality. Thai (Siamese) music (scale) is mentioned frequently throughout the book by way of illustration.

Young, Ernest. The Kingdom of the Yellow Robe: Being Sketches of the Domestic and Religious Rites and Ceremonies of the Siamese. London: Constable, 1907. 399 pp.

Zarina, Xenia. Classic Dances of the Orient. New York: Crown, 1967. 232 pp.

Discography

"Music of the Orient." A survey of the principal music of all high Oriental cultures compiled and arranged by Dr. E. M. von Hornbostel. (1951) Decca (Gold Label Series) DX-107. This was one of the first important albums to present recordings of non-Western music. The one band of Thai music contains an excerpt from a scene of the Thai version of the Indian Rama story. The album, unfortunately, has long been out of print.

"Thai Instrumental Music." Cornell Southeast Asia Program, 1719-1720. These two records, prepared and narrated by Carl Skinner, were released in the mid-1950s. Included are samples of the sounds of various instruments, played by Kamol Ketusiri, and excerpts of some of the traditional ensemble music. These records are no longer available.

"Music of Thailand." Recorded by Howard Kaufman. Ethnic Folkways Library, Folkways Records, FE 4463 (1959). Mr. Kaufman recorded a great deal of Thai music when he was stationed in Thailand. These tapes are in the Archives of Folk and Primitive Music at Indiana University (Bloomington, Indiana). While the sixteen bands of this record offer an assortment of samplings of various types of Thai music, excerpts of this type not containing the complete composition are useless for analysis of form.

"Musique de Thaïlande," Documents Sonores Recuillis et Enregistrés par Jean-Claude Berrier et Louis le Bourgeois. BAM (Boite à Musique) LD-388 (7"). Seven excerpts and selections including folk music, music of the theater, and one sēphā-type composition.

"Thailand, its Music and its People." Created and told by Cristobel Weerasinghe. Desto Records D-502 (mid-1960s). Some examples of the music and chanting style of the Buddhist monks (recorded in Bangkok by Dr. Diane K. Gordon) are woven into the spoken narrative.

"Traditional Music of Thailand." IER 7502. Issued by the Institute of Ethnomusicology, UCLA, Los Angeles, California 90024. 1968. A 2-record album of all the important genres of the traditional music, in simulated stereo made from the field tapes collected by David Morton in Thailand in 1958-1960. All compositions are complete. This is the only recording available outside of Thailand of complete Thai compositions of all the major types.

Recordings of Thai traditional music, recorded and released in Thailand are available there, but not outside the country.

Index

For the accurate pronunciation of Thai words, see the guide to pronunciation in Appendix A, page 231. Proper names are pronounced approximately as transliterated; exceptions are given in parentheses. The pagination for main entries for instruments, ensembles, terms, and so forth appears here italicized.

Angkor, 4, 12, 45, 54, 68, 78, 96, 196. *See also* Khmer music and instruments

"Ānū," 190

Arabic music. *See* Near Eastern music and instruments

Atchanarong, Chirat (či-rat), viii

Ayuthaya (a slight accent on the second syllable) period, 1, 3, 12-13, 20, 45, 54, 73, 90, 100, 102, 103, 105, 223

"Bai Khlang," 176

Balinese music and instruments, 11-12, 28, 46, 48, 62, 71, 73, 111, 227

Bandọ, 45, 101

Borrowed melodies, 15, 185

Bua lọi ensemble, 112-113

Burmese music and instruments, 1, 15, 45, 113-114

Cadences, 116, 117, 118-119, 126-128, 140, 169-172, 178, 181-182, 190, 198-199

Cambodian music and instruments, 1, 45, 55, 96. *See also* Angkor; Khmer music and instruments

Ceremonial music, 43, 52, 73, 89, 112, 180, *216*

Čhakhē, 3, 16, 44, *92-93*, 103, 108-111

Chakri (čha-kri), 15

Chan dio, 41, 43, 181

"Chāng Prasān NGā," 167-169

Chao Phaya river (čhao pha-yā), 15

Chāp, 44, 103, 105
    Chāp lek, *66-67*, 105, 107, 109-113
    Chāp yai, *67*, 105, 107, 110-113

Chinese music and instruments, 1, 2, 15, 45, 75, 76, 79, 98-100, 101, 119, 178, 190, 216, 223

Ching, 2-3, 40, 41, 44, *64-66*, 68, 75, 100, 103-113, 117, 119-121, 145, 178-179, 185, 186-188, 217

"Chom Suan Sawan," 175

Coda, *172-178*, 181, 205

Damrong Rachanubhap, Prince (dam-rong rā-čha-nu-phăp), 18, 102

Dance, 9, 12-14, 17

Department of Fine Arts, Bangkok, viii, 16-17, 212, 224, 226

Dhaninivat, Prince (tha-nī-ni-wāt), 3, 18

"Dọk Mai Sai," 159-161, 164

Drums, 5-8, 217. *See also* under individual names of drums

Dukdamban (theatrical form), 23

Duriyanga, (Phra) Chen (du-ri-yāng, [phra] čhēn; "phra" is a title), 18, 69

Dyaks of Borneo (Kalimantan), 92

Dynamics, 43

Fifth Polarities, *137*, 179

Finalis, 115-116, 130, 133, 137, 144, 165, 172, 174, 178-179, 210, 223

Flute. *See* Khlui

Folk music, 185, 229

Gong, 5, 40, 41, 67, 119-120. *See also* Mōng

Gong-kettles, 4, 6-7, 10, 13, 19, 24, 25, 29, 44, 46, 57, 217. *See also* names of instruments beginning with Khǫng

Harp, 9, 45-46

"Hok Bot," 171

"Hong Thǫng," 150-152

Indian music and instruments, 1, 2-3, 15, 22, 45, 48, 55, 68, 79-80, 89-92, 101, 115, 223

Iranian music. *See* Near Eastern music and instruments

Japanese music, 1

Javanese music and instruments, 3, 4, 11, 15, 19, 20, 28, 45, 48, 54, 62-63, 64, 73, 89-90, 92, 96, 103, 110, 111-112, 115, 119, 223

Kemanché, 96

Kep, 56, 93, 97, 100

"Khāek Lopburī," 177

"Khāek Mǭn Bāng Chāng," 161-164

"Khāek Mǭn Bāng Khun Phrom," 171, 211

"Khāek Sai," 42, 121, 123-126, 133, 137, 188-189, 191-194

"Khāek Thǭn Sāi Bua," 153

"Khāek Tǫi Mǭ," 34, 205-210, 214-215, 216

"Khamāe Thom," 141-144, 196-204, 214

"Khamēn Klāng," 196

"Khamēn La Ǭ Ong," 58, 172, 173, 186

"Khamēn Nǫi," 196

"Khamēn Pak Thǭ," 217-221

"Khamēn Sai Yōk," 30-32, 36, 216

"Khamēn Yai," 196-204, 214

Khap Mai ensemble, 101

Khim, 2

Khlui, 23, 37, 39, 44, *77-78*, 102, 103, 105-106, 108-111

Khmer music and instruments, 1, 3-10, 45, 54, 78, 102, 196. *See also* Angkor

"Khōm Song Khrūang," 172

Khōn, 13, 14, 23, 75, 79, 104-105, 206

Khǫng, 44

Khǫng hui, 67

Khǫng khū, 104

Khǫng mēng, 103-104, 112

Khǫng mǭn, *52-53*, 90, 113

Khǫng rabēng, 44

Khǫng rāng, 46, 103

Khǫng rāo, 67

Khǫng (wong) klāng, *51*, 109-111

Khǫng wong, 44, 52, 104

Khǫng wong lek, *50-51*, 103, 105, 107, 109-113

Khōng wong yai, 23, *45-50*, 60, 105-107, 109-113, 138

Khrp̄ang Sāi (string) ensemble, 23, 51, 77, 78, 93, 96, 97, 104, 105, 108, 111

Klǫng, 44

Klǫng chātrī, 44, 104-105

Klǫng khāek, 45, 72, *73-74*, 89-90, 103-104, 110, 111, 112

Klǫng Khāek ensemble, *103-104*

Klǫng malāyū, 45, 111-112

Klǫng marigan, 45

Klǫng that, 2, 72-73, *74-75*, 104-107

Klǫng yāo, 44

Krajappi, 45, 91, *92*, 102, 103

Krāo ram, 71

Krap, 44
    Krap phuang, 102-103
    Krap sēphā, 54-55

Krǫ, 44

Krǭ, 34, 36, 56, 93, 205

Krōng, 44

"Lā," 180-185, 190, 196, 206

Lakhǫn, 23, 79, 89, 104-105, 206

Lakhǫn nōrā, 76, 105

"Lāo Chiang Tat Sǫi," 140

"Lāo Damnōen Sāi," 214-216

"Lāo Duang Duan," 214-216

"Lāo Kham Hǫm," 36, 214

"Lāo Khruan," 138-139, 140, 214, 216

"Lāo Sīang Thīan," 31, 134

Laos and Laotian music, 15, 45, 214

"Līlā K(r)athum," 129, 146-147

Luang Pradit Phai Rǫ (Sǫn Silapabanleng; both names pronounced according to this transliteration), 16, 56, 188, 214, 216, 217, 224

Lūk khat, 212

Lūk lǫ, 212

Mahōrī ensemble, 23, 51, 76, 78, 93, 96, 97, 102-105, 109-111

Malayan music and instruments, 1, 77, 111

Melodic species, 31, 116-121, 179, 181, 205

Metabole, 128-130, 141, 145, 147-148, 178, 181, 198, 212

Metallophones, 62, 217. *See also* Ranāt ēk lek; Ranāt thum lek

Metric emphasis, *39-43*, 65, 117, 120-121, 178-179

Mode, 115-117

Modulation, 24, 32, 37, 39, 116, 123, 126, 128, 187. *See also* Metabole

"Mǫn Chom Čhan," 174

Mǫn style, 32-33, 117, 123-128, 130, 145, 147, 150, 170, 179, 205-212

Mōng, *67-68*, 75, 105, 107, 110-113

"Mulōng," 170

Musicians, 15-16, 17, 18

"Nāk Phan," 171

"Nāng Khruan," 176

Nāng yai. *See* Shadow plays

"Nārāi Plāeng Rūp," 165

Narit, Prince (sometimes spelled "Prince Naris"), 216

Near Eastern music and instruments, 76, 78-79, 89, 96, 116

"Nok Khao Khamāē," 141, 188, 195

Notation, 1, 18, 19, 65, 100, 123, 147, 161, 225-226

Oral tradition, 15, 18-19

Ornamentation, 34-36, 50, 51, 56, 59-60, 67, 79, 87-89, 97, 144, 169, 205, 217

"Pae," 170

Passing tones, 24, 32, 121, 123-125, 128-130, 139, 145, 147-150, 159, 178

Persian music. *See* Near Eastern music and instruments

Phakavali Institute of Dance and Music, 14, 16, 17, 25, 28, 232

"Phat Chā," 158

"Phayā Ram Phyng," 174

Phia, 44, 91

Phīn, 5, 45, 91-92

Phlēng chā, 40

Phlēng reo, 40, 41, 43, 70, 180-181, 196, 206

Phra Chen Duriyanga. *See* Duriyanga, Phra Chen

"Phrarām Dōen Dong," 32

Phrase-block, 120, 122

Phrase-unit, 42, 120, 122

"Phrayā Khruan," 153-155

"Phuang Rǫi," 129

Pī, 36, 39, 78-79, 104

Pī chanai, 20, 45, 79

Pī chawā, 23, 36, 45, 73, *88-90*, 103-104, 112

Pī mǫn, *90-91*, 113

Pī nai, 23, 79, *80-88*, 91, 104-107, 109-110

Pī nǫk, 23, 79, 105, 107

Pī Phāt ensemble, 18, 23, 37, 38, 68, 71, 78, 79, 99, 104-107

Pī Phāt Mǫn ensemble, 113

Pī Phāt Nāng Hong ensemble, 24, 112-113

Pitch levels, *37-39*, 115, 128, 145

Pitch outline, 121

Pōeng māng (khǫk), 113-114

Polyphonic stratification, 21

Prisadang, Prince (prit-sa-dāng), 22

Prop kai, 40-42, 70, 119-120, 128, 180-181, 188-189, 196

Question-answer technique, 137, 174, 212

Rām(a) Khamhāēng, 3

Rammanā, 73, 76, 77, 102, 103, 108-111

Ranāt ēk, 24, 44, 54-57, 78, 93, 97, 100, 102, 104-107, 109-113, 137, 138, 177, 212

Ranāt ēk lek, 62, 103, 105, 107, 110-111

Ranāt kāeo, 102-103

Ranāt thǫng, 62-63

Ranāt thum, 54, *57-61*, 103, 105-107, 109-113

Ranāt thum lek, 62, *63-64*, 103, 105, 107, 110-111

"Rasam Rasāi," 167

"Rātrī Pradap Dāo," 186

Rebab, 96, 110

Rhythmic emphasis. *See* Metric emphasis

Rua, 43

Rụ̄ang (suites), 32, 37, 38, 40, 50, 60, 63, 71, 129-130, 140, 141, 145, 172

"Rụ̄ang Chin Sāe Mai," 190

"Rụ̄ang Khāek Sai," 188, 196

"Rụ̄ang Khamēn Yai," 196

"Rụ̄ang Mǭn Plāeng," 205-206

"Rụ̄ang Phlēng Ching Prač̌han," 30

"Rụ̄ang Tao Kin Phak Bung," 181

Sabat, 39, 50

Sām chan, 40, 43, 115, 119-120, 172, 196, 212-213

"Sām Mai Nai," 148-149

Sang, 45

"Sāo Sǭt Wāen," 40

Sēphā, 23, 30, 54, 61, 71-72, 105, 130, 214, 229

Shadow plays (nāng yai), 23, 75, 76, 79

Sī chan, 216

Silapabanleng, Sǭn. See Luang Pradit Phai Rǭ

Sǭ, 44, 94

Sǭ duang, 2, 37, 97, 100, 103, 108-111

"Sǭi Mayurā," 165-166

"Sōm Sǭng Sāeng," 39, 214-216

Sǭng chan, 41, 115, 119, 138, 145, 188, 196, 214-216

Sǭng mai, 41, 70, 119, 180-181, 186, 188-189, 196

Sǭng nā, 44, 71-72, 105, 113

Sǭ sām sāi, 16, 44, 94-97, 101, 102, 103, 109-111

Sǭ thai, 94

Sǭ ū, 37, 92, 97-100, 103, 108-111

Stretto, 177, 212

String ensembles. See Khrụ̄ang Sāi ensemble; Mahōrī ensemble

Sukhothai period, 3, 78, 96, 103, 223

"Tao Kin Phak Bung" (Rụ̄ang), 181

Tap (suites), 138, 140, 145, 152, 212, 214, 216

"Tap Ābūhāsan," 153, 214

"Tap Khamēn," 214

"Tap Phralǭ," 139, 214

Taphōn, 68-71, 104-107

Taphōn mǭn, 68-69, 71, 90, 113

Tempo, 40, 43

Thao (fill-in phrase), 30, 34-35, 117, 119, 121, 122, 123-125, 130, 132-133, 138, 160, 188-189

Thao (form), 3, 38, 39, 40, 41, 115, 137, 172, 182-196, 216

Theater, 17, 43, 56, 73, 99, 104, 212, 216, 217. See also Khōn; Lakhǭn; Lakhǭn nōrā; Shadow plays

Thōn, 45, 73, 76-77, 100, 102, 103, 108-111
    Thōn chātrī, 76, 104
    Thōn mahōrī, 76-77

Thonburi, 15

Titles of songs, 180, 214-215

"Tǭi Rūp," 33

"(Ton) Nāng Nāk," 169

"Ton Phlēng Ching," 61

Tramote, Montri (tra-mōt), viii, 1, 13, 15, 18, 23, 206-210, 214, 225, 226, 227

"Tuang Phra Thāt," 131-133, 137

Tuning, 18, *22-29*, 45, 54, 57, 59, 62, 80, 93, 94, 97, 179, 223

Tuning levels, 24, *37-39*. *See also* Pitch levels

Vanij-Vadhana, Supachai (wa-nit-wa-ta-na, su-pa-chai), viii

Vichitr-Vadakarn (wi-chit-wa-ta-kān), 18

Vietnamese music, 128

Vocal music, *216-223*

"Wiwēk Wēhā," 170

Xylophones, 22, 25, 28, 29, 54, 217. *See also* the ranāt instruments

"Yǫng NGit," 153, 156-158

Yupho, Dhanit (yū-pho, tha-nit), 18, 44, 54, 68, 101